2

Compact
ACTUAL iBT Reading & Listening Book 2

Publisher Chung Kyudo
Editors Cho Sangik, Hong Inpyo
Authors Darakwon TOEFL Research Team
Proofreader Michael A. Putlack
Designers Zo Hwayoun, Park Sunyoung

First published in August 2011
By Darakwon, Inc.
Darakwon Bldg., 211, Munbal-ro, Paju-si, Gyeonggi-do 10881
Republic of Korea
Tel: 82-2-736-2031 (Ext. 250)
Fax: 82-2-732-2037

Price ₩10,000
ISBN 978-89-277-0598-7 18740
978-89-277-0581-9 18740 (set)

www.darakwon.co.kr

Components Main Book / Answer Book / 1 MP3 CD
12 11 10 9 8 7 6   21 22 23 24 25

2

DARAKWON

Contents

One of the most important standardized tests students of the English language may ever take is the TOEFL® iBT. Because getting a high score on the test is so crucial, it is important to prepare for the test as much as possible prior to taking it.

That is the purpose of *Compact Actual iBT Reading & Listening* series. This book focuses on two of the four sections on the TOEFL® iBT: the Reading and Listening sections. These are arguably the two most difficult parts of the TOEFL® iBT. In both the Reading and the Listening sections, test takers will face passages and lectures that cover a wide variety of topics. These include subjects in the arts, social sciences, physical sciences, and life sciences. For that reason, a familiarity with many of these topics is crucial. So is having an extensive vocabulary that includes knowledge of specialized words in each of the fields. Fortunately, *Compact Actual iBT Reading & Listening* provides exactly what students need. The Reading passages and Listening lectures cover many of the very topics that often appear on the TOEFL® iBT. In addition, the Listening conversations do the same: They cover topics that frequently appear on the TOEFL® iBT, which can only serve to assist test takers when they sit for the actual test.

Compact Actual iBT Reading & Listening has been designed to be used both in the classroom and by test takers working on an individual basis. Each compact test consists of one Reading passage, one Listening conversation, and one Listening lecture. All three of them are the standard length of actual TOEFL® iBT passages, conversations, and lectures. In addition, they all have the same number of questions and the same types of questions that are found on the actual test. By using this book, test takers will be more prepared for the test when they actually take it.

This book, however, is merely a tool. Both students and teachers must make use of this tool in the best possible manner so that test takers may do as well as possible when they take the TOEFL® iBT.

Compact Actual iBT Reading & Listening consists of ten units. Each unit consists of one compact test. A single compact test contains one Reading passage, one Listening conversation, and one Listening lecture. The passage, conversation, and lecture are followed by questions. These questions are of the same type and number that are found on the TOEFL® iBT.

In addition, the subjects of the passages in the Reading section are those that have all appeared on recent TOEFL® iBT tests. As many topics on the TOEFL® iBT Reading section tend to repeat, this can be a great benefit to test takers. By familiarizing themselves with the topics, subject matter, and vocabulary used in the passages in the Reading section of each compact test, test takers can be more confident when they take the Reading section of the TOEFL® iBT.

The same is true of the conversation and lectures in the Listening section. The Listening conversations contain situations that have appeared on recent TOEFL® iBT tests while the Listening lectures are all on topics that have occurred recently as well. By familiarizing themselves with the topics, subject matter, situations, and vocabulary used in the conversations and lectures, test takers can be more confident when they take the Listening section of the TOEFL® iBT.

The Reading section of each compact test consists of one full-length Reading passage followed by either thirteen or fourteen questions. Each passage covers a field that commonly occurs on the TOEFL® iBT. This includes fields such as history, archaeology, biology, and art.

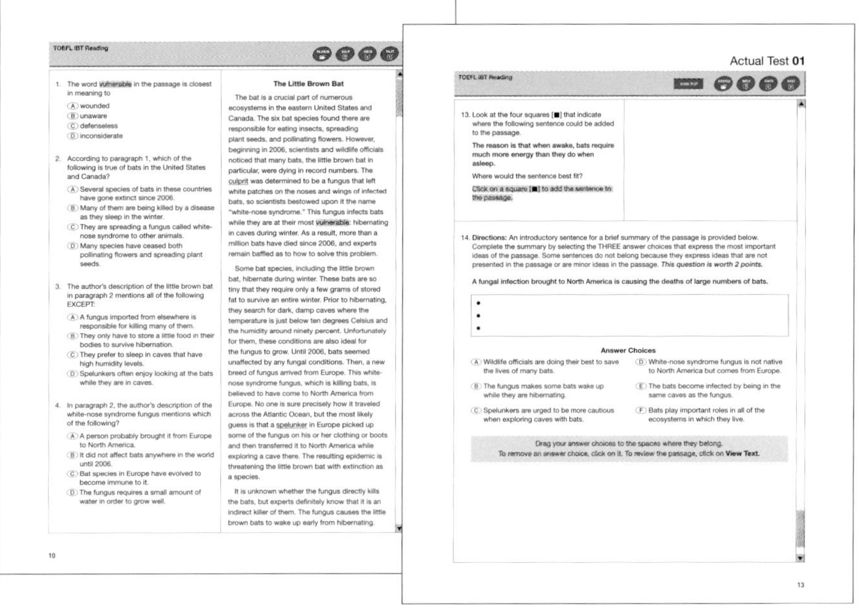

The Listening section of each compact test consists of one full-length Listening conversation followed by five questions and one full-length Listening lecture followed by six questions. Each conversation concerns either an office hours situation or a service situation whereas each lecture covers a topic that commonly occurs on the TOEFL® iBT. These topics are in the following four categories: arts, life sciences, physical sciences, and social sciences.

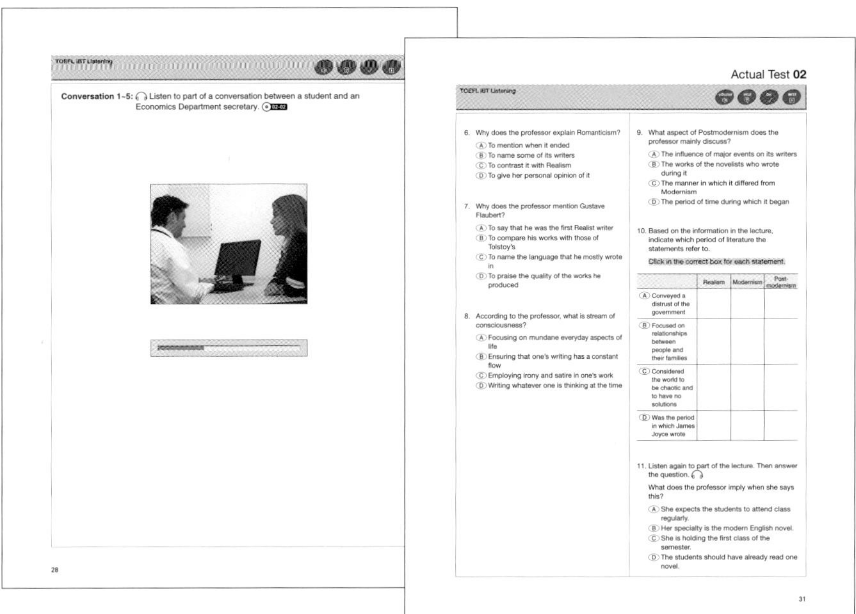

Actual Test 01

Reading
Section Directions

This section measures your ability to understand academic passages in English.

In this part, you will read 1 passage and answer reading comprehension questions about the passage. Most questions are worth one point, but the last question is worth more than one point. The directions indicate how many points you may receive.

Some passages include a word or phrase that is underlined in blue. Click on the word or phrase to see a definition or an explanation.

When you want to move on to the next question, click on **Next**. You may skip questions and go back to them later. If you want to return to previous questions, click on **Back**. You can click on **Review** at any time and the review screen will show you which questions you have answered and which you have not answered. From this review screen, you may go directly to any question you have already seen in the Reading section.

You may now begin the Reading section. You will read 1 reading passage. You will have **20 minutes** to read the passage and answer the questions.

Click on **Continue** to go on.

1. The word vulnerable in the passage is closest in meaning to

   (A) wounded
   (B) unaware
   (C) defenseless
   (D) inconsiderate

2. According to paragraph 1, which of the following is true of bats in the United States and Canada?

   (A) Several species of bats in these countries have gone extinct since 2006.
   (B) Many of them are being killed by a disease as they sleep in the winter.
   (C) They are spreading a fungus called white-nose syndrome to other animals.
   (D) Many species have ceased both pollinating flowers and spreading plant seeds.

3. The author's description of the little brown bat in paragraph 2 mentions all of the following EXCEPT:

   (A) A fungus imported from elsewhere is responsible for killing many of them.
   (B) They only have to store a little food in their bodies to survive hibernation.
   (C) They prefer to sleep in caves that have high humidity levels.
   (D) Spelunkers often enjoy looking at the bats while they are in caves.

4. In paragraph 2, the author's description of the white-nose syndrome fungus mentions which of the following?

   (A) A person probably brought it from Europe to North America.
   (B) It did not affect bats anywhere in the world until 2006.
   (C) Bat species in Europe have evolved to become immune to it.
   (D) The fungus requires a small amount of water in order to grow well.

The Little Brown Bat

The bat is a crucial part of numerous ecosystems in the eastern United States and Canada. The six bat species found there are responsible for eating insects, spreading plant seeds, and pollinating flowers. However, beginning in 2006, scientists and wildlife officials noticed that many bats, the little brown bat in particular, were dying in record numbers. The culprit was determined to be a fungus that left white patches on the noses and wings of infected bats, so scientists bestowed upon it the name "white-nose syndrome." This fungus infects bats while they are at their most vulnerable: hibernating in caves during winter. As a result, more than a million bats have died since 2006, and experts remain baffled as to how to solve this problem.

Some bat species, including the little brown bat, hibernate during winter. These bats are so tiny that they require only a few grams of stored fat to survive an entire winter. Prior to hibernating, they search for dark, damp caves where the temperature is just below ten degrees Celsius and the humidity around ninety percent. Unfortunately for them, these conditions are also ideal for the fungus to grow. Until 2006, bats seemed unaffected by any fungal conditions. Then, a new breed of fungus arrived from Europe. This white-nose syndrome fungus, which is killing bats, is believed to have come to North America from Europe. No one is sure precisely how it traveled across the Atlantic Ocean, but the most likely guess is that a spelunker in Europe picked up some of the fungus on his or her clothing or boots and then transferred it to North America while exploring a cave there. The resulting epidemic is threatening the little brown bat with extinction as a species.

It is unknown whether the fungus directly kills the bats, but experts definitely know that it is an indirect killer of them. The fungus causes the little brown bats to wake up early from hibernating.

5. The word **replenish** in the passage is closest in meaning to

   (A) replace
   (B) revert
   (C) reduce
   (D) reproduce

6. According to paragraph 3, the fungus kills bats because

   (A) it affects their respiratory systems, so they cannot breathe
   (B) it causes them to deplete their limited supplies of energy
   (C) it makes them more susceptible to cold winter weather
   (D) it reduces their ability to fly long distances to find food

7. The word **they** in the passage refers to

   (A) caves
   (B) homes
   (C) enormous numbers
   (D) white-nose infections

8. Which of the sentences below best expresses the essential information in the highlighted sentence in the passage? *Incorrect* answer choices change the meaning in important ways or leave out essential information.

   (A) Because of some people, the fungus moved from Europe to the North American continent.
   (B) When the fungus was transported to North America, people conspired to take it to other areas.
   (C) Incautious people probably brought the fungus to North America and then caused it to spread.
   (D) It was careless people who were responsible for the fungus appearing in caves all over North America.

The fungus is believed to cause an irritation in the bats' respiratory systems that interrupts their sleep. ■ The bats survive their time asleep by utilizing a finite amount of stored food, so waking up early causes them to expend too much of their energy. ■ They must then either find more food or die. ■ When the bats emerge from their caves, the harsh winter weather conditions kill them before they can replenish their fat supplies. ■ Wildlife officials have reported seeing thousands of dead bats lying either on cave floors or in the areas just outside cave entrances.

Not every cave is infected though. So far, the epidemic has spread only to caves in the eastern United States and in parts of southern Ontario and Quebec in Canada. Caves in the American South and Midwest, which are homes to enormous numbers of hibernating bats, have witnessed no white-nose infections as yet. But there still exists the possibility that they will occur as the fungus, which was first detected in a cave in New York, has spread significantly since its arrival in the United States. The primary issue regarding its spread is human explorers. Not only did a careless person most likely import the fungus to North America, but a number of others are probably also responsible for broadening its reach throughout the continent. Spelunkers are being discouraged from entering caves in which bats are hibernating as wildlife officials have been installing barred gates at the entrances of many caves. Bats are still able to fly in and out by moving between the bars, but people are unable to pass through them.

Despite these safety measures, experts are still concerned that the epidemic may result in the extinction of some bat species such as the little brown bat. Since the reasons the fungus attacks the bats and kills them are currently unknown, scientists have no way to cure infected bats. The loss of these bat species would result in the upsetting of the delicate balance of the

9. According to paragraph 4, which of the following is true of the caves where the fungus is found?

   (A) They are located in every region of the United States and Canada.
   (B) The caves are primarily in the New York region of the United States.
   (C) The number of caves that contain the fungus has continually grown.
   (D) Almost all of the caves in eastern Canada contain the fungus.

10. In paragraph 4, the author implies that bats

   (A) in some regions are slowly building an immunity to the fungus
   (B) have no role in spreading the fungus from cave to cave
   (C) are found in greater numbers in Canada than in the United States
   (D) may refuse to enter a cave that has bars across its entrance

11. In stating that the possible extinction of the little brown bat does not bode well for the future, the author means that the future of the little brown bat

   (A) has potential
   (B) will be a disaster
   (C) is not positive
   (D) is unknown

12. In paragraph 5, the author's description of the short-term effects of the extinction of bat species mentions which of the following?

   (A) It would result in a permanent change in numerous ecosystems.
   (B) It would allow some other animal species to increase in number.
   (C) It would cause many ecosystems in Canada to collapse entirely.
   (D) It would make some forests grow at slower rates than before.

ecosystem. In the short term, the insects the bats consume in great numbers would increase their populations and spread out of control, plant seeds would not be spread to new locations, and some flowers would never get pollinated. The long-term consequences of such an event are unknown, but the possible extinction of the little brown bat and other bat species does not bode well for the future of the forested lands of eastern North America.

Glossary

culprit: a person or thing responsible for something bad; a guilty party

spelunker: a person who explores caves

barred: having bars

13. Look at the four squares [■] that indicate where the following sentence could be added to the passage.

    The reason is that when awake, bats require much more energy than they do when asleep.

    Where would the sentence best fit?

    Click on a square [■] to add the sentence to the passage.

14. **Directions:** An introductory sentence for a brief summary of the passage is provided below. Complete the summary by selecting the THREE answer choices that express the most important ideas of the passage. Some sentences do not belong because they express ideas that are not presented in the passage or are minor ideas in the passage. *This question is worth 2 points.*

    A fungal infection brought to North America is causing the deaths of large numbers of bats.

    -
    -
    -

Answer Choices

(A) Wildlife officials are doing their best to save the lives of many bats.

(B) The fungus makes some bats wake up while they are hibernating.

(C) Spelunkers are urged to be more cautious when exploring caves with bats.

(D) White-nose syndrome fungus is not native to North America but comes from Europe.

(E) The bats become infected by being in the same caves as the fungus.

(F) Bats play important roles in all of the ecosystems in which they live.

Drag your answer choices to the spaces where they belong.
To remove an answer choice, click on it. To review the passage, click on **View Text**.

Listening
Section Directions

This section measures your ability to understand conversations and lectures in English.

In this part, you will listen to 1 conversation and 1 lecture. You will hear the conversation or lecture only **one** time. After the conversation or lecture, you will answer some questions about it. The questions typically ask about the main idea and supporting details. Some questions ask about a speaker's purpose or attitude. Answer the questions based on what is stated or implied by the speakers.

You may take notes while you listen. You may use your notes to help you answer the questions. Your notes will **not** be scored.

If you need to change the volume while you listen, click on the **Volume** icon at the top of the screen.

In some questions, you will see this icon: ∩ This means that you will hear, but not see, part of the question.

Some of the questions have special directions. These directions appear in a gray box on the screen.

Most questions are worth one point. If a question is worth more than one point, it will have special directions that indicate how many points you can receive.

You must answer each question. After you answer, click on **Next**. Then click on **OK** to confirm your answer and go on to the next question. After you click on **OK**, you cannot return to previous questions.

A clock at the top of the screen will show you how much time is remaining. The clock will not count down while you are listening. The clock will count down only while you are answering the questions.

Now you may begin the Listening section.

Conversation 1~5: Listen to part of a conversation between a student and a professor.

01-02

1. Why does the student visit the professor?

   Ⓐ To find out about the topic of a paper he must write

   Ⓑ To ask the professor some questions about the class

   Ⓒ To schedule another meeting with the professor

   Ⓓ To discuss a conflict he has with two of his classes

2. Where is the student going for his geology class?

   Ⓐ To a museum

   Ⓑ To a rock collector's home

   Ⓒ To a dig site

   Ⓓ To a geology laboratory

3. What is the professor's attitude toward the student?

   Ⓐ She is disappointed with his request.

   Ⓑ She is upset about his performance.

   Ⓒ She is considerate of his situation.

   Ⓓ She is pleased with his questions.

4. What will the professor probably do next?

   Ⓐ Get in touch with Professor Timber

   Ⓑ Teach her next class

   Ⓒ Give the student a homework assignment

   Ⓓ Go home for the day

5. Listen again to part of the conversation. Then answer the question.

   What does the professor imply when she says this?

   Ⓐ She accepts that the student will miss the exam.

   Ⓑ She wants the student to drop his geology class.

   Ⓒ The student is going to have to take a makeup exam.

   Ⓓ The student will get a low grade if he misses the test.

Lecture 6~11: Listen to part of a lecture in a geology class. 01-03

Geology

6. What aspect of abiotic oil does the professor mainly discuss?

   (A) How it is created
   (B) Where people have found it
   (C) Its relationship with synthetic oil
   (D) How it compares to biotic oil

7. How does the professor organize the information about the reasons people believe in abiotic oil that she presents to the class?

   (A) By citing some information from a leading journal on the topic
   (B) By focusing on her personal beliefs concerning the existence of abiotic oil
   (C) By describing the main theories and the possibility that they are correct
   (D) By giving the class a handout and then covering the information on it

8. What does the professor imply about methane?

   (A) It exists in small amounts on the Earth.
   (B) It takes many years for it to be created.
   (C) It is typically created by living organisms.
   (D) It can cause death or injury to people.

9. According to the professor, how is synthetic oil often made?

   (A) By a complicated laboratory process
   (B) By combining regular oil with methane
   (C) By making use of natural gas
   (D) By utilizing another fossil fuel

10. Listen again to part of the lecture. Then answer the question.

    What does the professor imply when she says this?

    (A) The possibility that she just mentioned is plausible.
    (B) She is a leading supporter of the theory of abiotic oil.
    (C) Oil is only produced from biological matter.
    (D) She has not made up her mind concerning the issue.

11. Listen again to part of the lecture. Then answer the question.

    Why does the professor say this?

    (A) To claim that methane has not been found on many planets
    (B) To try to explain the logic behind the main argument
    (C) To make a point about the presence of hydrocarbons in methane
    (D) To express her doubt concerning one theory on abiotic oil

Actual Test
02

Reading
Section Directions

This section measures your ability to understand academic passages in English.

In this part, you will read 1 passage and answer reading comprehension questions about the passage. Most questions are worth one point, but the last question is worth more than one point. The directions indicate how many points you may receive.

Some passages include a word or phrase that is underlined in blue. Click on the word or phrase to see a definition or an explanation.

When you want to move on to the next question, click on **Next**. You may skip questions and go back to them later. If you want to return to previous questions, click on **Back**. You can click on **Review** at any time and the review screen will show you which questions you have answered and which you have not answered. From this review screen, you may go directly to any question you have already seen in the Reading section.

You may now begin the Reading section. You will read 1 reading passage. You will have **20 minutes** to read the passage and answer the questions.

Click on **Continue** to go on.

1. The word drawbacks in the passage is closest in meaning to

  Ⓐ misunderstandings
  Ⓑ blunders
  Ⓒ shortcomings
  Ⓓ rejections

2. According to paragraph 1, which of the following is true of globalization?

  Ⓐ There are more people who oppose it than support it.
  Ⓑ One effect of it is the uniting of various financial markets.
  Ⓒ The industry that it has changed the most is communications.
  Ⓓ More workers are employed worldwide thanks to it.

3. Why does the author mention the Silk Road in paragraph 2?

  Ⓐ To describe the route that it took through Asia and Europe
  Ⓑ To name some of the goods which were traded on it
  Ⓒ To claim that it was the inception of economic globalization
  Ⓓ To explain why it was so important for many centuries

4. The word reaped in the passage is closest in meaning to

  Ⓐ spurned
  Ⓑ gained
  Ⓒ considered
  Ⓓ reported

5. The word hindrance in the passage is closest in meaning to

  Ⓐ barrier
  Ⓑ imposter
  Ⓒ inspiration
  Ⓓ rebuttal

The Economic Effects of Globalization

Globalization is the process through which the world is becoming integrated at all levels of society, particularly the economic one. It has been a slow process that began centuries ago, but, as improvements in technology, transportation, and communications have developed, the effects of global integration have spread more rapidly. Nowadays, the financial markets, trade, the sharing of technology, and the migration of workers are all highly globalized. This has resulted in an integrated global economy that has brought benefits to many places. Yet globalization has some drawbacks as well as detractors who do not support it.

Economic globalization has taken many centuries to attain its modern level of integration. Its beginnings can be traced back to the Silk Road, a fabled ancient trade route that started in China and passed through India, the Middle East, and Europe. Later, the constructing of large oceangoing ships and the European discoveries of new lands, such as the Americas, led to more integration of the world economy. By the eve of World War I in 1914, many countries were connected by fast ships and telegraph lines, and they reaped the benefits of free-trade policies. However, the fighting of wars on vast scales during the twentieth century brought globalization to a halt. Nations began jealously guarding their economies and imposing trade barriers. Starting in the mid-1940s, the Cold War divided the world into two armed camps, which served as a further hindrance to economic integration. Finally, the end of tensions in the 1990s and the development of computer communication systems such as the World Wide Web brought global economic integration to its current level.

The benefits of this integration have been substantial. Foremost is the creation of a worldwide financial market that is integrated at many levels. Stocks and bonds in one country

6. According to paragraph 3, after World War I began, globalization stopped for some time because

   (A) nations started to create impediments to trading with others

   (B) the Cold War focused more on politics than on economics

   (C) countries spent most of their efforts on fighting numerous wars

   (D) technology failed to advance at a rate that could support globalization

7. Which of the sentences below best expresses the essential information in the highlighted sentence in the passage? *Incorrect* answer choices change the meaning in important ways or leave out essential information.

   (A) There are many types of transportation available to distributers, so they can move products by sea, air, and land.

   (B) Until transportation systems improve, it is not possible to sell most products in places other than their local areas.

   (C) Globalization has advanced at a great pace so that it is now possible to sell products all around the world.

   (D) Because there is a global logistics system, goods that were once sold in local areas are now available worldwide.

8. The author's description of the benefits of globalization in paragraph 3 mentions all of the following EXCEPT:

   (A) It is possible for foreigners to purchase land in other countries.

   (B) There are fewer trade barriers since there are many free-trade zones.

   (C) Countries' financial systems have become connected to one another.

   (D) People are now more able to study in countries other than their own.

can be traded by individuals in others, currency rates are pegged against one another while money can be exchanged in numerous places, and people can buy and sell property in nations other than their own. Global trade has made products that were once sold in small regions available to the entire world thanks to the ships, airplanes, trains, and trucks that move products in a vast transportation system. The establishing of economic free-trade zones and trading <u>blocs</u> has freed the world of many of the trade restrictions that characterized the previous century.

■ Finally, as technology has advanced, its spread to other lands has resulted in improvements in the quality of life all around the world. ■ For instance, farmers currently employ modern methods to grow more food, improved medicines can cure numerous diseases, and advanced communication methods enable people to remain in touch with others no matter where in the world they are. ■ Another result is that people can work virtually anywhere in the world that they want. ■ Not only are workers often free to move to other countries to seek employment, but many of them also remain in their home countries while working for companies in other ones.

Despite all of these benefits, there are some negative issues concerning economic globalization. Financial markets have become so integrated that a problem in one nation can spread quickly around the world. This is especially true if the problem occurs in a financial <u>powerhouse</u> such as the United States. The economic downturn of 2008 and 2009 serves as a prime example of this danger. Additionally, while many nations and people are benefitting from economic globalization, there are tens of millions of people worldwide who still live in poverty and thus far have been unable to enjoy the advantages of economic globalization. These people are resentful of other individuals and nations that are better off and often feel as though they are being

9. The word ones in the passage refers to

   (A) advanced communication methods
   (B) workers
   (C) countries
   (D) companies

10. The word exploited in the passage is closest in meaning to

    (A) abandoned
    (B) abused
    (C) arrested
    (D) assumed

11. In paragraph 5, the author implies that the United States

    (A) has millions of people who are looking for jobs
    (B) has a powerful economy because of its technology
    (C) is the world's leader in encouraging globalization
    (D) witnessed a decline in its economy in 2008

12. According to paragraph 6, which of the following is true of the disadvantages of globalization?

    (A) Some countries have gone into debt because of globalization.
    (B) It has caused some trade wars to break out between nations.
    (C) Economic immigrants are sometimes disliked by the natives.
    (D) Many countries are losing their unique cultures because of it.

exploited.

Furthermore, while global trade enables people and companies to sell their products anywhere, some do not regard this as a positive feature. They claim that this has resulted in the world becoming too commercialized while more people are finding themselves in debt that they cannot repay because they made too many purchases. Likewise, individuals that move to new lands to find employment are not always welcomed by the native population, who accuse them of stealing jobs and importing problems to their societies.

Glossary

integration: the act of combining different parts to create a whole

bloc: a group that organizes for some purpose, often political or economic

powerhouse: someone or something that is very strong

VIEW TEXT  REVIEW  HELP  BACK  NEXT

13. Look at the four squares [■] that indicate where the following sentence could be added to the passage.

This is due to the existence of both the Internet and mobile phones.

Where would the sentence best fit?

Click on a square [■] to add the sentence to the passage.

14. **Directions:** An introductory sentence for a brief summary of the passage is provided below. Complete the summary by selecting the THREE answer choices that express the most important ideas of the passage. Some sentences do not belong because they express ideas that are not presented in the passage or are minor ideas in the passage. *This question is worth 2 points.*

The economic globalization of the world has resulted in both advantages and disadvantages.

-
-
-

Answer Choices

(A) During the Cold War, few people ever bothered to think much about globalization.

(B) Prior to 1914, free trade was a common feature in most of the world's countries.

(C) Millions of people have not benefitted from globalization, so they continue to live in poverty.

(D) Developments in transportation and technology have enabled globalization to spread.

(E) The integrating of financial markets worldwide has provided a number of benefits for people.

(F) The Silk Road was the first example of people trying to trade on a global scale.

Drag your answer choices to the spaces where they belong.
To remove an answer choice, click on it. To review the passage, click on **View Text**.

Listening
Section Directions

This section measures your ability to understand conversations and lectures in English.

In this part, you will listen to 1 conversation and 1 lecture. You will hear the conversation or lecture only **one** time. After the conversation or lecture, you will answer some questions about it. The questions typically ask about the main idea and supporting details. Some questions ask about a speaker's purpose or attitude. Answer the questions based on what is stated or implied by the speakers.

You may take notes while you listen. You may use your notes to help you answer the questions. Your notes will **not** be scored.

If you need to change the volume while you listen, click on the **Volume** icon at the top of the screen.

In some questions, you will see this icon: This means that you will hear, but not see, part of the question.

Some of the questions have special directions. These directions appear in a gray box on the screen.

Most questions are worth one point. If a question is worth more than one point, it will have special directions that indicate how many points you can receive.

You must answer each question. After you answer, click on **Next**. Then click on **OK** to confirm your answer and go on to the next question. After you click on **OK**, you cannot return to previous questions.

A clock at the top of the screen will show you how much time is remaining. The clock will not count down while you are listening. The clock will count down only while you are answering the questions.

Now you may begin the Listening section.

Conversation 1~5: Listen to part of a conversation between a student and an Economics Department secretary. 02-02

1. Why does the student visit the Economics Department office?

   (A) To ask about becoming an Economics major
   (B) To find out where a professor is
   (C) To get a schedule for the semester
   (D) To make a complaint about a class

2. Why does the student want to speak with Professor Hauser?

   (A) To submit an assignment to him
   (B) To discuss his most recent lecture
   (C) To talk about a test she is going to take
   (D) To ask him to be her student advisor

3. What is the student's opinion of Professor Hauser?

   (A) He is an easy grader.
   (B) He is an entertaining teacher.
   (C) He gives the right amount of homework.
   (D) He explains concepts clearly.

4. What does the man give the student?

   (A) An email address
   (B) A course catalogue
   (C) Some forms
   (D) A telephone number

5. Listen again to part of the conversation. Then answer the question.

   What does the student imply when she says this?

   (A) She will return to the office in the future.
   (B) She appreciates the help the man gave her.
   (C) She has some more questions for the man.
   (D) She needs to go to her next class now.

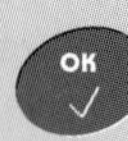

Lecture 6~11: Listen to part of a lecture in a literature class. 02-03

Literature

6. Why does the professor explain Romanticism?

   (A) To mention when it ended
   (B) To name some of its writers
   (C) To contrast it with Realism
   (D) To give her personal opinion of it

7. Why does the professor mention Gustave Flaubert?

   (A) To say that he was the first Realist writer
   (B) To compare his works with those of Tolstoy's
   (C) To name the language that he mostly wrote in
   (D) To praise the quality of the works he produced

8. According to the professor, what is stream of consciousness?

   (A) Focusing on mundane everyday aspects of life
   (B) Ensuring that one's writing has a constant flow
   (C) Employing irony and satire in one's work
   (D) Writing whatever one is thinking at the time

9. What aspect of Postmodernism does the professor mainly discuss?

   (A) The influence of major events on its writers
   (B) The works of the novelists who wrote during it
   (C) The manner in which it differed from Modernism
   (D) The period of time during which it began

10. Based on the information in the lecture, indicate which period of literature the statements refer to.

    Click in the correct box for each statement.

	Realism	Modernism	Post-modernism
(A) Conveyed a distrust of the government			
(B) Focused on relationships between people and their families			
(C) Considered the world to be chaotic and to have no solutions			
(D) Was the period in which James Joyce wrote			

11. Listen again to part of the lecture. Then answer the question.

    What does the professor imply when she says this?

    (A) She expects the students to attend class regularly.
    (B) Her specialty is the modern English novel.
    (C) She is holding the first class of the semester.
    (D) The students should have already read one novel.

Actual Test
03

Reading

Section Directions

This section measures your ability to understand academic passages in English.

In this part, you will read 1 passage and answer reading comprehension questions about the passage. Most questions are worth one point, but the last question is worth more than one point. The directions indicate how many points you may receive.

Some passages include a word or phrase that is underlined in blue. Click on the word or phrase to see a definition or an explanation.

When you want to move on to the next question, click on **Next**. You may skip questions and go back to them later. If you want to return to previous questions, click on **Back**. You can click on **Review** at any time and the review screen will show you which questions you have answered and which you have not answered. From this review screen, you may go directly to any question you have already seen in the Reading section.

You may now begin the Reading section. You will read 1 reading passage. You will have **20 minutes** to read the passage and answer the questions.

Click on **Continue** to go on.

The Humboldt Squid Expansion

One of the largest species of squid in the world is the Humboldt squid, which resides in the eastern part of the Pacific Ocean. It can grow to be the size of a man, is extremely fast, and has even been seen leaping high out of the water. At one time, the squid's range was the eastern coast of the Pacific from northern Chile to San Diego, California, USA. In recent years, however, the squid has been observed as far south as Tierra del Fuego, which is located at the southern tip of South America, and as far north as Alaska in North America. That has occurred because changes in the water in the Pacific have created numerous dead zones, which, while less suitable for many large marine life forms, are places where the Humboldt squid thrives.

The squid gets its name from the Humboldt Current, a cold, nutrient-rich stream of water that flows near the western coast of South America. The area covered by the current is the squid's primary territory. Around 2002, however, marine biologists observed that the squid's range was expanding. They noticed that this coincided with the rising number of dead zones in the ocean. These dead zones are regions where there is a severe lack of oxygen in the water. Commonly associated with coastal areas near river mouths that are polluted with industrial waste and chemicals used in agriculture, dead zones are currently being found in deeper waters. These deep-ocean dead zones are naturally occurring. Organic matter from dead fish and ocean plants falls to the bottom of the ocean, where it is consumed by bacteria that release carbon dioxide. If there is enough organic material, more bacteria grow, and thus more carbon dioxide is produced. The result is the creation of a dead zone.

These dead zones are not areas where large fish such as tunas and sharks, which need to extract

---

1. According to paragraph 1, which of the following is true of the Humboldt squid?

   (A) It consumes so many creatures that it creates dead zones in the water.

   (B) The main place where it can be found is off the coast of Alaska.

   (C) It is one of the largest of all marine creatures in the Pacific Ocean.

   (D) Its territory has increased considerably in the past few years.

2. Why does the author mention the Humboldt Current in paragraph 2?

   (A) To state which part of the Pacific Ocean it flows through

   (B) To explain how the Humboldt squid came to be named

   (C) To stress that the current has been changing lately

   (D) To describe the number of dead zones that are in it

3. According to paragraph 2, dead zones are created when

   (A) a great amount of organic matter begins to grow in the water and to use all the oxygen

   (B) companies dump large amounts of waste products into parts of the ocean

   (C) the amount of carbon dioxide in the water increases while the oxygen decreases

   (D) bacteria found in plants and fish release too much carbon dioxide into the water

4. In paragraph 2, the author implies that deep-ocean dead zones

   (A) permit nothing to live within them for a long time

   (B) are mostly found in cold water rather than warm water

   (C) were not known to any scientists until 2002

   (D) are not being created by the actions of people

5. The word copious in the passage is closest in meaning to

   (A) pure
   (B) continual
   (C) abundant
   (D) similar

6. Which of the following can be inferred from paragraph 3 about krill?

   (A) It is a primary source of food for the Humboldt squid.
   (B) It is a predator that hunts creatures smaller than it.
   (C) It is sometimes consumed by both sharks and tunas.
   (D) It does not need to breathe any oxygen to survive.

7. The word confounded in the passage is closest in meaning to

   (A) puzzled
   (B) interested
   (C) concerned
   (D) restricted

8. The author's description of dead zones in paragraph 4 mentions all of the following EXCEPT:

   (A) the depths at which the zones are currently being found at
   (B) some possible reasons why the zones are expanding in number
   (C) the year during which the dead zones began to increase
   (D) the countries whose waters contain the most dead zones

copious amounts of oxygen from the water, usually swim. The Humboldt squid, however, appears to be less affected by low oxygen levels, and, for some unknown reason, can remain in these dead zones for long periods of time. Additionally, small marine life forms, such as krill, are much less bothered by the low oxygen levels, so the squid still has a source of food in these dead zones. Finally, while the Humboldt squid is a favored food of tunas and sharks, since they are absent from these dead zones, it resides at the top of the food chain there.

The major issue that has scientists confounded is why the dead zones are expanding in the eastern Pacific Ocean. There are several possibilities, among them changes in climate, differences in water temperatures at various levels of the ocean, wind pattern changes, and current changes in the water. In warm waters, the dead zones extend from 200 to 1,000 meters beneath the surface, which is the prime feeding area of the squid. Prior to 2002, the dead zones started at much deeper levels—400 to 500 meters beneath the surface—which left a much smaller area for the squid to feed unmolested by large predators. But since 2002, the dead zones have increased in both size and spread, and the number and range of the Humboldt squid have also risen.

The resulting migrations of Humboldt squid to areas in which they never previously lived have caused great concern among marine biologists. Primary among these concerns are the amounts of marine life that the squid consume. Humboldt squid mostly exist on a diet of krill and other small marine life forms. However, recent examinations of some dead squid have discovered the remains of commercial fish such as hake and salmon within their digestive systems. Commercial fishermen fear that they will begin to catch fewer of these fish if the Humboldt squid expansions persist. Their worries have already become reality in Chile, where a hake fishery has suffered

9. The author discusses the deepness of the dead zones in paragraph 4 in order to

   (A) account for the lack of top predators in the ocean
   (B) note why the number of krill is declining
   (C) prove that the zones are harming the oceans
   (D) emphasize how it benefits the Humboldt squid

10. The word persist in the passage is closest in meaning to

   (A) remain
   (B) expand
   (C) return
   (D) continue

11. The word Their in the passage refers to

   (A) Hake and salmon
   (B) Commercial fishermen
   (C) These fish
   (D) The Humboldt squid expansions

12. According to paragraph 5, fishermen are concerned about the expansion of the Humboldt squid because

   (A) they eat too much krill, which the fishermen need to use for bait
   (B) the squid are consuming some fish species that the fishermen try to catch
   (C) several fisheries in South America have been severely depleted
   (D) some governments are considering banning both hake and salmon fishing

significant losses because of the squid. For the moment, that is the only fishery known to have been affected by the squid. Yet, should more squid continue to move to areas in which they do not traditionally go, parts of the eastern Pacific Ocean may undergo tremendous changes.

Glossary
coincide: to happen at the same time; to overlap
unmolested: not bothered or disturbed; alone
fishery: an area, often in an ocean or sea, where many fish live

VIEW TEXT REVIEW HELP BACK NEXT

13. **Directions:** Select the appropriate sentences from the answer choices and match them to the cause and effect of the Humboldt squid expansion to which they relate. TWO of the answer choices will NOT be used. *This question is worth 3 points.*

Cause
(Select 2)

-
-

Effect
(Select 3)

-
-
-

Answer Choices

(A) Sharks and tunas are two creatures that often consume the squid.

(B) Dead zones in the Pacific Ocean are becoming more prevalent.

(C) The squid has become the top predator in the food chain in the dead zones.

(D) Krill are regularly consumed by the Humboldt squid.

(E) Predators have fewer areas in which they can hunt the squid.

(F) A fishery in Chile has seen its fish population go down.

(G) The squid have expanded their range down to the tip of South America.

Drag your answer choices to the spaces where they belong.
To remove an answer choice, click on it. To review the passage, click on **View Text**.

Listening
Section Directions

This section measures your ability to understand conversations and lectures in English.

In this part, you will listen to 1 conversation and 1 lecture. You will hear the conversation or lecture only **one** time. After the conversation or lecture, you will answer some questions about it. The questions typically ask about the main idea and supporting details. Some questions ask about a speaker's purpose or attitude. Answer the questions based on what is stated or implied by the speakers.

You may take notes while you listen. You may use your notes to help you answer the questions. Your notes will **not** be scored.

If you need to change the volume while you listen, click on the **Volume** icon at the top of the screen.

In some questions, you will see this icon: This means that you will hear, but not see, part of the question.

Some of the questions have special directions. These directions appear in a gray box on the screen.

Most questions are worth one point. If a question is worth more than one point, it will have special directions that indicate how many points you can receive.

You must answer each question. After you answer, click on **Next**. Then click on **OK** to confirm your answer and go on to the next question. After you click on **OK**, you cannot return to previous questions.

A clock at the top of the screen will show you how much time is remaining. The clock will not count down while you are listening. The clock will count down only while you are answering the questions.

Now you may begin the Listening section.

Conversation 1~5: Listen to part of a conversation between a student and a professor.

1. What are the speakers mainly discussing?
   - (A) The student's plans for the upcoming semester
   - (B) The student's academic and personal life
   - (C) The student's decision on what her major will be
   - (D) The student's need to improve her grades

2. Why does the professor apologize to the student?
   - (A) Because he is late for their meeting
   - (B) Because he did not respond to her email
   - (C) Because his office is too cluttered
   - (D) Because he lost one of her documents

3. According to the student, in which class is she getting her best grade?
   - (A) Biology
   - (B) Latin
   - (C) Microeconomics
   - (D) Anthropology

4. Why does the student explain about her life before college?
   - (A) To note that she has no problems adjusting to school
   - (B) To let the professor know why she has not chosen a major
   - (C) To explain why she has to find a part-time job
   - (D) To tell the professor why she studies so much

5. What can be inferred about the professor?
   - (A) He is the student's anthropology teacher.
   - (B) He wants the student to major in biology.
   - (C) He rarely has any contact with the student.
   - (D) He believes the student should work less.

Lecture 6~11: Listen to part of a lecture in an environmental sciences class. 03-03

6. According to the professor, what are biofuels typically made of?

   Click on 2 answers.

   (A) Cellulose
   (B) Sugarcane
   (C) Soybeans
   (D) Coal

7. How does the professor organize the information about the manner in which cellulose is transformed into ethanol that she presents to the class?

   (A) She focuses on the explanation in the textbook.
   (B) She shows some illustrations and describes them.
   (C) She covers the process step by step.
   (D) She shows the students a short film clip.

8. According to the professor, what is the first step in processing cellulose into ethanol?

   (A) Conducting acid hydrolysis treatment
   (B) Breaking down the sugar molecules
   (C) Allowing the material to ferment
   (D) Employing enzymes to break down the wood

9. What does the professor imply about ethanol made from cellulose?

   (A) It is used primarily in Brazil.
   (B) It costs more than regular gasoline.
   (C) It is produced in the United States.
   (D) A new way to make it has been discovered.

10. Listen again to part of the lecture. Then answer the question.

    What does the professor imply when she says this?

    (A) Making ethanol takes too long.
    (B) The creation process is complicated.
    (C) She made a mistake in her description.
    (D) It is a waste of time to make ethanol.

11. Listen again to part of the lecture. Then answer the question.

    What can be inferred about the professor when she says this?

    (A) She is a supporter of making ethanol from plant matter.
    (B) She is working on a process to make ethanol from cellulose.
    (C) She thinks cellulose ethanol will never be economically viable.
    (D) She is worried about people cutting down too many trees.

Actual Test
04

Reading
Section Directions

This section measures your ability to understand academic passages in English.

In this part, you will read 1 passage and answer reading comprehension questions about the passage. Most questions are worth one point, but the last question is worth more than one point. The directions indicate how many points you may receive.

Some passages include a word or phrase that is underlined in blue. Click on the word or phrase to see a definition or an explanation.

When you want to move on to the next question, click on **Next**. You may skip questions and go back to them later. If you want to return to previous questions, click on **Back**. You can click on **Review** at any time and the review screen will show you which questions you have answered and which you have not answered. From this review screen, you may go directly to any question you have already seen in the Reading section.

You may now begin the Reading section. You will read 1 reading passage. You will have **20 minutes** to read the passage and answer the questions.

Click on **Continue** to go on.

1. The phrase partake in in the passage is closest in meaning to

   (A) observe
   (B) consider
   (C) participate in
   (D) plan for

2. The word they in the passage refers to

   (A) people
   (B) these mistakes
   (C) other times
   (D) others

3. In paragraph 1, the author implies that people

   (A) join large numbers of groups throughout their lives
   (B) have a general dislike for being by themselves
   (C) perform better when they belong to a group of peers
   (D) make more mistakes when alone than when in a group

4. Which of the sentences below best expresses the essential information in the highlighted sentence in the passage? *Incorrect* answer choices change the meaning in important ways or leave out essential information.

   (A) Parents, teachers, and the police regularly urge teenagers to be on their best behavior at all times.
   (B) If teenagers get caught by their parents or the police, they will cease doing certain activities.
   (C) Because of their moral values, many teenagers do not break the law or do any immoral activities.
   (D) For various reasons, some teenagers do not engage in activities that could get them in trouble.

Peer Pressure

Humans are instinctively social in that the vast majority of them desire companionship and contact with other people. The needs to belong to a group, to be accepted, and to have friends are feelings that most people experience. But part of this urge to belong to a group can lead individuals to feel pressured by others to partake in certain actions that make them uncomfortable. This pressure can cause people to make mistakes in judging what is right and what is wrong. While these mistakes tend to be innocent and cause no harm, at other times, they can be dangerous and may hurt others as well as the people doing these particular actions.

Peers are the people who belong to a person's age group. In many cases, they are individuals with whom a person grows up and attends school. People often become friends with their peers and, accordingly, socialize together and frequently establish bonds that may last a lifetime. As children age, however, they begin to be exposed to activities that are immoral, forbidden, and possibly even against the law. Young people—teenagers in particular—regularly engage in contests of the will against adults such as their parents and teachers. They attempt to see what actions they can get away with without getting into any trouble. As they push the boundaries between right and wrong, they may want their friends to go along with them. However, in every peer group, not all of its members will agree to engage in immoral, forbidden, or illegal activities. Some young people have a sense of morality, fear parental authority, or are afraid of being punished by their parents, the school system, or the police, so they decline to partake in certain activities.

This is when peer pressure comes into play. The others in a peer group may encourage the reluctant individuals until they agree to follow everyone else. When this happens, a person has succumbed to peer pressure. This occurs for a

5. The author's description of teenagers in paragraph 2 mentions which of the following?

    (A) Most of their closest friends are the people they met during their childhood.
    (B) The majority of them commit at least one illegal activity at some time in their lives.
    (C) Their fear of being caught by the police prevents them from illicit behavior.
    (D) When challenging the authority of adults, they often like to be with others.

6. The word derided in the passage is closest in meaning to

    (A) mocked
    (B) assaulted
    (C) rejected
    (D) amused

7. The word ostracized in the passage is closest in meaning to

    (A) repulsed
    (B) excluded
    (C) obtained
    (D) divulged

8. According to paragraph 3, which of the following is NOT true of peer pressure?

    (A) Teenagers face peer pressure more than any other group of people.
    (B) It may result in people being teased for not going along with a group.
    (C) Group members often try to coerce others to act in a similar manner.
    (D) There are a number of reasons people give in to peer pressure.

number of reasons. First, many people want to avoid being derided by their peers. Few people are willing to act by themselves, and most enjoy the comfort of knowing that they belong to a group. One aspect of being in a peer group is that its member must all act as one lest they be ostracized from the group. For children and teens, an unwillingness to follow the group may result in teasing and mockery from the other members. Boys are often ridiculed by having their manhood or bravery questioned while girls are typically insulted for their clothing or appearance. In many cases, the treatment is hurtful and can cause emotional distress. To avoid being taunted, many children and teens yield to peer pressure and act as others do.

A second reason people give in to peer pressure is that they are unwilling to be seen as letting their friends down even if the activity these individuals are doing is illegal or dangerous. This is particularly true for boys, who may have their loyalty to a group questioned should they resist following the others. If they fail to go along, they may be expelled from their peer group and thus will no longer be invited to take part in any activities, legal or otherwise. In this regard, boys may feel that they must remain with their group to avoid becoming outcasts. Being excluded from a peer group is perhaps the biggest fear that compels young people—especially boys—into doing activities that are not permitted to them.

Finally, many young people engage in forbidden acts because they want to be popular with others in their peer groups. ■ Drinking alcohol and smoking cigarettes are activities frequently associated with this aspect of peer pressure. ■ Young people see their parents and other adults drinking and smoking, so they come to consider these actions as both grown up and glamorous. ■ They then seek to imitate adults by partaking in these activities themselves even though they know that their actions might be dangerous to

9. According to paragraph 3, why do some girls have their appearances mocked by others?

   (A) The mockers are hoping to cause the girls emotional stress.

   (B) The way that the girls look is different from the current popular style.

   (C) Other females are upset that those girls are better looking than them.

   (D) The girls are unwilling to engage in behavior being done by a group.

10. The phrase expelled from in the passage is closest in meaning to

   (A) kicked out of

   (B) mistrusted by

   (C) confused by

   (D) abandoned by

11. According to paragraph 4, which of the following is true of boys with regard to peer pressure?

   (A) Some of them, such as star athletes, have no need to join any peer groups.

   (B) They have to decide whether or not to belong to a group or to become outcasts.

   (C) They may do illegal acts so that they do not disappoint their group members.

   (D) They are encouraged to engage in group behavior much more than girls are.

12. In paragraph 5, why does the author mention Drinking alcohol and smoking cigarettes?

   (A) To name two activities that people are often encouraged to do by their peers

   (B) To claim that they are dangerous and can wind up harming many teenagers

   (C) To state that most parents forbid their children from doing either of these activities

   (D) To blame adults for engaging in activities that teenagers like to imitate

themselves or others. ■ In many instances, one member of a group—the leader perhaps—may pressure the others to join him or her in doing these actions. In order to retain their popularity and status in the group, the other members must give in and follow the leader.

Glossary
ridicule: to make fun of
distress: pain; suffering, often of an emotional nature
outcast: a person who is not welcome among others

13. Look at the four squares [■] that indicate where the following sentence could be added to the passage.

For instance, some teens drink and drive and then die in automobile accidents.

Where would the sentence best fit?

Click on a square [■] to add the sentence to the passage.

14. **Directions:** An introductory sentence for a brief summary of the passage is provided below. Complete the summary by selecting the THREE answer choices that express the most important ideas of the passage. Some sentences do not belong because they express ideas that are not presented in the passage or are minor ideas in the passage. *This question is worth 2 points.*

Peer pressure happens when individuals, especially teenagers, are encouraged by others in their groups to do activities that they do not want to.

-
-
-

Answer Choices

(A) Teenagers often face intense pressure to act like the other members of their peer groups.

(B) Some people give in to peer pressure so that they are not expelled from their groups and made outcasts.

(C) The desire to be popular with others often induces teenagers to partake in certain adult activities.

(D) Girls regularly mock one another for their clothes or appearances when they are upset with each other.

(E) Children and teenagers usually make friends with their peers and may remain friends for their entire lives.

(F) Adults frequently have trouble convincing young people not to succumb to peer pressure.

Drag your answer choices to the spaces where they belong.
To remove an answer choice, click on it. To review the passage, click on **View Text**.

 04-01

Listening
Section Directions

This section measures your ability to understand conversations and lectures in English.

In this part, you will listen to 1 conversation and 1 lecture. You will hear the conversation or lecture only **one** time. After the conversation or lecture, you will answer some questions about it. The questions typically ask about the main idea and supporting details. Some questions ask about a speaker's purpose or attitude. Answer the questions based on what is stated or implied by the speakers.

You may take notes while you listen. You may use your notes to help you answer the questions. Your notes will **not** be scored.

If you need to change the volume while you listen, click on the **Volume** icon at the top of the screen.

In some questions, you will see this icon: This means that you will hear, but not see, part of the question.

Some of the questions have special directions. These directions appear in a gray box on the screen.

Most questions are worth one point. If a question is worth more than one point, it will have special directions that indicate how many points you can receive.

You must answer each question. After you answer, click on **Next**. Then click on **OK** to confirm your answer and go on to the next question. After you click on **OK**, you cannot return to previous questions.

A clock at the top of the screen will show you how much time is remaining. The clock will not count down while you are listening. The clock will count down only while you are answering the questions.

Now you may begin the Listening section.

Conversation 1~5: 🎧 Listen to part of a conversation between a student and a housing office employee. ⊙ 04-02

1. Why does the student visit the housing office?

   (A) To request a change in his roommate
   (B) To apply for a single dormitory room
   (C) To complain about a problem in his dormitory
   (D) To ask about a meeting that will be held soon

2. According to the man, what is the school going to do for the students living in Keller Dormitory?

   Click on 2 answers.

   (A) Provide them with transportation to the school
   (B) Let them move into some other dormitories
   (C) Have them stay in a local hotel for a while
   (D) Give them a refund on their housing fees

3. What is the student's attitude toward the man?

   (A) He is upset that the man is not doing more to help.
   (B) He is thankful the man is trying to solve the problem.
   (C) He is respectful of the man's high position.
   (D) He is impatient with the man's stalling tactics.

4. Listen again to part of the conversation. Then answer the question.

   What is the purpose of the man's response?

   (A) To have the student tell him everything he knows about the issue
   (B) To let the student know that the problem will be solved soon
   (C) To admit that other students have told him what is happening
   (D) To encourage the student to trust what he is telling him

5. Listen again to part of the conversation. Then answer the question.

   What does the student imply when he says this?

   (A) He doubts what the man just told him.
   (B) He wants to give the man his opinion.
   (C) He thinks the problem is easy to fix.
   (D) He wants an immediate solution.

Lecture 6~11: Listen to part of a lecture in an archaeology class. 04-03

Archaeology

6. What is the main topic of the lecture?

   (A) The discovery of Troy by Heinrich Schliemann
   (B) The different cities that were found at the Troy site
   (C) Two of the major ancient cities of Troy
   (D) The epic poems *Iliad* and *Odyssey* written by Homer

7. According to the professor, which city was most likely the one involved in the Trojan War?

   (A) Troy Two
   (B) Troy Four
   (C) Troy Seven
   (D) Troy Nine

8. Why does the professor tell the class about the Mycenaeans?

   (A) To mention that they wrote many ancient Greek myths
   (B) To let them know who probably conquered ancient Troy
   (C) To claim that Homer was aware of a great deal about them
   (D) To focus on their responsibility for the Greek Dark Ages

9. What does the professor imply about the Greek Dark Ages?

   (A) The Trojan War was the reason that they began.
   (B) The Greeks made several advances during this time.
   (C) Most Greek myths were created in this period.
   (D) There is little known about what happened in them.

10. Why does the professor mention Alexander the Great?

    (A) To show that Alexander believed that Troy had been a real city
    (B) To claim that Alexander had looked for Troy in the wrong place
    (C) To state that Alexander felt a connection with the Trojans
    (D) To stress that Alexander knew a lot about ancient Greek history

11. What is the professor's attitude toward Frank Calvert?

    (A) He should also be given credit for the discovery of Troy.
    (B) He was only a treasure hunter much like Schliemann was.
    (C) He was responsible for the world's greatest archaeological discovery.
    (D) He was an authority on the ancient Greeks and Trojans.

Actual Test 05

Reading

Section Directions

This section measures your ability to understand academic passages in English.

In this part, you will read 1 passage and answer reading comprehension questions about the passage. Most questions are worth one point, but the last question is worth more than one point. The directions indicate how many points you may receive.

Some passages include a word or phrase that is underlined in blue. Click on the word or phrase to see a definition or an explanation.

When you want to move on to the next question, click on **Next**. You may skip questions and go back to them later. If you want to return to previous questions, click on **Back**. You can click on **Review** at any time and the review screen will show you which questions you have answered and which you have not answered. From this review screen, you may go directly to any question you have already seen in the Reading section.

You may now begin the Reading section. You will read 1 reading passage. You will have **20 minutes** to read the passage and answer the questions.

Click on **Continue** to go on.

1. According to paragraph 1, which of the following is true of chemicals that are released into the environment?

   (A) It is possible for some of them to create problems that last for years.

   (B) Most of them are intentionally released into the environment by companies.

   (C) The majority of them affect the soil rather than the water or air.

   (D) They are the main reason that people are worried about the environment.

2. In paragraph 2, the author discusses acute exposure and chronic exposure in order to

   (A) show how both of them are responsible for killing a large number of organisms

   (B) mention how long-term effects are more disastrous than short-term ones

   (C) note the side effects of chemical exposure that people can suffer from

   (D) describe two ways that organisms and the environment are affected by chemicals

3. The word them in the passage refers to

   (A) the water, soil, and air

   (B) these chemicals

   (C) various processes

   (D) living organisms

4. The author's description of chronic exposure in paragraph 2 mentions all of the following EXCEPT:

   (A) It infects organisms through the transmission of chemicals in the environment.

   (B) It often involves smaller amounts of chemical doses than does acute exposure.

   (C) The most common way in which organisms are affected is through plant matter.

   (D) Organisms can suffer from this through either direct or indirect exposure.

The Effects of Toxic Chemicals on the Environment

Chemicals are used in a wide variety of industrial, transportation, and agricultural processes as they allow people to manufacture many products, to move farther and faster, and to grow more crops than ever before. However, many of these chemicals can harm the environment and cause damage to the soil, water, and air. Once released into the environment, these chemicals may be absorbed by plants, humans, and other animals. The short-term results are devastating at times. Many chemicals also pose long-term threats that frequently require decades to bring under control. Resultantly, controlling chemicals and preventing them from entering the environment is a major concern.

A chemical's lethality is measured by its toxicity. Some are more toxic than others as a small dose of one chemical may be more harmful than a large dose of another. There are two primary ways in which the environment, as well as living organisms, becomes exposed to these toxic chemicals: acute exposure and chronic exposure. Acute exposure refers to the onetime exposure to a highly toxic chemical. This chemical may be directly absorbed by an organism through ingestion, absorption, or breathing, and ill health or death may quickly ensue. Chronic exposure, however, takes place over a long period of time and in smaller doses. In the environment, chronic exposure happens mostly due to chemicals found in the water, soil, and air. As these chemicals, which are typically diluted by various processes, enter the environment, living organisms get exposed to them. This may be direct or indirect exposure. Plants, for instance, may be directly exposed to chemicals while the animals that eat their leaves are subsequently indirectly exposed to them.

The harmful effects of toxic chemicals on the environment and organisms vary depending

5. The word prime in the passage is closest in meaning to

Ⓐ leading
Ⓑ initial
Ⓒ common
Ⓓ extensive

6. In paragraph 3, why does the author mention miscarriages, birth defects, and cancer?

Ⓐ To name some problems suffered by people due to exposure to chemicals
Ⓑ To explain three major side-effects that most chemicals have on people
Ⓒ To emphasize that the high rate of these problems is a natural phenomenon
Ⓓ To point out that the people of Hinkley suffered from these less than did others

7. According to paragraph 3, the people of Hinkley, California, suffered problems because

Ⓐ a company exposed them to lethal doses of chemicals
Ⓑ nearly half of them developed some kind of cancer
Ⓒ the government failed to warn them about chemical dumping
Ⓓ their water supply was tainted with harmful chemicals

8. In paragraph 4, the author implies that acid rain

Ⓐ has been known to cause cancer in humans
Ⓑ would decrease if people began to use more nuclear power
Ⓒ only began to be a problem when industrialization began
Ⓓ contains larger amounts of sulfur than of nitrogen

upon the toxicity levels and the amount of time that exposure to the chemicals takes. In many prominent cases involving toxic chemical waste dumps near towns, the effects took years to manifest themselves, but they proved to be deadly. For instance, the Love Canal neighborhood in Niagara Falls, New York, and the entire town of Hinkley, California, are prime examples of the disasters that can occur when chemicals enter the environment. In both towns, excessive amounts of chemicals were introduced into the local water systems. Over a period of years, their residents suffered higher than normal levels of miscarriages, birth defects, and cancer. Eventually, the residents successfully sued the companies responsible, but the harm had already been done.

In recent decades, two of the biggest problems concerning chemicals have been acid rain and agricultural runoff. ■ Acid rain is the result of the industrialization of the planet and of humanity's dependence on the internal combustion engine for transportation and electricity for power. ■ The burning of fossil fuels to operate the machinery used in the modern world has released massive amounts of sulfur and nitrogen into the atmosphere, where they proceed to form acidic compounds. ■ These compounds attach themselves to water vapor and later fall to the ground when it rains. ■ In the process, they damage plants and animals and can even erode the concrete structures of buildings.

As for agricultural chemicals, the primary issue with them is the nitrates that are used in fertilizers. These nitrates are absorbed by the soil and help plants grow, but they are also absorbed by the water system and eventually run off into rivers, lakes, and oceans. Concentrated amounts of nitrates can create algae blooms, which cause a sudden increase in the amount of algae growing in the water. The algae absorb most of the oxygen in the water, which suffocates fish and other

9. The word Concentrated in the passage is closest in meaning to

   (A) Potent
   (B) Restricted
   (C) Accumulated
   (D) Fertilized

10. Which of the sentences below best expresses the essential information in the highlighted sentence in the passage? *Incorrect* answer choices change the meaning in important ways or leave out essential information.

    (A) The oxygen is absorbed by the algae, so most aquatic life dies when dead zones are created.
    (B) The dead zones that are created permit only very small creatures to survive in the water.
    (C) Algae grow so quickly that fish and other animals are not able to get enough oxygen to live.
    (D) Algae, fish, and marine life need oxygen, but the dead zones kill all of the organisms in them.

11. In stating that people's efforts are often all for naught, the author means that people's efforts are

    (A) ridiculed
    (B) ineffective
    (C) inane
    (D) thoughtless

12. According to paragraph 6, it is difficult to keep chemicals out of the environment because

    (A) most companies prefer to dump chemicals rather than to dispose of them properly
    (B) chemicals that get burned enter the atmosphere and cause harm in that way
    (C) some nations do not have strict enough laws concerning chemical dumping
    (D) people are not aware of the environmental damage that chemicals can cause

marine life, thereby creating dead zones in the water where little, if any, life exists.

Efforts to prevent toxic chemicals from entering the environment are underway all around the world, but people's efforts are often all for naught. Additionally, much of the equipment and procedures for controlling chemical waste are expensive and not high priorities for many companies despite their protests to the contrary. Furthermore, rules and regulations concerning chemical usage and dumping differ from nation to nation; some have stringent rules while others are more lax. Yet the environment lacks borders, and chemical pollutants from one country can easily affect people and the land in another, which makes the need for stricter laws concerning toxic chemicals even greater.

Glossary
lethality: the deadliness of something
prominent: famous; well-known
algae bloom: the rapid increase in the amount of algae in a certain place

VIEW TEXT REVIEW HELP BACK NEXT

---

13. Look at the four squares [■] that indicate where the following sentence could be added to the passage.

    This acid rain often falls in countries other than where its pollutants were expelled into the air.

    Where would the sentence best fit?

    Click on a square [■] to add the sentence to the passage.

---

14. **Directions:** An introductory sentence for a brief summary of the passage is provided below. Complete the summary by selecting the THREE answer choices that express the most important ideas of the passage. Some sentences do not belong because they express ideas that are not presented in the passage or are minor ideas in the passage. *This question is worth 2 points.*

Many chemicals that are released into the environment can harm the land, air, and water as well as organisms.

-
-
-

Answer Choices

(A) There are not enough environmental regulations to prevent people and companies from polluting the land.

(B) Some people have successfully sued companies that released chemicals into the environment.

(C) Acute exposure and chronic exposure are two ways in which chemicals may affect the environment.

(D) Some fertilizers cause large amounts of chemicals to enter the water, where they can do great harm.

(E) Thanks to chemicals, the overall quality of most humans' lives has increased a great deal.

(F) Some chemicals cause immediate problems while others can harm the environment for decades.

Drag your answer choices to the spaces where they belong.
To remove an answer choice, click on it. To review the passage, click on **View Text**.

Listening

Section Directions

This section measures your ability to understand conversations and lectures in English.

In this part, you will listen to 1 conversation and 1 lecture. You will hear the conversation or lecture only **one** time. After the conversation or lecture, you will answer some questions about it. The questions typically ask about the main idea and supporting details. Some questions ask about a speaker's purpose or attitude. Answer the questions based on what is stated or implied by the speakers.

You may take notes while you listen. You may use your notes to help you answer the questions. Your notes will **not** be scored.

If you need to change the volume while you listen, click on the **Volume** icon at the top of the screen.

In some questions, you will see this icon: ⌒ This means that you will hear, but not see, part of the question.

Some of the questions have special directions. These directions appear in a gray box on the screen.

Most questions are worth one point. If a question is worth more than one point, it will have special directions that indicate how many points you can receive.

You must answer each question. After you answer, click on **Next**. Then click on **OK** to confirm your answer and go on to the next question. After you click on **OK**, you cannot return to previous questions.

A clock at the top of the screen will show you how much time is remaining. The clock will not count down while you are listening. The clock will count down only while you are answering the questions.

Now you may begin the Listening section.

Conversation 1~5: Listen to part of a conversation between a student and a professor.

1. According to the professor, what kind of poem was the student supposed to write?

    (A) A sonnet
    (B) A short poem
    (C) A haiku
    (D) A 100-line poem

2. What does the professor imply about the student's poem?

    (A) It needs to be shortened and rewritten.
    (B) Its subject matter is easy to understand.
    (C) It was the best poem in her class.
    (D) It uses many outstanding images.

3. Why does the professor mention *The Penfeather*?

    (A) To indicate that its editor wants to publish the student's work
    (B) To encourage the student to apply for a position with it
    (C) To ask the student to submit her poem to it
    (D) To have the student read the most recent edition to get some ideas

4. What will the student probably do next?

    (A) Call the editor of *The Penfeather*
    (B) Rewrite her poem for the professor
    (C) Go to Professor Killian's office
    (D) Talk to the professor about another topic

5. Listen again to part of the conversation. Then answer the question.

    What does the professor imply when she says this?

    (A) She and Professor Killian teach the same topic.
    (B) Professor Killian's classes are very popular.
    (C) There are few students in Professor Killian's classes.
    (D) The student will be a sophomore next year.

Lecture 6~11: Listen to part of a lecture in a marine biology class. 05-03

Marine Biology

6. What is the main topic of the lecture?

   (A) The migration habits of gray whales
   (B) Gray whales and humpback whales
   (C) Where in the oceans gray whales live
   (D) How gray whales manage to migrate

7. According to the professor, why do whales migrate?

   Click on 2 answers.

   (A) To seek access to food sources
   (B) To escape from predators
   (C) To be able to swim in cold water
   (D) To mate and bear young

8. Why does the professor explain how scientists track whales?

   (A) To emphasize why the tracking data can be trusted
   (B) To mention why they know where whale transit points are
   (C) To show how tracking methods have changed over time
   (D) To prove that some whales migrate more than 10,000 kilometers

9. Based on the information in the lecture, indicate whether the statements refer to gray whales or humpback whales.

   Click in the correct box for each statement.

	Gray Whales	Humpback Whales
(A) A group of them migrates to Hawaii yearly.		
(B) They have mottled skin and fins.		
(C) Some of them live in the water around Antarctica.		
(D) They migrate to Mexico in the winter.		

10. According to the professor, how do gray whales probably know when to migrate?

    (A) The local environment becomes different.
    (B) Less food becomes available.
    (C) The female whales give birth.
    (D) Predators move nearby in great numbers.

11. Listen again to part of the lecture. Then answer the question. 🎧

    What does the professor imply when he says this?

    (A) It takes one year for a baby whale to mature.
    (B) Gray whales have a long gestation period.
    (C) Females give birth once every two years.
    (D) Young whales are strong enough to migrate.

Actual Test 06

Reading
Section Directions

This section measures your ability to understand academic passages in English.

In this part, you will read 1 passage and answer reading comprehension questions about the passage. Most questions are worth one point, but the last question is worth more than one point. The directions indicate how many points you may receive.

Some passages include a word or phrase that is <u>underlined</u> in blue. Click on the word or phrase to see a definition or an explanation.

When you want to move on to the next question, click on **Next**. You may skip questions and go back to them later. If you want to return to previous questions, click on **Back**. You can click on **Review** at any time and the review screen will show you which questions you have answered and which you have not answered. From this review screen, you may go directly to any question you have already seen in the Reading section.

You may now begin the Reading section. You will read 1 reading passage. You will have **20 minutes** to read the passage and answer the questions.

Click on **Continue** to go on.

1. The word **it** in the passage refers to

   Ⓐ the Mayan Empire
   Ⓑ diffusion
   Ⓒ writing
   Ⓓ the present

2. Which of the following can be inferred from paragraph 1 about the first writing systems?

   Ⓐ It took hundreds of years for them to be made.
   Ⓑ They are too complicated for people to translate.
   Ⓒ No one is sure exactly how they were created.
   Ⓓ Their creators utilized diffusion to make them.

3. The author's description of the first writing systems in paragraph 1 mentions which of the following?

   Ⓐ All four of the first writing systems influenced one another.
   Ⓑ All of them were created several millennia in the past.
   Ⓒ The Chinese invented writing earlier than the Egyptians did.
   Ⓓ The writing of the Mayan Empire was the most complicated.

4. The word **them** in the passage refers to

   Ⓐ the wedge-shaped symbols
   Ⓑ the tablets
   Ⓒ thousands of years
   Ⓓ archaeologists

Early Forms of Writing

Writing is a means of communication and a way to keep records, to entertain people through stories, and to preserve the past with historical accounts. Mankind invented writing in several separate places at different times in the past. Thousands of years ago, people somehow took the spoken word and created symbols that represented those words. Historical linguists have indentified four places where cultures invented some form of writing: Sumer (modern-day Iraq), Egypt, China, and the Mayan Empire (Central America). While other cultures developed writing, their writing methods were derived from one of the four original systems of writing either directly or through diffusion. Slowly, but steadily, writing spread and evolved until the present, where **it** exists in some form virtually everywhere.

The first form of writing was cuneiform, which originated in Sumerian culture around 3000 B.C. The Sumerians had a system of pictorial symbols that they had used for accounting for hundreds of years. These symbols were developed into cuneiform. It started as pictures representing common everyday aspects of Sumerian life. It was not based on the sounds of Sumerian words and had little in the way of grammar. The pictures were drawn on soft clay tablets with a <u>stylus</u>. The wedge-shaped symbols then dried in the soft clay. The tablets were so well preserved that, thousands of years later, archaeologists have discovered hundreds of **them** at various sites throughout former Sumerian lands. Gradually, as the Sumerians began combining pictures to make new words, cuneiform became a phonetic writing system based on the sounds of the Sumerian language.

In its more evolved form, cuneiform contained three types of symbols that represented spoken language. First, there were logograms, which are symbols that stand for a complete word. Second were phonetic signs, which represent a syllable,

5. According to paragraph 2, which of the following is NOT true of cuneiform?

   (A) It developed over time to become a writing system based on phonetics.
   (B) The Sumerians used it to make records that they kept on clay tablets.
   (C) It utilized various symbols that were shaped in the form of wedges.
   (D) It was invented by the Sumerians sometime around 3,000 years ago.

6. The word ambiguity in the passage is closest in meaning to

   (A) dispute
   (B) recognition
   (C) uncertainty
   (D) remembrance

7. According to paragraph 3, cuneiform utilized logograms in order to

   (A) stand for various words in their entirety
   (B) add to the meanings of other symbols
   (C) represent parts of certain words
   (D) clarify the grammatical meanings of sentences

8. According to paragraph 4, the Sumerian bureaucracy created the first accounting system because

   (A) Sumerian leaders wanted to maintain tight control over their people
   (B) there was a need to monitor both the products and people in Sumer
   (C) the soldiers in the Sumerian army required an effective logistics system
   (D) it improved the economic viability of the entire region

letter, part of a word, or grammatical element. Finally, there are specialized marks that were added when there was some ambiguity as to the meaning of a symbol. These were utilized when a certain symbol or a combination of symbols could have more than one meaning. The Sumerians also organized their writing. They read it from top to bottom in rows and from left to right, a pattern which most writing systems in the Western world follow.

The evolution of writing in Sumer was not something that happened overnight. It took a long time to develop, and, fortunately for the Sumerians, the civilization that they built gave their scholars enough time to construct the language. In addition, the nature of Sumerian society called for a writing system in which both people and products were kept track of. In Sumer, there were a ruling elite, priests, and soldiers, all of whom were fed by the labor of a huge number of farmers. A bureaucracy to keep track of food and other supplies thus emerged. It was these bureaucrats who created the first accounting system.

Similar events happened in Egypt, China, and the Mayan Empire, all three of which also had enduring stable civilizations. In Egypt, hieroglyphics—a system of logograms—was used for thousands of years. Linguists believe that the Chinese writing system evolved from symbols scratched into soft seashells and turtle shells that were employed for divination. Like the Sumerians, the Mayans used both logograms and phonetic signs. However, linguists have had a harder time determining the origins and evolution of the Mayan writing system since few samples of it survived the European conquest of their lands, and they have not been deciphered in their entirety.

From these four places, writing later spread to other lands in one of two ways: blueprint copying or diffusion. Blueprint copying happens when one

9. The word **enduring** in the passage is closest in meaning to

   (A) peaceful
   (B) advanced
   (C) scholarly
   (D) long-lasting

10. The word **conquest** in the passage is closest in meaning to

    (A) defeat
    (B) invasion
    (C) assault
    (D) colonization

11. In paragraph 6, the author uses **the Latin alphabet** as an example of

    (A) how diffusion was employed to create several writing systems
    (B) an alphabet that was created by people in the Middle East
    (C) the utilization of blueprint copying by a number of cultures
    (D) a writing system that is quite similar to that used by the Greeks

12. Which of the sentences below best expresses the essential information in the highlighted sentence in the passage? *Incorrect* answer choices change the meaning in important ways or leave out essential information.

    (A) It was necessary for people to create their own writing systems based on those of other cultures by using diffusion.
    (B) Sometimes, people in one culture modeled their writing systems on those of other cultures, which is a process known as diffusion.
    (C) Diffusion occurred when people were aware of the existence of writing systems but did not know exactly how they were done.
    (D) It took a long time for writing to diffuse to other cultures because most people knew that it could be done but did not know how to do it.

group directly adopts another's writing system and then modifies it to fit its own culture. Most cultures which adapted the Latin alphabet for their languages used blueprint copying, and the Latin alphabet itself came from Greek and some Middle Eastern alphabets. Diffusion was a slightly more complex way of creating a writing system. In diffusion, people in a culture knew that writing was possible and had some basic ideas about how it was done, but they lacked a complete knowledge of another culture's writing system or the symbols that were used. Therefore, through the process of trial and error, a new writing system, one which may have had similarities to other writing systems but which was not a direct copy, was developed.

Glossary
stylus: an ancient instrument used for writing on wax tablets
divination: the practice of trying to tell the future through supernatural methods
decipher: to decode; to figure out the meaning of something hidden or encoded

VIEW TEXT    

13. **Directions:** Select the appropriate statement from the answer choices and match them to the early writing system to which they relate. TWO of the answer choices will NOT be used. *This question is worth 3 points.*

Sumerian
(Select 3)

- •
- •
- •

Egyptian, Chinese, and Mayan
(Select 2)

- •
- •

Answer Choices

(A) Utilized both logograms and phonetic symbols

(B) Was first created because of the effects of diffusion

(C) Used various symbols in a system known as cuneiform

(D) Had many early writing samples destroyed by invaders

(E) Developed from a system that was employed for divination

(F) Was created to help bureaucrats do accounting

(G) Made use of the Latin alphabet for many years

Drag your answer choices to the spaces where they belong.
To remove an answer choice, click on it. To review the passage, click on **View Text**.

Listening

Section Directions

This section measures your ability to understand conversations and lectures in English.

In this part, you will listen to 1 conversation and 1 lecture. You will hear the conversation or lecture only **one** time. After the conversation or lecture, you will answer some questions about it. The questions typically ask about the main idea and supporting details. Some questions ask about a speaker's purpose or attitude. Answer the questions based on what is stated or implied by the speakers.

You may take notes while you listen. You may use your notes to help you answer the questions. Your notes will **not** be scored.

If you need to change the volume while you listen, click on the **Volume** icon at the top of the screen.

In some questions, you will see this icon: 🎧 This means that you will hear, but not see, part of the question.

Some of the questions have special directions. These directions appear in a gray box on the screen.

Most questions are worth one point. If a question is worth more than one point, it will have special directions that indicate how many points you can receive.

You must answer each question. After you answer, click on **Next**. Then click on **OK** to confirm your answer and go on to the next question. After you click on **OK**, you cannot return to previous questions.

A clock at the top of the screen will show you how much time is remaining. The clock will not count down while you are listening. The clock will count down only while you are answering the questions.

Now you may begin the Listening section.

Conversation 1~5: Listen to part of a conversation between a student and the dean of students. 06-02

1. Why did the student receive an award?

   (A) She has the highest grades in her class.
   (B) She performed well on a standardized test.
   (C) An essay she wrote won first prize in a contest.
   (D) She was the best player on the soccer team.

2. What is the dean's opinion of the student?

   (A) He offers no opinion.
   (B) He wants her to work harder.
   (C) He thinks highly of her.
   (D) He has little respect for her.

3. Why did the dean ask the student to visit his office?

   (A) To name her the class valedictorian
   (B) To tell her about a new class the school is offering
   (C) To encourage her to apply for a grant
   (D) To discuss a special scholarship with her

4. In the conversation, the dean describes a number of facts about the Furman Prize. Indicate whether each of the following is a fact about the Furman Prize.

   Click in the correct box for each statement.

	Fact	Not a Fact
(A) It provides spending money for a student.		
(B) A student must write an essay to apply for it.		
(C) It pays a student's tuition for four years.		
(D) The winning student gets free room and board.		

5. What does the dean imply about the Furman Prize?

   (A) The student is likely to win it this year.
   (B) It will be discontinued after this semester.
   (C) The student could win it if she writes an essay.
   (D) It will soon permit a student to study in Asia.

Lecture 6~11: Listen to part of a lecture in an economics class. 06-03

6. What is the main topic of the lecture?

   (A) British and Spanish colonies in the Americas
   (B) The main aspects of mercantilism
   (C) The urge for home countries to gain colonies
   (D) The reason gold and silver were desired

7. Based on the information in the lecture, indicate whether the statements refer to home countries or colonies.

   Click in the correct box for each statement.

	Home Countries	Colonies
(A) They were needed for their natural resources.		
(B) Finished products were mostly made there.		
(C) They often heavily taxed various goods.		
(D) Black Africans were sent there as slaves.		

8. According to the professor, how did the Spanish treat the natives in their colonies?

   (A) They were treated as well as British colonists.
   (B) They were enslaved along with Africans.
   (C) They were mostly ignored by the Spanish.
   (D) They were exploited to a great extent.

9. What will the professor probably do next?

   (A) Discuss the American Revolution
   (B) Talk about some aspects of mercantilism
   (C) Describe the triangle trade some more
   (D) Lecture on the economics of colonialism

10. Listen again to part of the lecture. Then answer the question.

    What does the professor mean when he says this?

    (A) Mercantilism is a concept the students must know about.
    (B) He is going to spend his time lecturing on mercantilism.
    (C) The students do not understand what mercantilism is.
    (D) He would like the students to contribute to the discussion.

11. Listen again to part of the lecture. Then answer the question.

    What is the purpose of the professor's response?

    (A) To discuss the relevance of the question
    (B) To ignore the question
    (C) To get the student to answer her own question
    (D) To praise the student

Actual Test 07

Reading
Section Directions

This section measures your ability to understand academic passages in English.

In this part, you will read 1 passage and answer reading comprehension questions about the passage. Most questions are worth one point, but the last question is worth more than one point. The directions indicate how many points you may receive.

Some passages include a word or phrase that is <u>underlined</u> in blue. Click on the word or phrase to see a definition or an explanation.

When you want to move on to the next question, click on **Next**. You may skip questions and go back to them later. If you want to return to previous questions, click on **Back**. You can click on **Review** at any time and the review screen will show you which questions you have answered and which you have not answered. From this review screen, you may go directly to any question you have already seen in the Reading section.

You may now begin the Reading section. You will read 1 reading passage. You will have **20 minutes** to read the passage and answer the questions.

Click on **Continue** to go on.

1. The word harbored in the passage is closest in meaning to

   (A) promoted
   (B) grew
   (C) sheltered
   (D) expanded

2. In paragraph 1, the author's description of water on Mars mentions all of the following EXCEPT:

   (A) the places on the planet where it is located
   (B) when its presence on Mars was first proven
   (C) the amount of it that is located underground
   (D) the manner in which it was discovered to be there

3. The author discusses the *Viking* probes in paragraph 2 in order to

   (A) describe how they proved the existence of water on Mars
   (B) focus on how humans were studying Mars in-depth in the 1970s
   (C) explain how scientists learned about the topography of Mars
   (D) provide information on the composition of the atmosphere of Mars

4. The word it in the passage refers to

   (A) the second *Viking* probe
   (B) the surface of the planet
   (C) the thin atmosphere
   (D) water vapor

Water on Mars

Most organisms on Earth require water to survive, so scientists believe that any carbon-based life that exists on other worlds will have an identical need for water. The discovery of water on Mars in the early twenty-first century led some experts to speculate that life exists there; however, the satellites that flew by or landed on Mars have thus far found no evidence of any living organisms. Currently, the water on Mars is either frozen at the polar ice caps or lies deep underground, yet the fact that evidence exists that water flowed freely over the Martian surface in the past gives hope to some scientists that the planet once harbored life.

The first proof of water on Mars came from photographs taken by satellites that passed close by the planet's surface. These pictures revealed a topography that showed signs of water erosion. Broad formations that were similar to river valleys and river systems with numerous tributaries branching off extended for hundreds of kilometers all across the Martian landscape. Later, when the *Viking* probes landed on Mars in the mid-1970s, some experiments they conducted on the soil led scientists to conclude that water had once flowed freely on Mars' surface. The second *Viking* probe even transmitted pictures that looked as though there was frost on the surface of the planet, thereby suggesting that the thin atmosphere held water vapor. Unfortunately, it was unable to take any samples, so the pictures were inconclusive.

Later photographic evidence of Mars' north and south poles showed vast white-colored regions that appeared to be covered in snow and ice. The ice caps around both of the poles are believed to be approximately three kilometers thick. Readings from orbital satellites show that the white patches are indeed ice and are comprised mostly of frozen carbon dioxide but also of frozen water. It is suspected that the top layers are primarily frozen carbon dioxide while underneath is a much large

5. According to paragraph 2, which of the following is true of the second *Viking* probe?

   (A) It proved that water was once located on Mars' surface.

   (B) It transmitted photographic evidence of frost on Mars.

   (C) It supplied scientists with copious information on Mars' atmosphere.

   (D) It was specifically designed to map the planet's surface.

6. The phrase bathed in in the passage is closest in meaning to

   (A) rotated by

   (B) blockaded by

   (C) shown to

   (D) immersed in

7. According to paragraph 3, which of the following is NOT true of Mars' polar ice caps?

   (A) They change in size according to the seasons.

   (B) They contain carbon dioxide as well as ice.

   (C) They have been visited by several satellites.

   (D) They sometimes receive very little sunlight.

8. In paragraph 3, the author implies that the satellites sent to Mars

   (A) always orbit the planet rather than land on it

   (B) would be more productive if they landed at a polar ice cap

   (C) need to be upgraded in order to send back better information

   (D) will never be able to prove how much water Mars has

layer of frozen water. However, since no satellites have landed at either ice cap, the precise composition of the Martian polar caps remains a mystery. Scientists have learned, though, that both polar caps shrink and expand with the changing of the Martian seasons. As Mars' axis is tilted like Earth's, at times, one pole is in virtually complete darkness while the other is exposed to almost continual sunlight as the planet orbits the sun. The pole bathed in sunlight often has some of its carbon dioxide melt while the other sees an increase in its amount of frozen carbon dioxide.

Nevertheless, even though the carbon dioxide both freezes and thaws throughout the Martian year, there is no liquid water on Mars. The primary reason for this is that both the temperature and the pressure on Mars reduce any water either to its frozen or gaseous state virtually immediately. Still, there is evidence that water once flowed on the planet's surface. Scientists believe that Mars, like Earth, experienced many volcanic eruptions millions of years ago. This high level of volcanic activity gave Mars a thick, warm atmosphere full of water vapor. Rain fell, water accumulated, and rivers, lakes, and possibly even oceans existed. However, the atmosphere changed over time. Mars' weak magnetic field was unable to retain its atmosphere, which was gradually stripped away by solar winds. These exposed the surface water to high levels of radiation and low temperatures, so the water gradually evaporated or froze.

Since water once flowed on Mars' surface, astronomers wonder if life ever existed there. Most have decided that carbon-based life probably never lived on the planet. The reason is that Mars lies on the periphery of what astronomers call the life zone, which is the region of space that is neither too close to the sun nor too far from it for life to exist. A planet like Mercury, which is too close to the sun, receives a great amount of heat and radiation from the sun, thereby making it impossible for life to survive there. Meanwhile,

9. The word **thaws** in the passage is closest in meaning to

    (A) disappears
    (B) diffuses
    (C) evaporates
    (D) melts

10. The word **which** in the passage refers to

    (A) rivers, lakes, and possibly even oceans
    (B) Mars' weak magnetic field
    (C) its atmosphere
    (D) solar winds

11. According to paragraph 4, Mars used to have a thick atmosphere because

    (A) it experienced a great number of volcanic eruptions
    (B) it used to be closer to the sun than it currently is
    (C) the sun's solar winds were once not particularly harsh
    (D) the percentage of oxygen in the atmosphere was higher

12. The word **periphery** in the passage is closest in meaning to

    (A) extent
    (B) edge
    (C) region
    (D) topside

13. The author's description of the life zone in paragraph 5 mentions which of the following?

    (A) It covers an area extending millions of kilometers from the sun.
    (B) The only planet within it in the solar system is Earth.
    (C) It is possible for life to be discovered outside it.
    (D) Neither Mercury nor Jupiter lies within its boundaries.

planets such as Jupiter and Saturn are too far from the sun, so they do not receive enough heat to support life. Of course, it is possible that life may exist on Mars, but, if that is the case, it is likely different from the carbon-based organisms that thrive on Earth. Until future missions to Mars are carried out, scientists will not be able to know the truth.

Glossary
topography: the geographical features of an area of land
frost: a covering of tiny bits of ice created when dew freezes
axis: the line around which a planet revolves

VIEW TEXT  REVIEW  HELP  BACK  NEXT 

14. **Directions:** An introductory sentence for a brief summary of the passage is provided below. Complete the summary by selecting the THREE answer choices that express the most important ideas of the passage. Some sentences do not belong because they express ideas that are not presented in the passage or are minor ideas in the passage *This question is worth 2 points.*

The recent discovery of water on Mars has caused some scientists to wonder if the planet has ever had life on it.

-
-
-

Answer Choices

(A) Some government agencies are planning to send more satellites to Mars in the next few years.

(B) Scientists believe that Mars has a better chance of supporting life than do Mercury, Jupiter, and Saturn.

(C) Satellites sent to Mars in the 1970s were the first to confirm that there was water on the planet.

(D) The water that is found at the polar ice caps lies beneath a solid layer of frozen carbon dioxide.

(E) Much of the water that exists on Mars is either frozen in places or is found deep in the ground.

(F) Even though water once flowed freely on Mars, its location in the life zone makes the possibility of life being on it remote.

Drag your answer choices to the spaces where they belong.
To remove an answer choice, click on it. To review the passage, click on **View Text**.

Listening

Section Directions

This section measures your ability to understand conversations and lectures in English.

In this part, you will listen to 1 conversation and 1 lecture. You will hear the conversation or lecture only **one** time. After the conversation or lecture, you will answer some questions about it. The questions typically ask about the main idea and supporting details. Some questions ask about a speaker's purpose or attitude. Answer the questions based on what is stated or implied by the speakers.

You may take notes while you listen. You may use your notes to help you answer the questions. Your notes will **not** be scored.

If you need to change the volume while you listen, click on the **Volume** icon at the top of the screen.

In some questions, you will see this icon: This means that you will hear, but not see, part of the question.

Some of the questions have special directions. These directions appear in a gray box on the screen.

Most questions are worth one point. If a question is worth more than one point, it will have special directions that indicate how many points you can receive.

You must answer each question. After you answer, click on **Next**. Then click on **OK** to confirm your answer and go on to the next question. After you click on **OK**, you cannot return to previous questions.

A clock at the top of the screen will show you how much time is remaining. The clock will not count down while you are listening. The clock will count down only while you are answering the questions.

Now you may begin the Listening section.

Conversation 1~5: Listen to part of a conversation between a student and a professor.

07-02

1. What problem does the student have?

   Ⓐ She is not prepared to take her final exam.
   Ⓑ She has missed too many classes to pass the course.
   Ⓒ She does not understand the professor's lectures.
   Ⓓ She failed to submit one of her assignments.

2. Why has the student not been attending the professor's class?

   Ⓐ She was hospitalized for a few weeks.
   Ⓑ The class is held too early in the morning.
   Ⓒ She had a problem with her work schedule.
   Ⓓ She was taking care of a sick parent.

3. What does the student imply about her winter break?

   Ⓐ She is going to take a trip during it.
   Ⓑ She will enroll in vacation classes.
   Ⓒ She will spend it doing schoolwork.
   Ⓓ She is going to find a part-time job during it.

4. Listen again to part of the conversation. Then answer the question.

   What does the professor mean when she says this?

   Ⓐ She cannot solve the student's problem.
   Ⓑ Stress is a major issue for the student.
   Ⓒ It is all right for the student to be nervous.
   Ⓓ The student is worried for no reason.

5. Listen again to part of the conversation. Then answer the question.

   What does the student imply when she says this?

   Ⓐ She is disappointed by her grades this semester.
   Ⓑ She will ask her other professors for incompletes.
   Ⓒ She has already spoken with her other professors.
   Ⓓ She will have to work harder next semester.

Lecture 6~11: Listen to part of a lecture in a drama class. 07-03

Drama

6. What aspect of Jerzy Grotowski does the professor mainly discuss?

    (A) Konstantin Stanislavsky's influence on him
    (B) His work with the Poor Theater Group
    (C) His beliefs pertaining to the theater
    (D) The ten principles of acting that he wrote

7. What is the professor's opinion of Jerzy Grotowski?

    (A) He was an excellent theater director.
    (B) He was even more influential than Stanislavsky.
    (C) He wrote some of history's best plays.
    (D) He is the professor's least favorite director.

8. How does the professor organize the information about Jerzy Grotowski's life that he presents to the class?

    (A) By ignoring the time he spent in Italy
    (B) By focusing primarily on his time in the West
    (C) By closely examining his formative years
    (D) By covering it in chronological order

9. According to the professor, how did Grotowski view the members of the audience watching his plays?

    (A) As something necessary but not really desired
    (B) As people that should be involved in the performance
    (C) As extras that could be given minor speaking roles
    (D) As enlightened individuals who had contributions to make

10. Why does the professor mention the travel restrictions in Eastern Europe?

    (A) To explain why Grotowski was relatively unknown in Western Europe
    (B) To note the novelty of Grotowski's troupe traveling to the West
    (C) To give the reason that Grotowski sought asylum in the United States
    (D) To stress why Grotowski remained in Poland for most of his life

11. What will the professor probably do next?

    (A) Go over a handout with the class
    (B) Give the class a writing assignment
    (C) Cover the life of Stanislavsky
    (D) Start a discussion on Grotowski

Actual Test
08

Reading
Section Directions

This section measures your ability to understand academic passages in English.

In this part, you will read 1 passage and answer reading comprehension questions about the passage. Most questions are worth one point, but the last question is worth more than one point. The directions indicate how many points you may receive.

Some passages include a word or phrase that is underlined in blue. Click on the word or phrase to see a definition or an explanation.

When you want to move on to the next question, click on **Next**. You may skip questions and go back to them later. If you want to return to previous questions, click on **Back**. You can click on **Review** at any time and the review screen will show you which questions you have answered and which you have not answered. From this review screen, you may go directly to any question you have already seen in the Reading section.

You may now begin the Reading section. You will read 1 reading passage. You will have **20 minutes** to read the passage and answer the questions.

Click on **Continue** to go on.

1. In paragraph 1, the author uses the Renaissance as an example of

   (A) a period of time in which people studied Greek and Roman history
   (B) a reason why Greek and Roman styles became popular in the 1700s
   (C) the time in history when architects first began to imitate ancient styles
   (D) a period that developed as a response to the Rococo style of art

2. The word them in the passage refers to

   (A) the fifteenth and sixteenth centuries
   (B) Greek and Roman styles
   (C) the Roman cities Pompeii and Herculaneum
   (D) the drawings

3. The word opulence in the passage is closest in meaning to

   (A) resourcefulness
   (B) quality
   (C) lavishness
   (D) style

4. The word nostalgia in the passage is closest in meaning to

   (A) satisfaction
   (B) desire
   (C) pleasure
   (D) reminiscence

5. According to paragraph 2, which of the following is true of the Neoclassical Period?

   (A) It started prior to the Rococo Period but after the Baroque Period had begun.
   (B) It began in part due to the fact that people came to dislike the Rococo Period.
   (C) During it, some architects attempted to create models of the Athenian Parthenon.
   (D) The architects who started this period were based in both Italy and Greece.

Neoclassical Architecture

In the first half of the eighteenth century, the Western world of architecture was in the middle of the Rococo Period. Yet, as the century progressed, people began to desire something different. They looked back to the fifteenth and sixteenth centuries when the Renaissance was taking place in Italy and Greek and Roman styles were popular. Additionally, in the mid-1700s, the Roman cities Pompeii and Herculaneum, which had been buried during an eruption of the volcano Vesuvius in 79 A.D., were rediscovered. The drawings made of them captured the minds of many architects, and classical architecture once again became popular. From the middle of the 1700s all throughout the 1800s, the Neoclassical Period dominated architecture in both Europe and the United States.

Much of the virtually instant popularity of Neoclassical architecture had to do with a backlash against the opulence of Rococo, which belonged to the late Baroque Period. Rococo abandoned symmetry in its designs and instead relied upon ornate, flowing patterns that were intricately crafted. But Europeans began to tire of Rococo by the mid-1700s. Coupled with that was a feeling of nostalgia for ancient Greece and Rome as many Europeans hoped to recapture the lost grandeur of those two civilizations. Since many great works of the Greeks and Romans—including the Parthenon in Athens and the Coliseum in Rome—were still standing, people began to recognize and admire their simplicity and commanding presences. Thus began a longing for the past that greatly influenced the Neoclassical Period.

At the same time, the two lost Roman towns of Pompeii and Herculaneum were rediscovered buried beneath several meters of ash. They had been totally consumed by the eruption of Vesuvius nearly 1,700 years before. Slowly, the towns had vanished from people's memories, but, upon

6. In paragraph 3, the author implies that Vesuvius

   Ⓐ has erupted many times in the past 2,000 years
   Ⓑ is the highest mountain located on the Italian peninsula
   Ⓒ killed most of the people of Pompeii and Herculaneum
   Ⓓ lies near the coast of Italy along the Mediterranean Sea

7. According to paragraph 3, the rediscovery of Pompeii excited many Europeans because

   Ⓐ they were reintroduced to previously lost Roman styles
   Ⓑ they had been searching for the lost city for decades
   Ⓒ it enabled architects to make exact copies of Roman buildings
   Ⓓ their homes were able to be built in a more efficient manner

8. The word emphasized in the passage is closest in meaning to

   Ⓐ stressed
   Ⓑ preferred
   Ⓒ forced
   Ⓓ employed

9. The author's description of Andrea Palladio in paragraph 4 mentions all of the following EXCEPT:

   Ⓐ the Roman buildings which he liked the most
   Ⓑ the period of time during which he lived
   Ⓒ the part of Italy from which he came
   Ⓓ the influence that his writings had on others

being found, they fascinated many Europeans. Importantly, the towns had not been destroyed by lava but had instead been buried by ash. ■ As a result, many buildings were well preserved, so intricate details about Roman life, art, and architecture were rediscovered. ■ Drawings of the two towns created a sensation across Europe, and countless architects made sure to visit them to witness firsthand the ancient styles. ■ The designs of the interiors of Roman homes were particularly admired, and they were soon being copied in the villas of the rich. ■

Ancient Greek and Roman designs were not unfamiliar prior to the 1700s though. The Europeans had known a great deal about them since the Renaissance. This was the time when the Venetian architect Andrea Palladio had lived. Palladio had taught and written much about ancient architecture, and his works were primary sources for many European and American architects during the Neoclassical Period. Palladio had emphasized symmetry and balance in the overall designs of buildings, and he also favored columns and imposing facades. Columns, he felt, bestowed a profound sense of power and dignity upon a building.

But columns were not the only aspect from Greece and Rome utilized in the Neoclassical Period. Roman-style arches and domes were also incorporated into many Neoclassical structures. Stone, particularly granite and limestone for exteriors and marble for interiors, was commonly used by architects as well. During the Neoclassical Period, the interiors of buildings were incredibly simplistic, especially when compared to Rococo buildings. Neoclassical buildings emphasized space and light, so their interiors had a sense of strength. However, although this minimalist style was effective in libraries, university office buildings, and government structures, it served little purpose in family homes. For that reason, attempts to copy designs of Roman homes were

10. Which of the following can be inferred from paragraph 4 about the buildings designed by Andrea Palladio?

(A) Many of them were copies of past Roman and Greek structures.

(B) One of their features was that they often had columns.

(C) Some were built in North America many years later.

(D) They were constructed from the best building materials.

11. In paragraph 5, the author's description of buildings made in the Neoclassical Period mentions which of the following?

(A) The libraries built then were better looking than the office buildings made.

(B) They were typically made with a combination of granite and limestone.

(C) Their insides were less complicated than Rococo buildings.

(D) They always had either an arch or a dome in their structures.

12. Why does the author mention Thomas Jefferson in paragraph 6?

(A) To state that he became the president of the United States

(B) To describe the effects of Neoclassical architecture on him

(C) To point out his relationship with the University of Virginia

(D) To claim that there was no better American architect than he

13. Look at the four squares [■] that indicate where the following sentence could be added to the passage.

For instance, intact Roman murals were found there that provided details on many aspects of life in Roman times.

Where would the sentence best fit?

Click on a square [■] to add the sentence to the passage.

put aside for practical reasons.

The Neoclassical Period of architecture started in Europe, but, by the end of the 1700s, it was influential in the United States. Thomas Jefferson, perhaps the first true American architect, spent time in Paris examining the new style and then returned home full of ideas. Several buildings that he designed and built, particularly at the University of Virginia, are still used today. The Neoclassical Period remained popular throughout the 1800s, but it began to lose influence in the latter half of the century as more modern buildings made of concrete and steel were erected. Nevertheless, many aspects of the Neoclassical Period survived into the 1900s, and its influence can be seen both in the Soviet architecture of the mid-1900s and on many university campuses all across North America.

Glossary

backlash: a strong reaction against something

intricate: complicated; detailed

incorporate: to utilize; to make use of

VIEW TEXT    

14. **Directions:** An introductory sentence for a brief summary of the passage is provided below. Complete the summary by selecting the THREE answer choices that express the most important ideas of the passage. Some sentences do not belong because they express ideas that are not presented in the passage or are minor ideas in the passage *This question is worth 2 points.*

The Neoclassical Period was sparked by a revival of interest in both ancient Greek and Roman styles and culture.

-
-
-

Answer Choices

(A) The rediscovery of Pompeii and Herculaneum made people want to learn more about the past.

(B) People craved the simplicity of Neoclassical works, which emphasized both light and space.

(C) Andrea Palladio was the most well-known architect who lived during the time of the Renaissance.

(D) Thanks to standing structures from the past, architects in this period modeled their designs to resemble them.

(E) Neoclassical architecture emphasized ancient ideas such as the use of columns, arches, and domes.

(F) Thomas Jefferson brought the ideas that he learned in Europe back to the United States with him.

Drag your answer choices to the spaces where they belong.
To remove an answer choice, click on it. To review the passage, click on **View Text**.

Listening
Section Directions

This section measures your ability to understand conversations and lectures in English.

In this part, you will listen to 1 conversation and 1 lecture. You will hear the conversation or lecture only **one** time. After the conversation or lecture, you will answer some questions about it. The questions typically ask about the main idea and supporting details. Some questions ask about a speaker's purpose or attitude. Answer the questions based on what is stated or implied by the speakers.

You may take notes while you listen. You may use your notes to help you answer the questions. Your notes will **not** be scored.

If you need to change the volume while you listen, click on the **Volume** icon at the top of the screen.

In some questions, you will see this icon: 🎧 This means that you will hear, but not see, part of the question.

Some of the questions have special directions. These directions appear in a gray box on the screen.

Most questions are worth one point. If a question is worth more than one point, it will have special directions that indicate how many points you can receive.

You must answer each question. After you answer, click on **Next**. Then click on **OK** to confirm your answer and go on to the next question. After you click on **OK**, you cannot return to previous questions.

A clock at the top of the screen will show you how much time is remaining. The clock will not count down while you are listening. The clock will count down only while you are answering the questions.

Now you may begin the Listening section.

Conversation 1~5: Listen to part of a conversation between a student and a librarian.

1. Why does the student visit the library?

   (A) To renew some of his books
   (B) To return a piece of equipment
   (C) To ask about fixing a movie projector
   (D) To find the location of the AV room

2. What can be inferred about the librarian?

   (A) She was once a graduate student.
   (B) She is a part-time employee.
   (C) She has met the student before.
   (D) She knows how to fix the machinery.

3. Why does the student ask the librarian about checking out a movie projector?

   (A) He needs to borrow a machine for a class.
   (B) His professor asked him to find out about it.
   (C) He has to use a projector for a presentation.
   (D) He wants to watch some movies for fun.

4. According to the librarian, why are students not allowed to check out movie projectors?

   (A) One student stole a projector in the past.
   (B) The head librarian does not want them to do so.
   (C) The students often returned them too late.
   (D) They failed to take good care of them before.

5. Listen again to part of the conversation. Then answer the question.

   What does the student imply when he says this?

   (A) He is interested in meeting the woman again.
   (B) He thinks the woman has been very helpful.
   (C) He feels confident a professor will give him a note.
   (D) He wants to borrow a movie projector tomorrow.

Lecture 6~11: Listen to part of a lecture in a chemistry class. 08-03

6. What aspect of helium-3 does the professor mainly discuss?

   (A) Where on the Earth it can be found
   (B) How it can be used to create energy
   (C) Why humans have little access to it
   (D) What elements decay to create it

7. In the lecture, the professor describes a number of facts about helium-3. Indicate whether each of the following is a fact or not.

   Click in the correct box for each statement.

	Fact	Not a Fact
(A) It is formed mostly during nuclear reactions.		
(B) It contains two protons and two neutrons.		
(C) Little of it exists on the Earth.		
(D) It forms when an isotope of hydrogen decays.		

8. According to the professor, what can helium-3 react with to produce energy?

   (A) Tritium
   (B) Barium
   (C) Lithium
   (D) Deuterium

9. What can be inferred about the helium-3 that is found on the moon?

   (A) It originated on the sun.
   (B) It took many years to decay.
   (C) It contains some lithium.
   (D) It is trapped there by the moon's atmosphere.

10. Why does the professor discuss fossil fuels?

    (A) To claim that they can produce more energy than helium-3
    (B) To mention one reason helium-3 reactors do not exist yet
    (C) To state that the Earth is rapidly running out of them
    (D) To complain about how they harm the Earth's environment

11. Listen again to part of the lecture. Then answer the question.

    What does the professor imply when he says this?

    (A) He believes going to the moon is a waste of time.
    (B) He thinks that NASA will make a moon base first.
    (C) He would like to see a moon base in the future.
    (D) He thinks returning to the moon is too difficult.

Actual Test 09

Reading

Section Directions

This section measures your ability to understand academic passages in English.

In this part, you will read 1 passage and answer reading comprehension questions about the passage. Most questions are worth one point, but the last question is worth more than one point. The directions indicate how many points you may receive.

Some passages include a word or phrase that is <u>underlined</u> in blue. Click on the word or phrase to see a definition or an explanation.

When you want to move on to the next question, click on **Next**. You may skip questions and go back to them later. If you want to return to previous questions, click on **Back**. You can click on **Review** at any time and the review screen will show you which questions you have answered and which you have not answered. From this review screen, you may go directly to any question you have already seen in the Reading section.

You may now begin the Reading section. You will read 1 reading passage. You will have **20 minutes** to read the passage and answer the questions.

Click on **Continue** to go on.

1. The word insidious in the passage is closest in meaning to

   (A) slow-moving
   (B) contagious
   (C) stealthy
   (D) deadly

2. According to paragraph 1, which of the following is NOT true of Alzheimer's disease?

   (A) People often said that those with it were suffering from dementia.
   (B) There are millions of people around the world who have the disease.
   (C) Doctors are not quite sure what causes people to get the disease.
   (D) It is possible for some people to survive the disease upon catching it.

3. The word evinces in the passage is closest in meaning to

   (A) remarks on
   (B) shows
   (C) identifies
   (D) proves

4. In paragraph 2, the author uses high-blood pressure and head trauma as examples of

   (A) problems that may make people more likely to get Alzheimer's
   (B) symptoms that the majority of Alzheimer's patients get
   (C) medical issues that are more common for women than for men
   (D) genetic problems that increase the rate at which people get Alzheimer's

5. According to paragraph 2, people may come down with Alzheimer's disease when

   (A) they reach the age of ninety
   (B) their genes have certain proteins in them
   (C) their brothers or sisters get it as well
   (D) they engage in certain risky behavior

Alzheimer's Disease

From time to time, people forget things. But there are instances where people forget their names, their loved ones, and virtually every event from their lives. That is what living with Alzheimer's disease is like. In the past, it was referred to as dementia or senility, but today it is recognized as an insidious disease of the brain. Although the precise cause of Alzheimer's is unknown, scientists suspect that both genetic and environmental factors are to blame. Not knowing the cause has made finding a cure difficult, so the disease is currently fatal to all whom it afflicts. While around twenty-five million people worldwide are believed to suffer from the disease, as the global population continues to age, the problem will only worsen in the future.

Alzheimer's disease is named after the German psychiatrist who first theorized its existence in 1906. Thanks to decades of research, doctors now understand that it is a physical disease that affects the brain. The risk factors for getting Alzheimer's increase as people age, which is evidenced by the fact that most cases occur in people over the age of sixty. But not every elderly person gets Alzheimer's, so factors other than age must be involved. Doctors speculate that it may be genetic since a person whose parents or their siblings had Alzheimer's is more likely to succumb to the disease than a person whose family history evinces no presence of Alzheimer's. Recent research also indicates that certain protein combinations in the genes increase the likelihood of a person getting Alzheimer's. Other risk factors are high-blood pressure and head trauma, and women are more prone to the disease than men as well.

The main symptoms of Alzheimer's involve a person having difficulty with various aspects of his or her mental abilities, including memory, language, perception, emotions, and cognitive reasoning. The first warning signs of the onset of

6. In paragraph 3, why does the author mention pneumonia?

   Ⓐ To name a disease that frequently kills Alzheimer's patients

   Ⓑ To blame it for the pain that it causes many Alzheimer's patients

   Ⓒ To claim that it makes Alzheimer's patients' symptoms worse

   Ⓓ To state that it causes Alzheimer's patients to become forgetful

7. In paragraph 3, the author's description of the first warning signs of Alzheimer's disease mentions which of the following?

   Ⓐ A patient becomes more likely to catch other types of illnesses.

   Ⓑ A sufferer may start to forget who his or her family members are.

   Ⓒ A person may have trouble doing two activities at the same time.

   Ⓓ An individual has no more desire to do once-liked activities.

8. The author's description of the advanced stages of Alzheimer's disease in paragraph 3 mentions all of the following EXCEPT:

   Ⓐ People may not be able to communicate effectively with others.

   Ⓑ Some people spend most of their time sitting in wheelchairs.

   Ⓒ People's bodies may no longer work the way that they desire.

   Ⓓ Some individuals may not remember what they did in the past.

9. The word It in the passage refers to

   Ⓐ Early onset Alzheimer's

   Ⓑ Late onset Alzheimer's

   Ⓒ The age of sixty

   Ⓓ A relatively slow pace

the disease are an inability to remember recent events, trouble solving problems, and difficulty multitasking. As the disease progresses, sufferers forget where they placed things, get lost taking familiar routes, lose interest in doing activities that they once enjoyed, and have trouble doing slightly complicated tasks. In the disease's advanced stages, sufferers forget their personal history, no longer recognize their loved ones, become delusional, speak in convoluted sentences or forget language entirely, and lose control over many bodily functions, including the ability to swallow. Death often swiftly ensues, usually as a result of some other disease such as pneumonia, which sufferers are unable to resist.

Alzheimer's has two forms: early onset and late onset. Early onset Alzheimer's occurs before the person reaches the age of sixty. It sometimes affects people in their forties although this is rare. This form of the disease progresses rapidly and is believed to be genetic since it typically manifests in several members of the same family. Late onset Alzheimer's, on the other hand, occurs in people over the age of sixty and is the more common form of the disease. It progresses at a relatively slow pace and does not seem to run in families, making this form less likely to be caused by genetic factors. Late onset Alzheimer's often remains undiagnosed in its early stages due to its similarity to other mental diseases as well as the common perception that people are prone to forgetfulness as they age.

As of now, the only certain way to know if a person had Alzheimer's is to examine that individual's brain after death. Such an examination can reveal the presence of dead nerve cells in clusters, which is an indicator of Alzheimer's. These cells die because of the buildup of plaque in the brain as a result of an abnormal protein called beta-amyloid. Why this happens is currently unknown. Scientists once believed that excessive amounts of chemicals, including

10. The word prone in the passage is closest in meaning to

(A) forced
(B) restricted
(C) impressed
(D) inclined

11. According to paragraph 4, which of the following is true of early onset Alzheimer's disease?

(A) It kills most of its victims before they reach the age of sixty.
(B) Experts have a difficult time diagnosing it for a number of reasons.
(C) It happens much more often than late onset Alzheimer's disease.
(D) Doctors think that a person's genetics may be responsible for it.

12. Which of the sentences below best expresses the essential information in the highlighted sentence in the passage? *Incorrect* answer choices change the meaning in important ways or leave out essential information.

(A) All that can be done is to provide support for the victims and their families since the patients are going to die.
(B) By aiding the sufferers of Alzheimer's disease, doctors can help prolong their lives, which their families appreciate.
(C) Caregivers go to great efforts to make the families of Alzheimer's patients feel as comfortable as possible.
(D) Having a person with Alzheimer's disease in one's family can be a difficult and emotional time for everyone involved.

13. According to paragraph 5, doctors study some deceased individuals' brains because

(A) it enables them to find high amounts of lead and mercury in their brains
(B) they can inject beta-amyloid into the brains to conduct research on them
(C) it is the only way to determine if Alzheimer's disease killed those people
(D) they believe that it will help them find a cure for Alzheimer's disease

lead and mercury, caused this, but that is no longer believed to be true. Without a better understanding of what causes Alzheimer's, there can be no cure. Current attempts to utilize drugs to slow the progression of the disease have had limited results. The only thing that can be done at the present is to make sufferers as comfortable as possible and to ensure that their families have support to help them deal with these difficult and emotional situations as, ultimately, death is inevitable.

Glossary

afflict: to affect a person, as in a disease; to trouble or bother

delusional: having mistaken or erroneous beliefs

ensue: to follow; to result

14. **Directions:** An introductory sentence for a brief summary of the passage is provided below. Complete the summary by selecting the THREE answer choices that express the most important ideas of the passage. Some sentences do not belong because they express ideas that are not presented in the passage or are minor ideas in the passage *This question is worth 2 points.*

Alzheimer's disease typically affects the elderly and, since there is no cure, always results in the sufferer's death.

-
-
-

Answer Choices

Ⓐ Until medical experts find a cure, all they can do is make the patients more comfortable.

Ⓑ Doctors believe that genetics and other reasons are responsible for Alzheimer's disease.

Ⓒ Most Alzheimer's patients get the disease after they turn sixty, but some suffer from it earlier.

Ⓓ Alzheimer's disease was once misdiagnosed as dementia or senility in many elderly people.

Ⓔ There are several stages of the disease, all of which become progressively worse.

Ⓕ Scientists can only diagnose a patient with Alzheimer's once that person has passed away.

Drag your answer choices to the spaces where they belong.
To remove an answer choice, click on it. To review the passage, click on **View Text**.

Listening

Section Directions

This section measures your ability to understand conversations and lectures in English.

In this part, you will listen to 1 conversation and 1 lecture. You will hear the conversation or lecture only **one** time. After the conversation or lecture, you will answer some questions about it. The questions typically ask about the main idea and supporting details. Some questions ask about a speaker's purpose or attitude. Answer the questions based on what is stated or implied by the speakers.

You may take notes while you listen. You may use your notes to help you answer the questions. Your notes will **not** be scored.

If you need to change the volume while you listen, click on the **Volume** icon at the top of the screen.

In some questions, you will see this icon: ⌒ This means that you will hear, but not see, part of the question.

Some of the questions have special directions. These directions appear in a gray box on the screen.

Most questions are worth one point. If a question is worth more than one point, it will have special directions that indicate how many points you can receive.

You must answer each question. After you answer, click on **Next**. Then click on **OK** to confirm your answer and go on to the next question. After you click on **OK**, you cannot return to previous questions.

A clock at the top of the screen will show you how much time is remaining. The clock will not count down while you are listening. The clock will count down only while you are answering the questions.

Now you may begin the Listening section.

Conversation 1~5: Listen to part of a conversation between a student and a professor.

1. Why did the professor ask to see the student?

   (A) To tell him the results of his last test
   (B) To talk to him about his coursework
   (C) To assign some homework to him
   (D) To encourage him to come to class more

2. According to the student, how does he spend most of his free time?

   (A) Reading books at the library
   (B) Working at his part-time job
   (C) Doing research in a laboratory
   (D) Hanging out with his roommate

3. What does the student imply about his grades?

   (A) They are the best in his class.
   (B) They are lower than normal this semester.
   (C) They are always A's and B's.
   (D) They could be much higher.

4. Listen again to part of the conversation. Then answer the question.

   What can be inferred from the professor's response to the student?

   (A) She wants him to be more polite.
   (B) She thinks he is not trying hard enough.
   (C) She cannot understand what he is doing.
   (D) She is not satisfied with his answer.

5. Listen again to part of the conversation. Then answer the question.

   What does the professor mean when she says this?

   (A) She would like for the student to do well in her class.
   (B) The student needs to stop blaming others.
   (C) It is the student's fault that he cannot get an A.
   (D) The student may have to take her class again next semester.

Lecture 6~11: Listen to part of a lecture in a literature class. 09-03

Literature

6. Why does the professor explain transcendentalism?

   (A) To describe the major American philosophy during Thoreau's life
   (B) To give one of the reasons why Thoreau lived at Walden Pond
   (C) To contrast it with the beliefs of some environmentalists
   (D) To describe why the philosophy was so appealing to Thoreau

7. What does the professor imply about Ralph Waldo Emerson?

   (A) His works were better written than Thoreau's.
   (B) He traveled widely throughout the United States.
   (C) He helped Thoreau write part of *Walden*.
   (D) He had a major effect on Thoreau's life.

8. In the lecture, the professor describes a number of facts about Henry David Thoreau's life at Walden Pond. Indicate whether each of the following is a fact or not.

   Click in the correct box for each statement.

	Fact	Not a Fact
(A) Thoreau stayed at his cabin every night while he lived at the pond.		
(B) Thoreau wrote several works while he was there.		
(C) Thoreau survived by farming the land around Walden Pond.		
(D) Thoreau and his friends built his cabin there.		

9. Why does the professor mention the modern environmentalist movement?

   (A) To state that its members have misinterpreted the meaning of *Walden*
   (B) To express her admiration for the majority of its members' beliefs
   (C) To claim that its members need to read *Walden* much more carefully
   (D) To declare that many environmentalists try to imitate Thoreau's life

10. What will the professor probably do next?

    (A) Talk more about the paper the students must write
    (B) Let the students go for the day
    (C) Collect the students' homework papers
    (D) Ask questions to some of the students

11. Listen again to part of the lecture. Then answer the question.

    Why does the professor say this?

    (A) To mention that Thoreau attended church services
    (B) To emphasize how near civilization Thoreau's cabin was
    (C) To claim that Thoreau erred in where he built his cabin
    (D) To prove that Thoreau was not really living by himself

Actual Test 10

Reading
Section Directions

This section measures your ability to understand academic passages in English.

In this part, you will read 1 passage and answer reading comprehension questions about the passage. Most questions are worth one point, but the last question is worth more than one point. The directions indicate how many points you may receive.

Some passages include a word or phrase that is <u>underlined</u> in blue. Click on the word or phrase to see a definition or an explanation.

When you want to move on to the next question, click on **Next**. You may skip questions and go back to them later. If you want to return to previous questions, click on **Back**. You can click on **Review** at any time and the review screen will show you which questions you have answered and which you have not answered. From this review screen, you may go directly to any question you have already seen in the Reading section.

You may now begin the Reading section. You will read 1 reading passage. You will have **20 minutes** to read the passage and answer the questions.

Click on **Continue** to go on.

1. The word **encompassed** in the passage is closest in meaning to

   (A) included
   (B) conquered
   (C) established
   (D) divided

2. The word **squabbled** in the passage is closest in meaning to

   (A) tore apart
   (B) argued
   (C) destroyed
   (D) debated

3. According to paragraph 1, which of the following is true of Charlemagne?

   (A) He was responsible for founding several modern nation-states.
   (B) The Carolingian Dynasty was established by him.
   (C) His territory increased in size after he began to rule it.
   (D) Western European culture started during his reign.

4. The author discusses Carloman in paragraph 2 in order to

   (A) claim that he should have been king instead of Charlemagne
   (B) state that he was responsible for leading Charlemagne's armies
   (C) declare that Charlemagne may have been responsible for his death
   (D) note that he and Charlemagne had issues before Carloman died

5. The word **precursor** in the passage is closest in meaning to

   (A) evolution
   (B) ancestor
   (C) relative
   (D) forerunner

Charlemagne

The fall of the Roman Empire in the late fifth century left a power vacuum in Western Europe that lasted for centuries. Over time, small tribes of the people who had overrun the Romans established kingdoms in the former Roman lands. The most successful and important of these kingdoms was the one founded by the Frankish rulers of the Carolingian Dynasty. Its territory eventually encompassed the lands of modern-day France, Western Germany, Italy, Switzerland, Belgium, the Netherlands, and Luxembourg. Charlemagne was the most powerful of all the Frankish rulers. He was a warrior king who spent much of his life in battle, inherited a sizable kingdom from his father, secured his inheritance, and then expanded the size of his empire. Yet Charlemagne was also a ruler of vision, so, during his reign, a revival of Western European culture began. Following his death, however, Charlemagne's successors squabbled and divided his empire, which paved the way for the creation of the various nation-states that dominated Western Europe for more than a millennium.

Charlemagne was born in 742 and was the son of the Frankish ruler Pepin the Short. Little is known of Charlemagne's early life. He had at least one younger brother—Carloman—with whom he jointly ruled the kingdom when their father died in 768. The two brothers seemed set to clash over their inheritance, but Carloman died in 771, and Charlemagne became the sole ruler. ■ His early years in charge were spent putting down revolts against his rule and expanding his territory. ■ Charlemagne's armies were virtually always successful and suffered only one true defeat, when they attacked Spain in 778. ■ The Spanish border would remain a trouble spot throughout much of Charlemagne's reign. ■ The Franks often challenged the Moorish rulers of Spain yet were never able to move beyond the northern regions of the Pyrenees Mountains.

6. The author's description of Pope Leo III in paragraph 3 mentions which of the following?

    (A) He was the reason that Charlemagne was crowned emperor.
    (B) He granted Charlemagne most of the land on the Italian peninsula.
    (C) He failed to tell Charlemagne that he was going to crown him emperor.
    (D) He gave Charlemagne the opportunity to reject the gift he had been given.

7. The word it in the passage refers to

    (A) the Carolingian Renaissance
    (B) a revival of interest
    (C) Charlemagne's court
    (D) the city of Aachen

8. The word emulate in the passage is closest in meaning to

    (A) restructure
    (B) imitate
    (C) outdo
    (D) restore

9. According to paragraph 4, which of the following is true of the Carolingian Renaissance?

    (A) It resulted in Aachen becoming the grandest city in the West.
    (B) It affected everyone in the empire, from the nobility to the peasants.
    (C) One of its longest-lasting effects was Carolingian miniscule.
    (D) It was responsible for coins being introduced to Western Europe.

In the east, Charlemagne experienced many difficulties, particularly during his attempts to subdue the Saxons and other Germanic tribes, who frequently rebelled against his authority. Greater success was achieved in Italy, where Charlemagne was on good terms with the Church. It was in Rome on Christmas Day in 800 that Pope Leo III crowned Charlemagne "Emperor of the Romans," which was the precursor of the title "Holy Roman Emperor" that was used in the high Middle Ages. It was during the middle of a religious service in Rome while Charlemagne was kneeling to pray that the pope placed a crown on his head and declared him emperor. While historians disagree as to whether or not Charlemagne was aware of the pope's intentions, he accepted the title and thus established the Holy Roman Empire, which lasted until the early nineteenth century.

Charlemagne's rule did not solely involve warfare and bloodshed. He is also associated with what historians refer to as the Carolingian Renaissance. This was a period in which there was a revival of interest in culture, art, architecture, literature, language, education, and religious studies. It was centered on Charlemagne's court in the city of Aachen and was limited to the clergy, intellectuals, and nobility as commoners reaped few benefits from it. Charlemagne actively encouraged this revival; he sought to emulate the Roman Empire by supporting advances in learning, but little was accomplished that lasted long after his reign. The exceptions were the many architectural achievements and the standardized form of writing called Carolingian miniscule. Charlemagne did, however, experience more success with his economic and monetary reforms, his attempts to standardize trade, and the minting of coins for his empire.

Charlemagne had at least four wives and twenty children. Many died before him, and, when he died in 814 at the age of seventy-two, his only

10. Which of the following can be inferred from paragraph 5 about the reign of Louis the Pious?

   Ⓐ It was a period during which there was a great deal of infighting.

   Ⓑ The empire that Charlemagne had created became smaller.

   Ⓒ There were more wars with the Moors during his reign.

   Ⓓ It lasted almost a decade longer than Charlemagne's reign had.

11. According to paragraph 5, the Treaty of Verdun was necessary because

   Ⓐ Louis the Pious had not named an heir prior to his death in 840

   Ⓑ the sons of Louis the Pious could not agree on how to divide the empire

   Ⓒ the Germanic lands were less desirable than those in Italy

   Ⓓ Louis the Pious' sons felt that a divided empire would be more powerful

12. Look at the four squares [■] that indicate where the following sentence could be added to the passage.

They had been attempting to defeat the Muslim Moors, who were occupying Spain.

Where would the sentence best fit?

Click on a square [■] to add the sentence to the passage.

living legitimate son was Louis the Pious. Louis assumed power and kept the empire intact for many years in spite of frequent attempts to oust him from power. When Louis died in 840, his three sons fought over the inheritance, and the Carolingian Empire was separated into different parts. The Treaty of Verdun in 843 settled their dispute. As a result, one son took the Germanic lands in the east, another took the Frankish lands to the west, and the third received the lands in the middle. This became the blueprint for modern Europe as the nations of Germany, France, and several others eventually emerged from the empire Charlemagne had once ruled.

Glossary
power vacuum: an instance in which a region has no central authority
reign: the period of time in which a king or queen rules a land
bloodshed: violence; fighting

13. **Directions:** Select the appropriate sentences from the answer choices and match them to the period of time to which they relate. TWO of the answer choices will NOT be used. *This question is worth 3 points.*

During Charlemagne's Life
(Select 3)

-
-
-

After Charlemagne's Life
(Select 2)

-
-

Answer Choices

Ⓐ The title "Emperor of the Romans" was first used.

Ⓑ Many advances that had been made ceased to be practiced.

Ⓒ The Carolingian Dynasty was founded in Frankish lands.

Ⓓ There were economic reforms in the empire.

Ⓔ Islamic invaders were defeated while in Frankish territory.

Ⓕ People became more interested in studying religion.

Ⓖ The empire was split into three separate parts.

Drag your answer choices to the spaces where they belong.
To remove an answer choice, click on it. To review the passage, click on **View Text**.

Listening

Section Directions

This section measures your ability to understand conversations and lectures in English.

In this part, you will listen to 1 conversation and 1 lecture. You will hear the conversation or lecture only **one** time. After the conversation or lecture, you will answer some questions about it. The questions typically ask about the main idea and supporting details. Some questions ask about a speaker's purpose or attitude. Answer the questions based on what is stated or implied by the speakers.

You may take notes while you listen. You may use your notes to help you answer the questions. Your notes will **not** be scored.

If you need to change the volume while you listen, click on the **Volume** icon at the top of the screen.

In some questions, you will see this icon: 🎧 This means that you will hear, but not see, part of the question.

Some of the questions have special directions. These directions appear in a gray box on the screen.

Most questions are worth one point. If a question is worth more than one point, it will have special directions that indicate how many points you can receive.

You must answer each question. After you answer, click on **Next**. Then click on **OK** to confirm your answer and go on to the next question. After you click on **OK**, you cannot return to previous questions.

A clock at the top of the screen will show you how much time is remaining. The clock will not count down while you are listening. The clock will count down only while you are answering the questions.

Now you may begin the Listening section.

Conversation 1~5: Listen to part of a conversation between a student and a financial aid office employee. 

1. What problem does the student have?

    (A) She needs a loan to be able to pay her tuition for that semester.
    (B) She does not know when she needs to start repaying her loans.
    (C) She cannot afford to pay back her loans after she graduates.
    (D) She is no longer eligible to receive financial aid from the school.

2. Why does the student explain how much money in loans she has?

    (A) To answer a question that the man asks
    (B) To find out if she can receive a new loan
    (C) To complain about how much she owes
    (D) To complete a form the man is filling out

3. In the conversation, the student describes a number of facts about her student loans. Indicate whether each of the following is a fact or not.

    Click in the correct box for each statement.

	Fact	Not a Fact
(A) She has taken out a loan every semester.		
(B) She has started to pay back her loans.		
(C) She has around $8,000 in loans.		
(D) She owes 5% interest on her loans.		

4. What does the man imply about the form he gives the student?

    (A) It will take several minutes for her to fill the form out.
    (B) The student must give it to a bank official in person.
    (C) It has to be submitted before the student graduates.
    (D) The student has to provide several pages of information.

5. Listen again to part of the conversation. Then answer the question.

    What can be inferred about the student when she says this?

    (A) She dislikes the man's sense of humor.
    (B) She would like a more detailed explanation.
    (C) She does not want to begin repaying her loans.
    (D) She is going to graduate the following year.

Lecture 6~11: Listen to part of a lecture in a biology class. 10-03

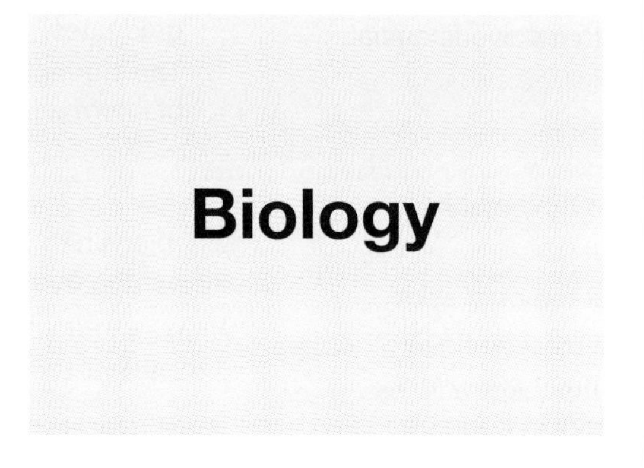

6. What is the lecture mainly about?

   (A) Upsetting the balance of nature
   (B) Gause's Hypothesis
   (C) Changes in ecosystems
   (D) Georgii Gause

7. What organisms did Georgii Gause use in his experiments to try to prove his hypothesis?

   Click on 2 answers.

   (A) Bacteria
   (B) Bears
   (C) Yeasts
   (D) Protozoa

8. Why does the professor tell the students about some species of plankton in the oceans?

   (A) To explain one species in nature that tries to outcompete similar species
   (B) To mention the types of resources that they need in order to survive
   (C) To talk about an experiment that Gause considered conducting with them
   (D) To provide an example of how Gause's Hypothesis has been proven false

9. What is the likely outcome of putting two similar bacteria in a controlled environment and providing them with the same resources?

   (A) One type of bacteria would die.
   (B) Both would share the resources.
   (C) They would expand at a similar rate.
   (D) Their numbers would both decrease.

10. What does the professor imply about Gause's Hypothesis?

    (A) It is more accurate for herbivores than for carnivores.
    (B) Animals in nature will adapt, so it does not apply to them.
    (C) The hypothesis has been rewritten several times in the past.
    (D) It has been proven correct in experiments by many scientists.

11. Listen again to part of the lecture. Then answer the question.

    What can be implied about the professor when he says this?

    (A) He often dreams about how to conduct various experiments.
    (B) He doubts that anyone can conduct an experiment in nature.
    (C) He believes that what he just described would be too difficult.
    (D) He has never been in an ecosystem with very few organisms.

DARAKWON

Reading Section p.9

Answers

1. Ⓒ [Vocabulary Question]
2. Ⓑ [Factual Question]
3. Ⓓ [Negative Factual Question]
4. Ⓐ [Factual Question]
5. Ⓐ [Vocabulary Question]
6. Ⓑ [Factual Question]
7. Ⓓ [Reference Question]
8. Ⓒ [Sentence Simplification Question]
9. Ⓒ [Factual Question]
10. Ⓑ [Inference Question]
11. Ⓒ [Vocabulary Question]
12. Ⓑ [Factual Question]
13. 2nd [Insert Text Question]
14. Ⓑ, Ⓓ, Ⓔ [Prose Summary Question]

Translation

작은갈색박쥐

박쥐는 미국과 캐나다 동부의 수많은 생태계에서 중요한 부분을 차지한다. 그곳에서 발견되는 여섯 종의 박쥐들은 곤충을 잡아먹고, 식물의 씨앗을 퍼뜨리며, 꽃을 수분시키는 역할을 한다. 하지만, 2006년부터, 과학자들과 산림 감시원들은 많은 박쥐들이, 특히 작은갈색박쥐들이, 기록적인 수치로 죽어 가고 있다는 사실을 알아냈다. 주범은 감염된 박쥐의 코와 날개에 하얀 반점을 남기는 진균류인 것으로 밝혀졌고, 과학자들은 이러한 증상에 "박쥐 괴질"이라는 명칭을 부여했다. 이 진균류는 박쥐가 가장 병에 걸리기 쉬울 때 이들을 감염시킨다: 바로 겨울 동안 박쥐들이 동굴에서 겨울잠을 잘 때이다. 그 결과, 2006년부터 백만 마리 이상의 박쥐들이 죽었고, 전문가들은 이러한 문제의 해결 방법을 찾는데 당혹스러워하고 있다.

작은갈색박쥐를 포함하여, 몇몇 박쥐의 종들은 겨울 동안 겨울잠을 잔다. 이러한 박쥐들은 너무 작아서 겨울 내내 살아남기 위해 겨우 몇 그램 정도의 저장 지방만을 필요로 한다. 겨울잠을 자기 전, 이들은 기온이 섭씨 10도보다 약간 낮고 습도가 90퍼센트 정도인 어둡고, 축축한 동굴을 찾는다. 이들에게는 불행하게도, 이러한 조건은 진균류가 자라기에도 이상적이다. 2006년까지, 박쥐들은 어떠한 종류의 진균류로 인한 병에도 걸리지 않았던 것 같다. 그 후, 새로운 진균류의 종자가 유럽으로부터 유입되었다. 박쥐를 죽이는

이 박쥐 괴질 진균류는 유럽에서 북미 지역으로 유입되었다고 생각된다. 이들이 대서양을 어떻게 건너왔는지에 대해서는 어느 누구도 확신하지 못하지만, 유럽의 동굴 탐험가가 약간의 진균류를 자신의 옷이나 신발에 묻힌 다음, 북미에서 동굴을 탐사하는 동안 이곳으로 진균류를 이동시켰을 가능성이 가장 높다. 이러한 결과로 생겨난 전염병이 작은갈색박쥐를 위협하고 있어서 종 자체가 멸종될 위기에 처하게 되었다.

진균류가 직접적으로 박쥐들을 죽이는지에 대해서는 알려져 있지 않지만, 전문가들은 진균류가 간접적으로 박쥐들을 죽인다는 사실에 대해서는 확신하고 있다. 진균류는 작은갈색박쥐가 겨울잠에서 일찍 깨도록 한다. 진균류는 박쥐의 호흡기계에 염증을 일으킴으로써 이들의 잠을 방해한다고 생각된다. 박쥐들은 한정된 양의 저장 지방을 활용하여 잠든 시간 동안 살아가기 때문에, 일찍 잠에서 깨게 되면 너무 많은 양의 에너지를 써 버리게 된다. (그 이유는, 박쥐들이 잠에서 깨면 잠을 잘 때보다 훨씬 더 많은 에너지를 필요로 하기 때문이다.) 이렇게 되면 그들은 더 많은 먹이를 찾아야만 하며 그렇지 못하면 죽게 된다. 박쥐들이 동굴에서 나올 때, 혹독한 겨울의 날씨로 인하여 이들은 지방의 양을 보충할 수 있기 전에 죽는다. 산림 감시원들은 동굴의 바닥이나 동굴 입구 바로 앞의 지역에 놓여 있는 수천 마리의 죽은 박쥐들을 목격한 사실을 보고한 바 있다.

하지만 모든 동굴이 감염된 것은 아니다. 지금까지, 전염병은 미국 동부 및 캐나다의 온타리오 주와 퀘백 주 남부 지역의 동굴에서만 퍼졌다. 엄청나게 많은 수의 박쥐들의 서식지인 미국 남부와 중서부 지역의 동굴에서는 아직까지 박쥐 괴질이 발견되었던 적이 없다. 하지만 뉴욕 주에서 처음으로 발견된 진균류들이 미국에 도달한 이후로 눈에 띄게 퍼져 나갔기 때문에 괴질이 발생할 가능성은 여전히 남아있다. 괴질의 확산과 관련하여 가장 문제가 되는 것은 인간 탐험가들이다. 부주의한 사람이 북미 지역으로 진균류를 유입시켰을 가능성이 가장 높을 뿐만 아니라, 다수의 다른 사람들도 진균류가 대륙 전역으로 퍼져 나간 원인이 되었을 것이다. 산림 감시원들은 많은 동굴의 입구에 가로대로 만든 출입구를 설치해서 박쥐들이 겨울잠을 자는 동굴에 동물 탐험가들이 들어가는 것을 저지하고 있다. 박쥐들은 이러한 가로대 출입구 사이를 통과하여 동굴로 드나들 수 있지만, 사람들은 이곳을 통과할 수 없다.

이러한 안전 대책에도 불구하고, 전문가들은 여전히 전염병에 의하여 작은갈색박쥐와 같은 몇몇 종의 박쥐들이 멸종할 수도 있다는 우려를 하고 있다. 진균류가 박쥐를 공격하여 죽이는 원인이 알려져 있지 않기 때문에, 과학자들이 감염된 박쥐들을 치료할 수 있는 방법은 없다. 이러한 박쥐의 종들이 사라지면 미묘한 생태계의 균형이 무너지게 될 것이다. 단기적으로는, 박쥐들이 잡아먹는 엄청난 양의 곤충들의 수가 통제할 수 없을 정도로 증가하여 퍼져 나갈 것이고, 식물의 씨앗이 새로운 장소로 퍼져 나가지 못할 것이며, 몇몇 꽃들은 수분되지 못할 것이다. 이러한 현상의 장기적인 결과에 대해서는 알려진 것이 없지만, 북미의 동부 지역 삼림 지대에서 작은갈색박쥐와 다른 종의 박쥐들이 앞으로 멸종할 가능성은 적지 않다.

Answers

1. D [Gist-Purpose Question]
2. B [Detail Question]
3. C [Understanding Attitude Question]
4. A [Making Inferences Question]
5. A [Understanding Function Question]
6. A [Gist-Content Question]
7. C [Understanding Organization Question]
8. C [Making Inferences Question]
9. D [Detail Question]
10. A [Understanding Attitude Question]
11. D [Understanding Function Question]

Script

| 01-02 |

W Professor: Sam, I heard from your TA that you've been looking for me. He said you need to talk about something urgent. Is that right?

M Student: Ah, that's correct, Professor Lawson. I've got something, uh, rather important about which I need to speak with you. Do you have a few moments right now?

W: Sure. Go ahead. I'm all ears.

M: Great. Thanks. You see, I have to talk about the upcoming midterm exam.

W: Okay. Do you need to know what's going to be on the exam or something? I can fill you in on that rather easily.

M: No, it's not that. You see, um . . . I've got a minor, er, make that a major, conflict with our midterm exam. I don't think I'm going to be able to take the test during our class.

W: And why not? You do realize that your midterm exam is worth thirty percent of your final grade, don't you? I hope you have a really, really good excuse for not being able to take the test. What is it?

M: See, um . . . I'm currently enrolled in a geology class. That class has a lot of extracurricular activities. You know, such as visiting the museum, going on digs, uh, stuff like that. Well, Professor Timber—he's my geology professor—he scheduled a field trip to a local rock collector's house on the day of the exam.

W: ⁵What time is the trip?

M: We leave at eleven in the morning and come back around three or so.

W: Hmm . . . It sounds like you're going to miss the exam in that case. So what do you propose that we do about that?

M: Is there any way that I can, uh, I don't know . . . take a makeup exam either before or after the exam? Or maybe I could write a paper instead.

W: I prefer having you take a makeup exam instead of writing a paper. It wouldn't be fair to the other students if you don't have to take the midterm exam when they do. That seems rather, um, wrong. You know what I'm saying?

M: Yes, ma'am. I agree with you.

W: You can see my office hours posted right here. Which of these times will you be able to come and take the exam here in my office?

M: Let me see . . . I think Friday afternoon at two works perfectly. I'll be done for the day, so there will definitely be no conflict.

W: No trips to the museum or anything else like that?

M: Er . . . No, none of those. Thank you for your understanding, ma'am. I really appreciate it. And I'm sorry about the problem. But if I don't go on that field trip, I'll lose a lot of points in the class. Still, I'm sorry I had to ask you for this favor.

W: It's not a problem, Sam. But I think I'm going to have a chat with Professor Timber in a moment. He shouldn't be scheduling field trips during prime class hours. He knows that he's supposed to schedule that kind of thing for the evening or the weekend.

Translation

W Professor: *Sam*, 학생이 저를 찾고 있다고 조교로부터 이야기를 들었어요. 무언가 급한 일 때문에 저와 이야기를 해야 할 필요가 있다고 하더군요. 맞나요?

M Student: 아, 맞아요, *Lawson* 교수님. 교수님과 이야기를 해야 할, 어, 다소 중요한 문제가 있어요. 지금 잠시 시간을 내주실 수 있나요?

W: 물론이에요. 이야기해 봐요. 들어 볼게요.

M: 잘 되었군요. 감사합니다. 아시겠지만, 다가오는 중간고사에 대해 이야기를 나누어야 해서요.

W: 좋아요. 시험에 무엇이 나올 것인지를 알아야 하는 것과 같은 건가요? 그 점에 대해서는 쉽게 알려 줄 수 있죠.

M: 아니오, 그런 것이 아니고요. 아시겠지만, 음… 중간고사와 충돌할 수 있는 사소한, 어, 클 수도 있는 문제가 하나 있어요. 수업 시간에 시험을 볼 수가 없을 것 같아요.

W: 왜 그렇죠? 중간고사는 기말 성적의 30%를 좌우한다는 것을 알고 있죠, 그렇지 않나요? 시험을 볼 수 없는 것에 대한, 정말로 충분한 이유가 있기를 바라요. 이유가 무엇인가요?

M: 그것이, 음… 저는 현재 지리학 수업을 수강하고 있어요. 그 수업에는 많은 과외 활동들이 있죠. 아시겠지만, 박물관을 방문하고, 유적지를 찾아 다니고, 어, 그러한 것들이에요. 음, *Timber* 교수님께서 — 지리학 교수님이신데 — 시험 당일 날 인근 암석 수집가의 집을 찾는 현장 학습을 계획하고 계세요.

W: 현장 학습이 언제인가요?

M: 오전 11시에 출발해서 3시 정도에 돌아올 거예요.

W: 흠… 그런 경우라면 시험을 보지 못할 것으로 들리는군요. 그러면 그에 대해 어떻게 했으면 하나요?

M: 어, 잘 모르겠지만… 시험 전이나 그 후에 보충 시험을 치는 것과 같이 제가 할 수 있는 다른 방법이 있을까요? 아니면 그 대신에 보고서를 쓸 수도 있을 것 같고요.

W: 보고서를 쓰는 것보다 보충 시험을 보는 것이 나을 것 같네요. 다른 학생들은 시험을 보는데 학생만 시험을 보지 않는다면, 공정하지 않게 될 것이에요. 그건 다소, 음, 옳지 못한 것처럼 보이고요. 무슨 말인지 알죠?

M: 네, 교수님. 동의해요.

W: 여기에 게시된 제 사무실 근무 시간을 볼 수 있을 거예요. 여기제 사무실로 와서 시험을 볼 수 있는 때가 언제인가요?

M: 볼게요… 금요일 오후 2시가 적당할 것 같아요. 수업이 다 끝나기 때문에, 분명 시간이 충돌할 일은 없을 거예요.

W: 박물관으로 현장 학습을 가는 등의 그런 일은 없죠?

M: 어… 아니에요, 없어요. 이해해 주셔서 고맙습니다, 교수님. 정말 감사드려요. 그리고 그러한 문제에 대해서는 죄송하고요. 하지만 현장 학습을 가지 않으면, 그 수업에서 점수가 많이 깎일 거예요. 어쨌든, 이러한 부탁을 드리게 되어 죄송하고요.

W: 문제가 되는 것은 아니에요, *Sam*. 하지만 잠시 *Timber* 교수님과 이야기를 나누어볼 생각이에요. 시험 기간이 한창일 때 현장 학습을 계획해서는 안 되는 것이죠. 그런 일은 저녁이나 주말에 계획해야 한다는 점을 그 분이 알고 계실 거예요.

Script

| 01-03 |

W Professor: Since the nineteenth century, humans have utilized one energy source more than any other. I'm talking, of course, about oil. The common belief is that oil is a nonrenewable source of energy that was created over a period of millions of years. During that time, plant and animal matter died, was buried in the ground, and was subjected to a tremendous amount of pressure, thereby transforming it into oil. [10]As a result, people claim, Earth contains a finite amount of oil. However, what would you say if I told you that there's actually an infinite supply of oil? Hold on . . . It's not as outlandish as you may think. Some experts believe that oil is not only made by biological matter but that it can also be created by non-biological forces deep within the Earth's mantle. This is referred to as abiotic oil.

There are two main theories that explain how oil could be made without the presence of biological matter. One posits that huge amounts of carbon in the mantle can be converted into oil. How . . . ? According to this theory, the carbon combines with hydrogen to form methane. Then, through reactions with rocks and while under intense pressure, the methane transforms into other hydrocarbons and forms oil. The second theory proposes that microbes deep within the Earth release methane through an internal process. Later, this methane combines with other materials to produce oil.

M Student: Microbes? Aren't they living organisms like, uh, bacteria?

W: That's right, but supporters of the abiotic theory consider them non-biological. They state that these microbes are different from plant and animal matter because, while they produce methane, they don't physically transform into oil.

Now, about biotic oil. People originally believed that oil came from plants and animals because they discovered the remains of plant and animal matter after closely expecting some oil deposits. These are known as biomarkers and indicate that, uh, the oil was somehow created from plant and animal matter. Abiotic oil supposedly lacks biomarkers. Yet no one has ever discovered any oil lacking biomarkers. Of course, those who support the theory of abiotic oil declare that just because deposits of abiotic oil haven't been found doesn't mean that they don't exist. They state that abiotic oil is found deep within the Earth and will require intensive drilling efforts to reach it. As of now, however, we lack the technology to drill deep enough to reach where abiotic oil is supposed to be.

Despite their failure to find any deposits, there are two main reasons why supporters of abiotic oil believe it must exist on the Earth. The first reason is the large amounts of methane found on some other planets and moons in our solar system. These planets have no life forms, so, they ask, where does the methane come from? [11]The theory is that this methane comes from a transformation that involves carbon and hydrogen. If this occurs on other planets, they reason, then why can't it happen on the Earth as well? However, as of yet, only methane, not the hydrocarbons that make up oil, has been discovered elsewhere in the solar system, so this leap of logic is not terribly convincing to me.

I am, however, more intrigued with the second theory. There is something strange that happens in some old abandoned oil wells. You see, um, sometimes these supposedly dry oil fields start to fill up with oil again. This has happened in, let's see, Texas, Oklahoma, the Middle East, and numerous other places all around the world. Abiotic oil supporters cite this as proof that there's oil deep within the Earth. They claim that since the oil formed from living creatures is only located in the upper crust, any oil coming from deeper regions such as the mantle, where there's no life, must be made by an abiotic process. These people claim that abiotic oil is slowly seeping toward the surface, which is why some oil fields are starting to fill up again. It's an interesting theory. I mean, the fields really were empty once, but now they're not.

Anyway, the theory of abiotic oil has been around for a while, but it got a lot of support in the Soviet Union during the Cold War. Soviet scientists were searching for new sources of oil, and many believed in abiotic oil. They thought it would solve their energy needs if the country was ever cut off from outside supplies of oil. However, the Soviets later discovered massive deposits of oil and natural gas within their borders, so they pretty much stopped searching for abiotic oil when they had so much easily extractable biotic oil available to them. Yes, Joseph? You have a question?

M: What about synthetic oil? Isn't that abiotic?

W: Hmm . . . Not really. We've been able to produce synthetic oil since the middle of the twentieth century, but it's typically derived from another fossil fuel—usually coal—and the process isn't particularly economical. But that's a good question. I like the fact that you came up with that.

Translation

W Professor: 19세기 이후로, 인간은 다른 무엇보다 하나의 에너지원을 활용해 왔습니다. 물론, 석유에 대해 말씀드리고 있는 것입니다. 일반적인 믿음에 따르면, 석유는 수백만 년의 기간에 걸쳐 생성된, 재생이 불가능한 에너지원입니다. 그러한 기간 동안, 식물과 동물이 죽어서, 땅 속에 묻히고, 막대한 양의 압력을 받아, 그렇게 해서 석유로 변하게 되는 것이죠. 그 결과, 지구에는 한정된 양의 석유가 있다고 사람들이 주장을 합니다. 하지만, 실제 석유가 무한히 존재한다고 말씀드리면, 여러분들은 어떻게 말하실 건가요? 잠시만요… 여러분이 생각하는 것만큼 이상한 이야기는 아닙니다. 일부 전문가들은 석유가 생물적인 물질로부터 뿐만 아니라 지구 맨틀의 깊숙한 곳에 있는 비생물적인 요인들로부터도 만들어 질 수 있다고 믿고 있습니다.

생물학적인 물질 없이 어떻게 석유가 만들어 질 수 있는지를 설명해 주는 두 개의 주요한 이론이 있습니다. 하나는 맨틀에 있는 막대한 양의 탄소가 석유로 바뀔 수 있다고 가정합니다. 어떻게요…? 이 이론에 따르면, 탄소는 산소와 결합하여 메탄을 만들어 냅니다. 그런 다음, 암석과 반응하고 막대한 압력을 받아, 메탄이 다른 탄화수소로 변하여 석유를 생성해 냅니다. 두 번째 이론은 지구 깊은 곳에 있는 미생물들이 내부 프로세스를 통해 메탄을 방출해 낸다는 것입니다. 이후, 이러한 메탄이 다른 물질과 결합하여 석유가 만들어 지는 것이죠.

M Student: 미생물이요? 미생물들은, 어, 박테리아와 마찬가지로 생물이 아니지 않나요?

W: 그렇기는 하지만, 비생물적 이론을 지지하는 사람들은 그것들을 생물적 요인이 아니라고 생각합니다. 그들은 그러한 미생물들이 식물 및 동물과는 다른 것이라고 주장을 하는데, 그 이유는, 메탄을 생성해 내는 동안, 이들이 물리적으로 석유가 되지는 않기 때문입니다.

자, 생물적 석유에 대해 알아보죠. 석유가 매장되어 있다고 예상이 되면 식물과 동물의 유해들이 발견되기 때문에, 처음부터 사람들은 석유가 식물과 동물로부터 나온다고 믿었습니다. 이는 바이오마커라고 알려져 있으며, 어, 석유가 어느 정도 동식물로부터 만들어 진다는 점을 나타내 줍니다. 비생물적 석유에는 바이오마커가 없다고 생각됩니다. 하지만 바이오마커가 없는 석유를 발견한 적은 없었습니다. 물론, 비생물적 석유 이론을 지지하는 사람들은 비생물적 석유의 매장지가 발견된 적이 없다는 점이 비생물적 석유가 존재하지 않는다는 것을 의미하는 것은 아니라고 주장합니다. 비생물적 석유는 지구 깊숙한 곳에서 발견되며 이를 발굴하기 위해서는 강력한 시굴이 필요

할 것이라고 주장을 합니다. 하지만, 현재로서는, 비생물적 석유가 있다고 생각되는 곳까지 깊이 도달할 수 있는, 시굴 기술이 존재하지 않습니다.

매장된 곳을 찾는 데는 실패했지만, 비생물적 석유를 믿는 사람들이 그것이 지구상에 존재한다고 생각하는 두 가지 주된 이유가 있습니다. 첫 번째 이유는 태양계의 다른 행성 및 달에서 많은 양의 메탄이 발견되었기 때문입니다. 이러한 행성에는 생명체가 없는데, 따라서, 그들이 질문하기를, 그러한 메탄은 어디로부터 나온 것일까요? 이 이론에 따르면 그러한 메탄은 탄소와 수소가 연관된 변화 과정으로부터 나오는 것입니다. 이러한 일이 다른 행성에서 일어난다면, 그들이 생각하기에, 왜 지구상에서는 일어날 수 없는 것일까요? 하지만, 아직까지, 메탄만이, 석유를 구성하는 탄화수소가 아니라, 태양계의 다른 곳에서 발견되고 있기 때문에, 이러한 논리적인 비약은 제게 큰 설득력이 없습니다.

저는, 하지만, 두 번째 이론에 보다 흥미를 느낍니다. 오래 전에 폐쇄된 일부 유전에서 때때로 이상한 일이 일어납니다. 아시겠지만, 음, 때때로 고갈되었다고 생각되는 이러한 유전에서 석유가 다시 채워지기 시작하는 것이죠. 이는, 봅시다, 텍사스, 오클라호마, 중동, 그리고 지구상의 수많은 다른 지역에서도 발생하고 있습니다. 비생물적 석유를 믿는 사람들은 지구 깊숙한 곳에 석유가 존재한다는 증거로서 이를 언급합니다. 생물로 만들어진 석유는 지각의 상부에만 위치해 있기 때문에, 생물이 존재하지 않는 맨틀과 같은, 보다 깊은 지역에서 만들어 지는 석유는 반드시 비생물적 프로세스에 의해 만들어 지는 것이라고 주장을 합니다. 이러한 사람들은 비생물적 석유가 천천히 지표면으로 스며 나와, 일부 유전이 다시 채워지는 이유가 된다고 주장합니다. 흥미로운 이론입니다. 제 말은, 유전이 실제로 한때 고갈되었지만, 현재는 그렇지 않다는 것입니다.

어쨌든, 비생물적 석유 이론은 한동안 유행했으나, 냉전 시대 소련에서 많은 지지를 받았습니다. 소련 과학자들은 석유에 대한 새로운 출처를 찾고 있었고, 많은 학자들이 비생물적 석유의 존재를 믿었습니다. 그들은 외부로부터 석유의 공급이 차단되는 경우, 비생물적 석유가 에너지 수급 문제를 해결해 줄 수 있을 것으로 생각했습니다. 하지만, 이후 소련 사람들은 자신의 국경 근처에서 석유 및 천연 가스가 매장되어 있는 거대한 지역을 발견하여, 생물적 석유를 쉽게 시추하여 이용할 수 있게 되자, 비생물적 석유를 찾는 것을 중단했습니다. 네, *Joseph*? 질문이 있나요?

M: 합성유는 어떤가요? 그것은 비생물적이 아닌가요?

W: 흠… 꼭 그렇지는 않습니다. 20세기 중반 이후로 합성유를 생산해 낼 수 있게 되었지만, 이는 전형적으로 또 다른 화석 연료로부터 – 보통 석탄으로부터 – 만들어 지며 그 과정은 그렇게 경제적이지가 않습니다. 하지만 좋은 질문이었어요. 그와 같은 것을 생각해 내다니 기분이 좋군요.

Actual Test 02

Reading Section
p.21

Answers

1. C [Vocabulary Question]

2. B [Factual Question]

3. C [Rhetorical Purpose Question]

4. B [Vocabulary Question]

5. A [Vocabulary Question]

6. A [Factual Question]

7. D [Sentence Simplification Question]

8. D [Negative Factual Question]

9. C [Reference Question]

10. B [Vocabulary Question]

11. D [Inference Question]

12. C [Factual Question]

13. 3rd [Insert Text Question]

14. C, D, E [Prose Summary Question]

Translation

세계화의 경제적인 영향

세계화란 전 세계가 사회의 모든 차원, 특히 경제적인 차원에서 동일화 되는 과정이다. 이는 수세기 전에 시작된 천천히 진행되던 과정이었지만, 기술, 교통, 그리고 통신의 진보가 일어나면서, 세계적인 통합의 영향이 보다 빠르게 퍼져 나가고 있다. 오늘날, 금융 시장, 무역, 기술 공유, 그리고 노동자들의 이주가 모두 상당히 세계화 되어 있다. 그 결과, 많은 지역에 혜택을 가져다 주고 있는 통합된 세계 경제가 등장했다. 하지만 이를 지지하지 않는 사람들과 함께 세계화에는 몇몇 단점들도 있다.

경제적인 세계화로 인하여 많은 국가들이 현재 수준의 통합을 이루었다. 경제적인 세계화의 시작은 실크로드로 거슬러 올라갈 수 있는데, 이는 중국에서 시작하여 인도, 중동, 그리고 유럽에 이르는 전설적인 고대의 무역로이다. 그 후, 거대한 외항선의 건조와 유럽인들의 신대륙 발견으로 인하여, 세계의 경제는 더욱 통합되었다. 1914년 제1차 세계 대전 직전, 많은 국가들은 빠른 배들과 전신선으로 연결되어 있었으며, 이 국가들은 자유 무역 정책으로 혜택을 얻었다. 하지만, 20세기 대규모 전쟁들로 인하여 세계화는 중지되었다. 국가들은 몹시 경계하며 자국의 경제를 보호했고 무역 장벽을 설치했다. 1940년대 중반에 시작된 냉전으로 인하여, 전 세계는 두 군사 기지로 분할되었는데, 이는 경제적인 통합에 더욱 큰 방해가 되었다. 마침내, 1990대에 긴장이 해소되었고 월드 와이드 웹과 같

은 컴퓨터 통신 체계가 개발되면서 현재 수준의 세계 경제 통합이 이루어졌다.

이러한 통합의 이익은 상당했다. 가장 중요한 것은 전 세계의 금융 시장이 여러 차원에서 통합되었다는 것이다. 한 나라의 주식과 채권이 다른 나라의 사람들에 의해서 거래될 수도 있고, 여러 장소에서 화폐가 교환될 수 있기 때문에 환율이 서로 억제되며, 사람들은 자국 이외의 다른 국가의 재산을 사고 팔 수 있다. 세계 무역을 통하여, 한때 좁은 지역에서만 판매되던 제품들이 전 세계 모든 곳에서 사용 가능해졌는데, 이는 광대한 수송 체계를 통해서 제품을 수송하는 선박, 비행기, 그리고 트럭 덕분이다. 경제 자유 구역과 무역 블록의 설치로 인하여, 세상은 이전 세기의 특징이었던 여러 무역 규제로부터 자유로워졌다.

마지막으로, 기술이 발달하고 다른 지역으로 전파됨에 따라, 전 세계적으로 삶의 질이 향상되었다. 예를 들어, 보다 많은 식량을 기르기 위해서 농부들이 현재 현대적인 기법들을 채택하고 있고, 진보된 의학으로 인하여 수많은 질병들이 치료되고 있으며, 발달된 통신 수단으로 인하여 사람들은 다른 사람들이 어느 곳에 있는지에 관계 없이 그들과 연락을 취할 수 있다. (이는 인터넷과 핸드폰이 존재하기 때문이다.) 또 다른 결과는 사람들이 사실상 전 세계 어느 곳이든 자신이 원하는 지역에서 일을 할 수 있다는 것이다. 노동자들은 일자리를 찾아서 다른 국가로 자유롭게 이동할 수 있을 뿐만 아니라, 이들 중 많은 사람들은 자국에 머무르면서 다른 나라의 회사 업무를 할 수도 있다.

이러한 모든 이익에도 불구하고 경제의 세계화와 관련된 몇 가지 부정적인 문제들이 있다. 금융 시장이 통합되면서 한 나라의 문제가 전 세계로 빠르게 전파될 수 있다. 이는 특히 미국과 같은 금융 강국에서 문제가 생겼을 경우에 더욱 그러하다. 2008년과 2009년의 경제적인 침체가 이러한 위험의 좋은 사례이다. 또한, 많은 국가들과 사람들이 경제의 세계화의 혜택을 보고 있지만, 여전히 빈곤하게 생활하기 때문에 경제의 세계화의 혜택을 누릴 수 없는 사람들도 수천만 명이나 된다. 이러한 사람들은 한층 더 나은 생활을 하는 국가의 사람들에게 분노를 느끼며 자신들이 착취당한다고 느끼는 경우가 많다.

뿐만 아니라, 국제 무역을 통하여 사람들과 회사들은 어느 곳에서나 제품을 판매할 수 있지만, 몇몇 사람들은 이를 긍정적인 것으로 생각하지 않는다. 그들은 이러한 상황이 전 세계를 지나치게 상업화하여 보다 많은 사람들이 너무 많은 구매를 하게 됨으로써 부채를 떠안게 된다고 주장한다. 마찬가지로, 일자리를 찾아 새로운 지역으로 이주한 사람들은 현지인들에게 항상 환영을 받는 것은 아닌데, 현지인들은 이 사람들이 자신들의 일자리를 빼앗아 가며 자신들의 사회에 문제를 일으킨다고 비난한다.

Listening Section
p.27

Answers

1. B [Gist-Content Question]

2. D [Detail Question]

3. B [Understanding Attitude Question]

4. C [Detail Question]

5. (A) [Understanding Function Question]

6. (C) [Gist-Content Question]

7. (A) [Understanding Organization Question]

8. (D) [Detail Question]

9. (C) [Gist-Content Question]

10.

	Realism	Modernism	Post-modernism
(A)		X	
(B)	X		
(C)			X
(D)		X	

[Connecting Content Question]

11. (C) [Making Inferences Question]

Script

| 02-02 |

M Economics Department Secretary: Good afternoon, young lady. Is there something that I can help you with today?

W Student: Uh, hi. Yes, please. I'm looking for Professor Hauser.

M: Have you tried visiting his office? It's located on the fifth floor. It's room, um . . . room 504 I believe.

W: Yes, I was just up there and knocked on the door, but there was no answer. And the light in his office was off, so I'm pretty certain that he wasn't in there.

M: Okay, hold on and let me check his schedule for a moment.

W: Sure.

M: All right . . . He's supposed to have office hours, um . . . oh, not until Friday. And today's Wednesday. I know for sure that he doesn't have class on Thursday, so he's probably not going to be at school until Friday. Sorry.

W: Oh, I see . . . That's too bad.

M: Is this something urgent? I can give you his email address if you need it. I can't let you know his phone number. He doesn't like it when students call him since some of them have been known to do that rather late at night, but he's really good about answering his email. So, um, would you like to have his email address?

W: Ah, no, I've already got it. But thanks for the offer.

M: Do you mind if I ask why you need to see him?

W: Not at all. I'm a student in one of his classes, and I'm thinking of majoring in Economics. In fact, I'm hoping to declare that as my major even though I'm only a freshman. So, er, I was planning to ask Professor Hauser if he'd serve as my advisor. I took a class with him last semester, and I'm taking another one with him right now. I just love the way that he teaches class. He

totally makes economics so much fun.

M: Yeah, he's one of the most popular professors in the entire department. But just so you know, Professor Hauser gets lots of requests from students to serve as their advisor every semester. For your sake, I hope that your grades are fairly good because he doesn't always accept all of the students that ask him to be their advisor. If he did, he'd have way too many advisees.

W: He doesn't take everyone? Oh, no. What if he says no? I don't know any other professors in the department.

M: How are your grades?

W: I got an A in his class last semester, and I just aced the midterm exam. So I'd say that I've been doing a good job in his classes.

M: You're getting A's? Then you've got nothing to worry about.

W: That's a relief.

M: Oh, do you have all of the forms that you need to fill out in order to declare a major?

W: Forms?

M: I'll take that as a no. Just a sec . . . Here . . . and here . . . These are the two required forms. You need to fill out both of these and have Professor Hauser sign them. Uh, assuming that he takes you on as an advisee, that is. [5]Then, you need to turn them in to the Registrar's Office, and you'll be an Economics major.

W: Excellent. Thanks for your help. **And I'll see you around.**

Translation

M Economics Department Secretary: 안녕하세요. 제가 도와 드릴 일이 있을까요?

W Student: 어, 안녕하세요. 네, 그래요. 저는 *Hauser* 교수님을 찾고 있어요.

M: 사무실에 가보았나요? 5층에 위치해 있죠. 사무실이, 음… 504호일 거에요.

W: 네, 방금 전에 그곳에 가서 노크를 해보았지만, 아무런 대답이 없더군요. 그리고 교수님 사무실의 불이 꺼져 있는 것으로 보아, 그분이 그곳에 계시지 않다는 점은 확실해요.

M: 알겠어요. 기다리시면 제가 잠시 그분의 스케줄을 확인해 볼게요.

W: 네.

M: 좋아요… 그분은, 음… 오, 금요일까지는 사무실 근무 시간이 없으시군요. 그리고 오늘은 수요일이고요. 목요일에는 수업이 없으시다고 확실히 알고 있는데, 아마 금요일까지는 학교에 오지 않으실 것 같아요. 유감이네요.

W: 오, 알겠어요… 안 되었군요.

M: 급한 일인가요? 필요하다면, 그분의 이메일 주소를 알려줄 수 있어요. 전화번호는 알려드릴 수 없지만요. 일부 학생들이 밤늦게 전화를 한다고 알려져 있기 때문에 학생들의 전화를 받는 것은 좋아하지 않으시지만, 이메일에는 정말로 답을 잘 해주세요. 그래서, 음, 이메일 주소를 알고 싶나요?

W: 아, 아니에요. 이미 알고 있어요. 하지만 말씀해 주셔서 고마워

요.

M: 왜 그분을 만나야 하는지 물어봐도 될까요?

W: 물론이에요. 저는 그분의 수업 중 하나를 듣고 있는 학생인데, 경제학을 전공하려고 생각하고 있어요. 사실, 저는 신입생일 뿐이지만 전공으로 경제학을 선택할 수 있기를 바라고 있죠. 그래서, 어, *Hauser* 교수님께서 제 지도 교수님이 되어 주실 수 있는지 여쭤볼 생각이었어요. 지난 학기에 그분의 수업을 들었고, 현재 하나 더 들을 예정이에요. 그분이 수업하는 방식을 정말로 좋아하거든요. 경제학을 정말 재미있게 가르쳐 주세요.

M: 네, 그분께서는 학과 전체에서 가장 인기 있는 교수님 중의 한 분이시죠. 하지만, 알고 있는 대로, *Hauser* 교수님께서는 매 학기마다 자신의 지도 교수가 되어달라는 학생들의 요구를 많이 받고 계세요. 학생을 위해 말을 하면, 그분은 지도 교수가 되어달라는 학생들의 요구를 항상 받아들이시지는 않기 때문에 학생의 성적이 매우 좋기를 바라요. 만약 모두 받아들이신다면, 지도 학생들이 정말로 많게 될 거에요.

W: 모든 사람들을 받지는 않으신다고요? 오, 이런. 거절하시면 어떻게 하죠? 경제학과의 다른 교수님들은 모르고 있는데요.

M: 학점이 어떻게 되나요?

W: 지난 학기 그분의 수업에서 A를 받았는데, 중간고사에서는 최고 점수를 받았어요. 그래서 그분 수업에서의 성적은 좋은 편이라고 말씀드릴 수 있죠.

M: A를 받았다고요? 그러면 걱정할 것이 없어요.

W: 마음이 놓이는군요.

M: 오, 전공을 정하기 위해 기입해야 하는 양식들을 모두 가지고 있나요?

W: 양식이요?

M: 없다는 것으로 받아들일게요. 잠시만요… 여기… 그리고 여기… 필요한 두 양식이 이것이에요. 두 양식에 기입을 해서 *Hauser* 교수님의 서명을 받아야 해요. 어, 그분이 학생의 지도교수님이 된다고 가정하면, 그렇죠. 그런 다음, 학적과에 제출을 해야 하는데, 그러면 경제학 전공이 될 거에요.

W: 정말 잘 되었군요. 도와주셔서 감사합니다. 나중에 또 뵐게요.

Script

| 02-03 |

W Professor: All right, everyone. [11]Let's settle down, please . . . Now, during the course of this term, we're going to examine the modern novel, which means we're going to look at works from the 1800s and 1900s. In order to do this well, we need to understand three basic terms: Realism, Modernism, and Postmodernism. These refer to eras of writing. Certain novels and novelists are often placed into these categories. But before I talk about all three of them, I really need to stress one thing: These are not clearly defined literary movements, so there is often disagreement among literary critics as to whether a certain novel or novelist belongs in one period or another.

That having been said, let's jump right in and take a look at all three periods. If you took my class last semester, you'll remember that we explored Romanticism, which utilized flowery language and had rather unrealistic stories. Realism arose after the Romantic Period, and it was largely a reaction against Romanticism. Writers in the Realist Period began looking at the world around them. They saw the mundane everyday lives of the common people and wrote stories about them. They focused on the small things in life . . . um, what people did in the morning, at their jobs, and with their friends. They also examined the relationships people had with their friends and families and how they dealt with problems in their lives. There were no grand adventures or mystical quests in their works like there were in those of the Romantics.

Pardon me. During the mid-nineteenth century, several European writers started to experiment with the ideas of Realism. This was particularly true of writers in France and Russia. Gustave Flaubert from France is considered the first true writer of this period. But note that his novels often crossed the line between Romanticism and Realism. Additionally, the great Russian novelists of the nineteenth century—Tolstoy, Dostoyevsky, and Turgenev—are considered Realists. We'll examine them more closely this term just so you know. As for the English-speaking world, English author George Elliot's novel *Middlemarch* is often regarded as the first work of the Realist Period in English literature. It was published in 1871. Basically, the late nineteenth century was the time of Realism in literature.

By the early twentieth century, a new movement had begun. It was called Modernism. Much like Realism was a reaction to Romanticism, Modernism was a reaction to Realism. Modernist writers wanted to break free from the bonds of Realism so that they could use new literary techniques. Chief among them were timelines that didn't flow from one day to the next. Modernist stories often jumped around by going back and forth in time. Modernist writers also utilized stream of consciousness when they wrote. Uh, this means that they wrote whatever they were thinking at the time. It didn't matter if the words they wrote related to the overall plot or any unifying themes in their works. Irony and satire are two more characteristics of the Modernist Period. Works from this time are largely pessimistic, show a distrust of the government and social order, and display the authors' needs to get across to their readers their opinions on various social issues of the day. Modernism is regarded as arising partly as a reaction to the horrors of World War I. Modernist writers typically saw themselves as the ones who needed to . . . wake up society and alert it to the dangers of trusting authority, namely, uh, the government.

As for Modernist writers, I'd say that James Joyce is the most famous, and his novel *Ulysses* is seen as the epitome of Modernist writing. Other novelists who belonged to this period are T.S. Eliot, John Steinbeck, Marcel Proust, Ezra Pound, D.H. Lawrence, William Faulkner, and Ernest Hemingway. I'm sure you all have heard of most of these writers and have probably read a few of their books. We'll cover some—but not all—of them this semester.

Now, what about Postmodernism . . . ? Well, first, it's somewhat difficult to determine when Modernism ended and Postmodernism began, but most critics use World War II in the 1940s as a dividing point. Also, Postmodernism is rather difficult to define, and many critics actually disagree as to, well, what exactly it is. Let me compare it with Modernism. That might help you understand. The key difference between the two is that while Modernist writers believed they could find an answer to the chaos in the world, Postmodernist writers simply gave up. They regarded the world as a chaotic place where there were no answers to the problems plaguing it. Postmodernist writers were content to have their stories and characters fit into this world. They weren't on any great quests, nor did they seek to solve the world's problems. They were just living and playing in the world as it was. Postmodernist writers were greatly influenced by the extreme violence of World War II, the start of the Cold War, and the growth of technology in the 1950s and 1960s. Now, as for Postmodernist writers, there are quite a few notable ones.

Translation

W Professor: 좋아요, 여러분. 자리에 앉아 주세요… 자, 이번 학기 동안, 우리는 현대 소설에 대해 알아볼 것인데, 이는 1800년대와 1900년대의 작품들을 살펴볼 것이라는 점을 의미합니다. 그렇게 하기 위해서는, 세 가지 기본적인 용어를 이해해야 합니다: 사실주의, 모더니즘, 그리고 포스트모더니즘입니다. 이들은 작품들의 시대를 의미합니다. 특정 소설 및 소설가들이 이러한 범주에 따라 종종 구분되기도 하죠. 하지만 이 세 시기에 대해 언급하기에 앞서, 한 가지를 강조해야 할 것 같습니다: 이들이 명확히 정의된 문학 운동은 아니기 때문에, 따라서 특정 소설이나 소설가가 어떤 시기에 속하는지 혹은 다른 시기에 속하는지에 대해서는 문학 비평가들 사이에 종종 의견이 일치하지 않고 있습니다.

어쨌든, 넘어가서 이 세 시기 모두를 살펴보도록 합시다. 지난 학기 때 제 수업을 들으셨다면, 우리가 낭만주의를 살펴보았다는 점을 기억할 것인데, 낭만주의는 미사여구를 활용했고 다소 비현실적인 이야기를 담고 있었습니다. 사실주의는 낭만주의 시대 이후에 일어난 사조였으며, 대체적으로 낭만주의에 대한 반발의 성격을 띠고 있었습니다. 사실주의 시대의 작가들은 주위의 세상을 살펴보기 시작했습니다. 이들은 평범한 사람들의 세속적인 일상 생활을 보고 그러한 사람들의 주변 세상에 대한 글을 썼습니다. 삶에 있어서의 작은 것들에 초점을 맞췄는데… 음, 아침에, 일터에서, 그리고 친구들과 함께, 사람들이 하는 일에 초점을 맞추었습니다. 또한 친구들 및 가족들과의 관계와, 삶에서 문제들을 처리하는 방식을 관찰했습니다. 낭만주의 작품에서와 달리, 대단한 모험이나 신화적인 탐색도 그들의 작품 속에서는 존재하지 않았습니다.

죄송합니다. 19세기 동안, 유럽의 몇몇 작가들은 사실주의

의 아이디어로 실험을 시작했습니다. 이는 특히 프랑스와 러시아 작가들에게 있어서 사실이었죠. 프랑스 출신의 귀스타브 플로베르가 이러한 시기를 나타내는 최초의 작가로 생각되고 있습니다. 하지만 그의 소설에는 종종 낭만주의와 사실주의 간의 경계가 모호하게 나타나고 있다는 점에 주목해 주십시오. 또한, 19세기 러시아의 위대한 소설가들도 — 톨스토이, 도스토예프스키, 그리고 투르게네프도 — 사실주의 작가로 여겨지고 있습니다. 여러분도 알겠지만, 이번 학기에는 이들을 보다 면밀히 살펴볼 것입니다. 영어권 국가에서, 영국인 작가 조지 엘리어트의 소설 미들마치는 종종 영국 문학에 있어서 사실주의 작품의 효시로 간주되고 있습니다. 이 소설은 1871년에 출판되었습니다. 기본적으로, 19세기 후반은 문학에 있어서 사실주의의 시대였습니다.

20세기 초반이 되자, 새로운 사조가 시작되었습니다. 모더니즘이라고 불리는 것이었죠. 사실주의가 낭만주의에 대한 반발이었던 것처럼, 모더니즘 역시 사실주의에 대한 반발이었습니다. 모더니즘 작가들은 새로운 문학적 기교를 사용하기 위해 사실주의의 속박으로부터 벗어나고자 했습니다. 그 중 중요한 것이 시간 순서에 관한 것이었는데, 특정한 날 다음 그 다음 날로 이어지는 것이 아니었습니다. 종종 모더니즘의 이야기들은 시간 상 앞뒤로 왔다갔다함으로써 시간을 뛰어 넘었습니다. 모더니즘 작가들은 또한 글을 쓸 때 의식의 흐름을 활용했습니다. 어, 이는 순간적으로 생각나는 무엇이든 쓰는 것을 의미합니다. 그들이 적는 단어가 작품의 전체적인 구성이나 통일된 주제와 연관이 되는지는 중요하지 않았습니다. 반어와 풍자는 모더니즘 시대의 또 다른 두 가지 특징이었습니다. 이 시기의 작품들은 대체적으로 염세적이었고, 정부와 사회 질서에 대한 불신을 나타내었으며, 그리고 작품을 통해 당시의 다양한 사회적 이슈에 대한 자신들의 의견을 독자들에게 전달하고자 했습니다. 모더니즘은 부분적으로 세계 1차 대전이라는 공포에 대한 반작용으로 나타났다고 생각됩니다. 전형적으로 모더니즘 작가들은 스스로를, 어, 사회를 일깨워서 사회에 정권에 대한 믿음이, 즉, 어, 정부에 대한 믿음이 위험할 수 있다는 점을 경고해 주는 사람으로 바라보았습니다.

모더니즘 작가에 대해 말씀드리면, 제임스 조이스가 가장 유명하다고 해야 할 것 같은데, 그의 소설 율리시스는 모더니즘 작품의 정수라고 간주되고 있습니다. 이러한 시대에 속하는 다른 작가들로는 T.S. 엘리어트, 존 스타인벡, 마르셀 프루스트, 에즈라 파운드, D.H. 로렌스, 윌리엄 포크너, 그리고 어니스트 헤밍웨이가 있습니다. 여러분 모두가 이러한 대부분의 작가들의 이름을 들어보고, 아마 이들의 몇몇 작품들은 읽어보셨을 것으로 확신합니다. 이 중 일부를 – 전부는 아니고 – 이번 학기에 다루어 볼 예정입니다.

자, 포스트모더니즘은 어떨까요…? 음, 우선, 모더니즘이 언제 끝나서 포스트모더니즘이 언제 시작되었는지를 정하는 것은 다소 어려운 일이지만, 대부분의 비평가들은 1940년대의 세계 2차 대전을 그러한 분기점으로 바라보고 있습니다. 또한, 포스트모더니즘은 정의를 내리기가 꽤 어려우며, 많은 비평가들 사이에서 실제로, 음, 정확히 그것이 무엇인지에 관한 의견은 엇갈리고 있습니다. 포스트모더니즘을 모더니즘과 비교해 보도록 합시다. 그러면 여러분의 이해에 도움이 될 것입니다. 이 둘의 중요한 차이점은 모더니즘 작가들이 세상의 혼돈에 대해 답

을 찾아낼 수 있으리라고 믿었던 반면, 포스트모더니즘 작가들은 그것을 포기했다는 점입니다. 세상을 어지럽히는 문제들에 대해 그들은 그에 대한 해답이 존재하지 않는 세상에서 살고 있다고 생각했습니다. 포스트모더니즘 작가들은 자신의 이야기와 극중 인물들이 이러한 세상에 적응토록 하는데 만족했습니다. 대단한 탐구도 하지 않았고, 세상의 문제들을 해결하려고 하지도 않았습니다. 단지 있는 그대로의 세상 속에서 살면서 즐기려고 했습니다. 포스트모더니즘 작가들은 세계 2차 대전의 극단적인 폭력성, 냉전의 시작, 그리고 1950년대와 1960년대의 기술 발전에 의해 막대한 영향을 받았습니다. 자, 포스트모더니즘 작가들에 대해 말씀을 드리면, 주목해야 할 것들이 상당히 많습니다.

Actual Test 03

Reading Section p.33

Answers

1. Ⓓ [Factual Question]

2. Ⓑ [Rhetorical Purpose Question]

3. Ⓒ [Factual Question]

4. Ⓓ [Inference Question]

5. Ⓒ [Vocabulary Question]

6. Ⓐ [Inference Question]

7. Ⓐ [Vocabulary Question]

8. Ⓓ [Negative Factual Questionn]

9. Ⓓ [Rhetorical Purpose Question]

10. Ⓓ [Vocabulary Question]

11. Ⓑ [Reference Question]

12. Ⓑ [Factual Question]

13.

HUMBOLDT SQUID EXPANSION	
Cause	Ⓑ, Ⓔ
Effect	Ⓒ, Ⓕ, Ⓖ

[Fill in a Table Question]

Translation

훔볼트오징어의 확산

세상에서 가장 큰 오징어의 종 중 하나는 훔볼트오징어인데, 이들은 태평양 동부 지역에서 서식한다. 이 오징어는 사람과 비슷한 크기까지 자라기도 하고, 매우 빠르며, 수면 위로 높이 뛰어오르는 것이 목격된 적도 있다. 한 때, 이 오징어의 분포 지역은 칠레의 북부 지역에서부터 미국 캘리포니아의 샌디에고에 이르는 태평양 동부 해안이었다. 하지만, 최근 몇 년 동안, 이 오징어가 남쪽으로는 남미 최남단에 위치해 있는 티에라 델 푸에고에서, 북쪽으로는 북미의 알래스카에서도 발견되었다. 이는 태평양 해수의 변화로 인하여 수많은 죽음의 해역이 형성되었기 때문인데, 죽음의 해역이란, 커다란 많은 해양 생명체들에게는 적합하지 않지만, 훔볼트오징어들이 번성하고 있는 장소이다.

이 오징어는 훔볼트 해류의 이름을 따서 그 이름이 붙여졌는데, 이 해류는 남미 서해안 해변 인근에서 흐르는 차갑고, 영양분이 풍부한 해류이다. 이 해류가 흐르는 지역이 훔볼트오징어가 주로 서식하는 영역이다. 하지만, 2002년경, 해양 생물학자들은 오징어의 분포 지역이 확장되고 있다는 사실을 발견했다. 그들은 이러한 현상이 바다에서 죽음의 해역이 증가하는 것과 일치한다는 사실을 알게 되었다. 죽음의 해역은 수중 산소량이 극히 부족한 지역이다. 일반적으로 산업 폐기물과 농업에 사용되는 화학 물질들에 의하여 오염된 해안 인근의 강어귀와 관련이 있었던 죽음의 해역은 최근 수심이 깊은 지역에서도 발견되고 있다. 이러한 심해의 죽음의 해역은 자연스럽게 생겨나고 있다. 죽은 물고기와 해양 식물들의 유기 물질이 바다의 밑바닥으로 떨어지는데, 이곳에서 이산화탄소를 배출하는 박테리아들이 이러한 유기 물질을 먹는다. 유기 물질이 풍부하면, 박테리아의 수가 급증하여, 따라서 더욱 많은 이산화탄소가 생겨난다. 그 결과 죽음의 해역이 생성된다.

이러한 죽음의 해역에서는 물속의 막대한 양의 산소를 활용해야 하는 참치나 상어 같은 큰 물고기들이 좀처럼 헤엄쳐 다니지 않는다. 하지만, 훔볼트오징어는 낮은 산소 수준에 영향을 덜 받는 것으로 보이며, 어떤 이유인지는 모르겠지만, 장기간 죽음의 해역에 머무를 수 있다. 게다가, 크릴새우와 같은 작은 해양 생물들도 낮은 산소 수준의 영향을 덜 받기 때문에, 이 오징어는 죽음의 해역에서 지속적인 먹이를 확보할 수 있다. 마지막으로, 훔볼트오징어는 참치와 상어가 좋아하는 먹이이지만, 죽음의 해역에는 이들이 없기 때문에, 이 오징어가 먹이사슬의 가장 위를 차지한다.

과학자들이 혼란스러워 하는 주요한 문제는 태평양 동부 지역에서 죽음의 해역이 확장되고 있는 원인이다. 여기에는 여러 가능성이 존재하는데, 기후의 변화, 해양의 여러 층에서의 온도의 차이, 바람의 패턴의 변화, 그리고 해류의 변화가 그것이다. 난류 지역에서, 죽음의 해역은 해수면으로부터 200에서 1,000미터 아래의 지역에 걸쳐있는데, 이 지역이 바로 훔볼트오징어의 주된 먹이 활동 장소이다. 2002년 이전, 죽음의 해역은 이 오징어가 커다란 포식자들에게 방해를 받지 않고 먹이 활동을 할 수 있는 정도인 — 해수면에서 400에서 500미터 정도의 — 매우 깊은 곳이 시작 지점이었다. 하지만 2002년 이래로, 죽음의 해역은 그 크기와 범위가 증가했고, 훔볼트오징어의 수와 서식 범위 또한 증가하게 되었다.

이전에는 서식하지 않았던 지역으로 훔볼트오징어가 이동을 하게 되면서, 해양 생물학자들 사이에서는 상당한 우려의 목소리가 나오고 있다. 이들 중 가장 우려되는 것은 이 오징어가 먹는 해양 생물의 수이다. 훔볼트오징어는 주로 크릴새우와 다른 작은 해양 생물들을 먹으며 살아간다. 하지만, 몇몇 오징어의 사체에 대한 최근 연구에 따르면, 이들의 소화 기관 내에서 대구나 연어와 같은 상업용 어류의 일부분이 발견되었다. 수산업 종사자들은 훔볼트오징어의 확산이 지속될 경우, 이러한 물고기의 어획량이 감소하기 시

작할 것이라고 우려하고 있다. 그들의 우려는 칠레에서 이미 현실
화되었는데, 이 지역에서는 훔볼트오징어 때문에 대구의 수가 상당
히 감소했다. 지금은, 오직 수산업만이 오징어의 영향을 받는 것으
로 알려져 있다. 하지만, 이 오징어가 일반적으로 서식하지 않았던
지역으로 계속해서 이동해 나간다면, 태평양 동부의 여러 지역들도
상당한 변화를 겪게 될 것이다.

Listening Section p.39

Answers

1. B [Gist-Content Question]

2. C [Understanding Function Question]

3. C [Detail Question]

4. A [Gist-Purpose Question]

5. C [Making Inferences Question]

6. B, C [Detail Question]

7. C [Understanding Organization Question]

8. A [Detail Question]

9. B [Making Inferences Question]

10. B [Understanding Function Question]

11. A [Understanding Attitude Question]

Script

| 03-02 |

W Student: Professor Gilbert, good afternoon. I'm here for our three thirty meeting. Do you mind if I come in?

M Professor: Not at all, Susan. Long time no see. Please make yourself comfortable in my office. I'm terribly sorry about the mess in here. I'm doing some research for a book that I'm writing, so I've got all of these books and articles spread out all over the place. It looks bad, but I like having my research materials easily available.

W: Wow, it sounds great that you're writing a book. Are you almost done with it?

M: Hmm . . . I've probably got about another month of writing, and then it will be done. Then, of course, I'll have to proofread it, do rewrites . . . So, anyway, our meeting . . .

W: Ah, yes. Our meeting.

M: Now, you're a freshman in your first semester here, and I'm your student advisor, so the school mandates that we have a meeting during the middle of this semester. So tell me . . . how are you finding your classes? Any problems?

W: Well, I'd say that they're going pretty well so far. Let me see . . . My best class is microeconomics. I got an A on the midterm.

M: Well done. And your other classes?

W: I'm getting an A⁻ in my calculus class, an A⁻ in my Latin class, and a B⁺ in my biology class. As for my anthropology class, I'm not sure about my grade in that one.

M: Why's that?

W: We just took the midterm exam last week, but the professor hasn't returned our exams to us. So I haven't got the slightest idea what my grade is. I think I did well, but I don't know for sure.

M: All right. It sounds like your grades are not a problem at all. How would you say that you're, uh, adjusting to college life?

W: Hmm . . . I don't think I'm having any problems. I mean, I attended a boarding school during my senior year of high school, so I'm already used to living away from home. And my roommate is the same girl that I roomed with at that school, so we get along really well. We, um, actually chose to be roommates. And I don't have any early morning classes either, which is a good thing since I'm a night person. So, uh, I haven't missed a class the entire year. Oh, and I've got a part-time job at the music library. It's nice and quiet there, and I don't have to do that much work while I'm on the job. I rather like that.

M: Outstanding. I must say that it sounds like you're doing very well. Oh, uh, have you decided on a major yet?

W: No, not really. I mean, I'm considering both economics and biology. But I'm going to take some classes in other departments during the spring semester. That way, I can get rid of a few requirements and also see if I have an interest in any other fields. I don't have to choose a major until my sophomore year, right?

M: That's correct. You should definitely be sure to experiment around and take some other classes next semester. I like that idea. Okay, um, I think we're done here. Drop by anytime during the semester if you have any questions or need help.

W: I shall. Thanks a lot. I'll be sure to visit your office in a few weeks when I have to register for next semester's classes. Until then, I'll see you around.

Translation

W Student: *Gilbert* 교수님, 안녕하세요. 3시 반에 만나기로 해서 왔는데요. 안으로 들어가도 될까요?

M Professor: 어서 들어와요, *Susan*. 오랜만이군요. 제 사무실에서는 편안하게 있어도 돼요. 여기 안이 지저분해서 정말 미안해요. 지금 쓰고 있는 책에 대한 조사를 하고 있는 중이어서, 이 모든 책들과 글들이 어질러져 있죠. 좋아 보이지는 않지만, 연구 자료들을 쉽게 찾을 수가 있어서 좋아요.

W: 와, 책을 쓰고 계신다니 멋지게 들리는군요. 거의 다 쓰셨나요?

M: 흠… 아마 쓰는데 한 달은 더 걸릴 것 같은데, 그 후에는 다 되겠죠. 그런 다음에는, 물론, 교정을 보고, 고쳐 쓰고… 그래서, 어쨌든, 만나자고 한 것이…

W: 아, 네. 만나자고 하신 것이요.

M: 자, 학생은 여기서 첫 학기를 보내고 있는 신입생이고, 저는 학생의 지도 교수이기 때문에, 학교측에서는 우리가 이번 학기 중간에 만날 것을 요구하고 있죠. 그래서 말을 해보세요… 수업이 어떤 것 같나요? 문제라도 있나요?

W: 음, 지금까지는 꽤 잘 되어가고 있는 것 같다고 말씀드리고 싶어요. 생각해 보면… 가장 좋은 수업은 미시경제학이에요. 중간고사에서 A를 받았죠.

M: 잘 했군요. 다른 수업은요?

W: 미적분학 수업에서는 A⁻를 받았고, 라틴어 수업에서도 A⁻를, 그리고 생물학 수업에서는 B⁺를 받았어요. 오, 인류학 수업에 대해서 말씀을 드리면, 이 수업에서의 성적은 확실하지가 않고요.

M: 왜 그렇죠?

W: 지난 주에 중간고사를 봤지만, 교수님께서 저희에게 시험지를 돌려주지 않으셨어요. 그래서 제 성적이 어떤지 전혀 알 수가 없어요. 잘 봤다고 생각은 하지만, 확실하게는 모르겠어요.

M: 좋아요. 학생의 성적에는 전혀 문제가 없는 것 같이 들리는군요. 대학 생활에 적응하는 것에 대해서는, 어, 어떻게 말하고 싶나요?

W: 흠… 문제가 있다고 생각하지는 않아요. 제 말은, 고등학교 3학년 때 기숙 학교에 다녔기 때문에, 이미 집에서 멀리 떨어져 사는 것에는 익숙해 있어요. 그리고 고등학교 때 방을 같이 썼던 학생이 제 룸메이트여서, 정말로 잘 지내고 있어요. 우리는, 음, 실제로 서로를 룸메이트로 선택했어요. 그리고 오전 일찍 시작하는 수업도 없는데, 제가 저녁형 인간이라 잘 된 것 같아요. 그래서, 어, 학기 내내 수업에 빠진 적도 없고요. 오, 그리고 음악 도서관에서 아르바이트를 하고 있어요. 그곳이 조용하고 좋아서, 일하는 동안 그렇게 많은 일을 할 필요는 없어요. 잘 된 일이죠.

M: 훌륭하군요. 학생이 매우 잘 하고 있다고 해야 할 것 같아요. 오, 어, 전공은 결정했나요?

W: 아니오, 사실 그렇지는 않아요. 제 말은, 경제학과 생물학 모두를 생각하고 있어요. 하지만 봄학기 동안 다른 학과의 수업을 들어볼 거예요. 그렇게 하면, 몇몇 필수 과목들을 이수할 수도 있을 것이고, 또한 제가 다른 분야에 흥미를 갖고 있는지도 확인해 볼 수 있을 거예요. 2학년 때까지 전공을 정할 필요는 없죠, 그렇죠?

M: 맞아요. 잊지 말고 잘 살펴서 다음 학기에는 다른 수업도 들어보도록 해요. 그것이 좋을 것 같아요. 좋아요, 음, 이야기가 끝난 것 같군요. 질문이 있거나 도움이 필요한 경우에는 학기 중어느 때라도 들러 주세요.

W: 그렇게 할게요. 정말 고맙습니다. 몇 주 후 다음 학기 수업을 신청해야 할 때 교수님 사무실에 꼭 들리도록 할게요. 그 때까지, 안녕히 계세요.

Script

| 3-03 |

W Professor: The search for alternative energy has taken scientists to new areas. One that shows promise is that of biofuels. Biofuels are similar to oil and gasoline except for the fact that they come from the processing of organic materials. Some examples of these materials are crops that we normally eat, like corn, sugarcane, wheat, beets, and soybeans. Through special techniques, these organic products can be converted into fuels such as ethanol and biodiesel, which can run cars, trucks, and other machines. The main reason to use biofuels is that they're cleaner and produce fewer contaminants than fossil fuels. They do this because they contain a higher percentage of oxygen, so they burn more cleanly than traditional fossil fuels. This benefits the environment since, well, fewer contaminants being released results in less air pollution.

However, most of the products utilized in the creating of biofuels are important parts of the human food chain. In some places, uh, take Brazil for example . . . Well, Brazil has an abundant supply of sugarcane, so it's possible to produce enough biofuels in the form of ethanol to make the process economical there. But that's not typically the case elsewhere, so most of the world still relies on fossil fuels to supply the energy people need. But there's something else that we can convert into ethanol. I'm talking about cellulose. It comes from the parts of plants that are not edible, such as the wood, leaves, and stalks.

Obviously, we have an abundant supply of cellulose, yet there are many problems involved in processing it. First, all biofuels are made by converting the sugar in the organic material into ethanol. That's usually done by using specially engineered microorganisms that break down the sugar molecules, which are then distilled to create ethanol. But with plant matter, the sugar molecules are surrounded by other material. So it takes a lot of processing just to get to the sugar molecules in the plant matter. You see, um, the sugar in plants is contained in cellulose, but the cellulose itself is protected by a material called lignin, which is what enables plants to have such rigid internal structures. So, first, the plant matter has to be treated in order for the cellulose to be available so that its sugar can be converted. The most common treatment method uses acid hydrolysis.

Here's what happens . . . First, the workers cut the plant matter into very small pieces. Then, they subject it to the acid hydrolysis treatment. Basically, they soak the wood chips, leaves, branches, stalks, uh, whatever, in acid. It's usually sulfuric acid. The acid hydrolysis process frees the cellulose from its bonds to the plant matter. The next step involves using another hydrolysis process to break down the cellulose into sugar molecules. This second hydrolysis process is rather complex. Several methods can be used. Uh, some use chemicals while others employ enzymes.

Once the second hydrolysis process is complete, the sugar has to be fermented. During this stage, the most common method is to use specially engineered microorganisms to break down the sugar. The most common of these microorganisms are certain strains of yeast, which has long been used in various fermentation processes. From this step, the sugar is then distilled much in the same manner that alcohol gets distilled. [10]Finally, the ethanol is produced. But note that the ethanol isn't pure at this stage, so more steps have to be taken to get virtually one-hundred-percent pure ethanol. Once this happens, the ethanol can be used for fuel. Phew. **That's a lot of steps, isn't it?** Tom? Yes?

M Student: So if we can make ethanol from wood products, and, uh, obviously there's an ample supply of wood, which is a renewable resource, then why doesn't every car run on cellulose ethanol?

W: It pretty much all comes down to money. The primary issue is that, for the amount of effort that's put into making ethanol from cellulose, the returns aren't that great. So it's pretty much not economical at the moment. Basically, it's costly because the process is complex. To compare, it's much more complicated than making ethanol from corn or soybeans, both of which have rather easily accessible sugar molecules. In addition, it's much cheaper to search for, locate, and then drill for oil and natural gas. Just so you know, there are only a few places in the world where ethanol is made from plant cellulose. Many governments are funding scientists and research institutes to find improved methods to make the creation of ethanol from cellulose into a viable industry, but there haven't been any breakthroughs yet.

[11]Scientists are hoping for one because, as I explained earlier, ethanol burns much cleaner than fossil fuels. And since plant matter comprises around, oh, about eighty percent of all the Earth's biomass, this means that there's a tremendous supply of raw materials that could be used. **So you can see why we're excited by its potential.** Of course, the tradeoff is that lots of plants and trees would get cut down in the process. However, as Tom pointed out, trees are renewable resources, so it's not like they would permanently disappear from the landscape.

Translation

W Professor: 대체 에너지를 찾기 위한 노력은 과학자들로 하여금 새로운 분야에 다다르도록 만들었습니다. 그 중 유망한 것 중의 하나가 생물 연료입니다. 생물 연료는 그것이 유기 물질의 처리를 통해 만들어 진다는 사실을 제외하고는 석유 및 가솔린과 유사합니다. 이러한 물질의 몇 가지 예로는 옥수수, 사탕수수, 밀, 사탕무, 그리고 콩과 같이 우리가 통상적으로 먹는 작물들이 있습니다. 특별한 기술을 통해, 이러한 유기 물질들은 에탄올과 바이오디젤과 같은 연료로 전환될 수 있는데, 이러한 연료들은 자동차, 트럭, 그리고 기타 기기들을 작동시킬 수 있습니다. 생물 연료를 사용하는 주된 이유는 이들이 화석 연료보다 더 깨끗하고 오염 물질을 더 적게 생산해 내기 때문입니다. 이는 생물 연료에 산소가 많이 포함되어 있기 때문인데, 따라서 생물 연료는 기존의 화석 연료보다 더 깨끗하게 연소됩니다. 오염 물질이 보다 적게 배출되면, 대기 오염이 개선되기 때문에, 이러한 사실은, 음, 환경에 도움이 됩니다.

하지만, 생물 연료를 만들어 내는데 사용되는 대부분의 원료들은 인간의 먹이 사슬에서 중요한 부분을 차지하고 있습니다.

일부 지역에서, 어, 브라질을 예로 들어 봅시다… 음, 브라질에서는 사탕수수가 풍부하게 생산되기 때문에, 그러한 처리 과정을 경제적으로 만들기에 충분한, 에탄올 형태의 생물 연료를 생산해 내는 것이 가능합니다. 하지만 이것이 다른 곳에서도 일반적인 경우는 아니기 때문에, 세계 대부분의 지역에서는 아직도 화석 연료에 의존하여 필요한 에너지를 공급받고 있습니다. 하지만 에탄올로 변환시킬 수 있는 또 다른 물질이 있습니다. 셀룰로오스를 말씀드리고 있는 것입니다. 셀룰로오스는 나무, 잎, 그리고 줄기와 같이 먹을 수 없는 식물의 부분으로부터 나옵니다.

분명, 셀룰로오스는 풍부하지만, 그것을 처리하는 것에는 여러 문제들이 관련되어 있습니다. 먼저, 모든 생물 연료들은 유기 물질 상태의 당을 에탄올로 변환시킴으로써 만들어 집니다. 당 분자를 분해시키도록 특별히 마련된 미생물을 사용함으로써 보통 그렇게 하는데, 그 후 당 분자는 증류를 거치게 되고 이로써 에탄올이 만들어 집니다. 하지만 식물에서, 당 분자는 다른 물질들로 둘러싸여 있습니다. 따라서 식물에 있는 당 분자를 얻기 위해서는 많은 과정이 필요합니다. 아시겠지만, 음, 식물에 있는 당은 셀룰로오스에 포함되어 있지만, 셀룰로오스 자체는 리그닌이라고 불리는 물질에 의해 보호되고 있는데, 리그닌은 식물로 하여금 튼튼한 내부 구조를 가질 수 있도록 해주는 부분입니다. 그래서, 우선, 당이 변환될 수 있도록 셀룰로오스를 이용 가능한 것으로 만들기 위해서는 식물을 처리해야 합니다. 가장 일반적인 처리 방법은 산성 가수 분해를 이용하는 것입니다.

어떤 일이 일어나는지 알려드리죠… 먼저, 작업자들이 식물을 잘라 매우 작은 조각들로 만듭니다. 그런 다음, 산성 가수 분해 처리를 합니다. 기본적으로, 나무 조각, 잎, 가지, 줄기, 어, 그러한 무엇이던지 산에 적십니다. 보통은 황산입니다. 산성 가수 분해 과정으로 셀룰로오스는 식물에서 분리됩니다. 다음 단계는 또 다른 가수 분해 처리를 사용하여 셀룰로오스를 당 분자로 분해시키는 것입니다. 이러한 두 번째 가수 분해 과정은 다소 복잡합니다. 몇 가지 방법들이 사용될 수 있습니다. 어, 화학 물질이 사용되기도 하고, 효모가 사용되기도 합니다.

두 번째 가수 분해 과정이 완료되면, 당을 발효시켜야 합니다. 이러한 단계에서, 가장 일반적인 방법은 당을 분해시키기 위해 특별히 마련된 미생물들을 이용하는 것입니다. 이러한 미생물 중 가장 일반적인 것은 특정 종류의 효모인데, 이들은 다양한 발효 과정에서 오랫동안 사용되어 왔습니다. 이러한 단계에서, 당은 알코올이 증류되는 것과 거의 동일한 방법으로 증류됩니다. 마침내, 에탄올이 생산됩니다. 하지만 이러한 단계에서의 에탄올은 순수한 형태가 아니며, 따라서 실제적으로 100%의 순수한 에탄올을 얻기 위해서는 보다 많은 단계를 거쳐야 한다는 점에 주목해 주십시오. 그렇게 한 후에, 에탄올은 연료로 사용될 수 있습니다. 휴. 많은 단계가 있군요, 그렇지 않나요? Tom? 네?

M Student: 그러면 나무로부터 에탄올을 얻을 수 있고, 어, 충분한 양의 나무가 있다면, 나무는 재생 가능한 자원인데, 왜 모든 차량들이 셀룰로오스 에탄올로 운행되지 않나요?

W: 결국 비용 문제 때문입니다. 가장 중요한 문제는, 셀룰로오스로 에탄올을 만드는 노력의 크기에 비해, 그에 대한 보수가 그렇게 크지는 않다는 점입니다. 따라서 지금 당장으로서는 크게 경제적이지 못한 것이죠. 기본적으로, 처리 과정이 복잡하기 때문에 비용이 많이 듭니다. 비교를 해보면, 이는 옥수수나 콩으로

에탄올을 만드는 것보다 훨씬 더 복잡한데, 옥수수와 콩에는 다소 쉽게 얻을 수 있는 당 분자들이 포함되어 있습니다. 또한, 석유와 천연 가스를 찾아, 위치를 정해서, 시추를 하는 것이 훨씬 더 저렴합니다. 아시는 대로, 식물의 셀룰로오스로부터 에탄올을 만들어 내는 곳은 전 세계에서 몇 군데 없습니다. 많은 정부들이 과학자들과 연구 기관에 투자하여 셀룰로오스로 에탄올을 만드는 방법을 개선시킴으로써 이를 유망한 산업으로 만들려고 하고 있지만, 아직까지는 커다란 진보가 없습니다.

과학자들은, 앞서 제가 설명했듯이, 에탄올이 화석 연료보다 더 깨끗이 연소되기 때문에, 한 가지는 희망하고 있습니다. 그리고 식물은 지구의 생물량 중, 오, 약 80%를 차지하고 있는데, 이는 사용될 수 있는 막대한 양의 원료가 존재한다는 점을 의미합니다. 따라서 왜 우리가 그 잠재력에 의해 흥분되어 있는지 여러분들도 알 수 있을 것입니다. 물론, 그에 대한 대가는 그러한 처리 과정에서 수많은 식물과 나무들이 베어질 것이라는 점입니다. 하지만, *Tom*이 지적했듯이, 나무는 재생 가능한 자원이기 때문에, 나무가 자연에서 영원히 사라질 것 같지는 않습니다.

Actual Test 04

Reading Section p.45

Answers

1. Ⓒ [Vocabulary Question]
2. Ⓑ [Reference Question]
3. Ⓑ [Inference Question]
4. Ⓓ [Sentence Simplification Question]
5. Ⓓ [Factual Question]
6. Ⓐ [Vocabulary Question]
7. Ⓑ [Vocabulary Question]
8. Ⓐ [Negative Factual Question]
9. Ⓓ [Factual Question]
10. Ⓐ [Vocabulary Question]
11. Ⓒ [Factual Question]
12. Ⓐ [Rhetorical Purpose Question]
13. 4th [Insert Text Question]
14. Ⓐ, Ⓑ, Ⓒ [Prose Summary Question]

동료 압박

대다수의 사람들이 친구들을 사귀고 싶어하고 다른 사람들과의 교제를 원한다는 점에서 인간은 본능적으로 사회적이다. 집단에 소속되고, 받아들여지며, 친구를 사귀고 싶어하는 욕구들은 대부분의 사람들이 경험하는 감정이다. 하지만 부분적으로는 이렇게 집단에 소속되고자 하는 충동으로 인하여, 타인들로부터 자신들의 마음을 편치 못하게 하는 특정한 행동에 참여하도록 압박을 받게 될 수도 있다. 이러한 압박으로 인하여 사람들은 무엇이 옳고 그른지를 판단하는데 있어서 잘못을 하게 된다. 이러한 잘못들은 악의가 없고 해를 끼치지 않을 수도 있지만, 어떤 경우, 위험할 수도 있으며, 행동에 가담하는 사람들뿐만이 아니라 다른 사람들을 다치게 할 수도 있다.

동료란 어떤 사람의 또래 집단에 속해 있는 사람들이다. 많은 경우, 그들은 함께 성장을 하며 학교에 다니는 이들이다. 사람들은 종종 그들의 동료와 친구가 되며, 이에 따라서, 함께 사회 활동을 하며 평생 지속될 수도 있는 유대 관계를 형성하는 경우가 많다. 하지만, 나이가 들면서, 어린이들은 비도덕적이고, 금지된, 심지어 법을 어기는 행동들에 노출되기 시작한다. 젊은이들은 — 특히 십대들은 — 일반적으로 부모님이나 선생님들과 같은 어른들에게 반항하는 시험적인 행동들을 해본다. 그들은 문제를 일으키지 않으면서 해낼 수 있는 행동들이 어떤 것인지 알아보기 위한 시도를 한다. 옳고 그름의 경계에 다가가면서, 그들은 자신의 친구들도 그들과 함께 하기를 원한다. 하지만, 동료 집단에서, 모든 이들이 비도덕적이고, 금지된 혹은 불법적인 활동에 참여하려고 하는 것은 아니다. 몇몇 젊은이들은 도덕심을 가지고 있고, 부모님, 학교 제도, 혹은 경찰의 권위를 두려워하여, 특정한 활동들에 참여하지 않는다.

이때가 바로 동료 압박이 가해지는 때이다. 동료 집단 내 다른 사람들은 모든 사람들이 따라 하는데 동의할 때까지 망설이는 이들을 부추긴다. 이러한 일이 일어나면, 이들은 동료 압박에 굴복하게 된다. 첫째로, 많은 사람들은 다른 동료들로부터 비웃음을 사는 것을 피하고자 한다. 혼자서 행동을 하려는 사람들은 거의 없으며, 대부분의 사람들이 집단에 속해있다는 것을 편안하게 생각한다. 동료 집단에 소속되어 있다는 것의 한 가지 측면은 구성원들이 집단에서 배척되지 않기 위해서 모두가 하나로서 행동해야 한다는 점이다. 어린이들과 십대들의 경우, 집단을 따르는 것을 꺼려하게 되면 다른 구성원들로부터의 놀림과 조롱이 뒤따르게 된다. 남자아이들은 그들의 남자다움이나 용기를 의심받으며 놀림을 당하는 반면에 여자아이들은 그들의 옷이나 외모에 대해서 모욕적인 말을 듣게 되는 경우가 일반적이다. 많은 경우, 이러한 대우는 고통스럽고 정신적인 고통을 일으킬 수도 있다. 조롱을 당하지 않기 위해서, 많은 어린이들과 십대들은 동료 압박에 굴복하고 다른 이들이 하는 대로 행동을 한다.

사람들이 동료 압박에 굴복하는 두 번째 이유는, 자신들이 하고 있는 행동이 불법적이거나 위험하다고 할지라도 친구들을 실망시키는 사람으로 보여지고 싶어하지 않기 때문이다. 이는 특히 남자아이들의 경우에 더욱 그러한데, 이들은 누군가가 다른 아이들을 따르지 않으면 그들의 집단에 대한 충성도를 의심하게 된다. 함께 하지 않으면, 그들은 아마도 동료 집단에서 쫓겨나게 될 것이며, 합법적이든 아니든, 어떠한 활동에도 더 이상 초대받지 못하게 될 것이다. 이러한 점에서, 남자아이들은 왕따가 되지 않기 위해 그들의 집단에 머물러야 한다고 느끼게 될 것이다. 동료 집단에서 쫓겨난다는 것은 아마도 젊은이들이 — 특히 남자아이들이 — 해서는 안될 행동들을 억지로 할 수 밖에 없게 만드는 가장 큰 두려움일 것이다.

마지막으로, 많은 젊은이들은 동료 집단 내의 다른 사람들로부터 인기를 얻고 싶어서 금지된 행동에 가담한다. 술을 마시고 담배를 피우는 것은 동료 압박의 이러한 측면과 관련이 있다. 젊은이들은 부모님들과 다른 어른들이 술을 마시고 담배를 피우는 것을 보고, 이러한 행동들이 어른스럽고 멋지다고 생각하게 된다. 그리고 나면 그들은, 이러한 행동들이 자신들과 다른 사람들에게 위험하다는 것을 알고 있다 하더라도, 이러한 행동들을 직접 하면서 어른들을 흉내 내려고 한다. (예를 들면, 몇몇 십대들은 음주운전을 하다가 자동차 사고로 사망하기도 한다.) 대부분의 경우, 집단의 어느 한 명이 — 아마도 그 집단의 리더가 — 다른 이들도 이러한 행동을 하도록 그들을 압박할 것이다. 집단 내에서 자신들의 인기와 지위를 유지하기 위해, 다른 사람들은 리더에게 굴복하고 그를 따를 수밖에 없다.

Listening Section

p.51

Answers

1. C [Gist-Purpose Question]
2. A, C [Detail Question]
3. B [Understanding Attitude Question]
4. C [Understanding Function Question]
5. A [Making Inferences Question]
6. B [Gist-Content Question]
7. C [Detail Question]
8. B [Understanding Function Question]
9. D [Making Inferences Question]
10. A [Understanding Organization Question]
11. A [Understanding Attitude Question]

Script

| 04-02 |

M1 Student: Pardon me, but I really need to talk to a person in this office about my housing situation. Are you someone that can help me?

M2 Housing Office Employee: I sure hope so. Otherwise, the school might not want to keep me working here any longer. Anyway, to be serious, sure, I can probably assist you with your problem.

M1: That's great. You see, I've got a single room in Keller Dormitory. You know where that is, right?

M2: Sure. It's next to Bronwin Hall. Oh . . . I think I know why you're here.

M1: You do?

M2: Well, I've got a good idea, but why don't you tell me first?

M1: Okay . . . It's the smell. There's an awful smell in that dorm.

M2: Yeah, that's what I thought you were going to say.

M1: [4]So you're already aware of this problem?

M2: Oh, yeah. You can trust me when I say that everyone here is definitely aware of the problem.

M1: So, uh, what's going on? Why does that place smell like, uh, to be blunt . . . a garbage dump?

M2: We're not really sure. I hate to admit that, but it's true. You see, as I'm sure you're already aware, the smell suddenly appeared . . . uh, what was it? Three days ago, right?

M1: Correct.

M2: Yes, that's it. It was three days ago when we received the first complaint here. [5]Anyway, we thought that a construction crew working down in the basement might have hit a sewer line or something, but that doesn't seem to be the case. It just appears that, well, the smell appeared out of nowhere.

M1: Oh, come on. There has to be some reason.

M2: Believe me. We're trying to find out what the cause of the smell is. We've got two separate work crews there currently searching for the source. Once we pinpoint it, we should be able to eliminate the smell, and then everything will go back to normal.

M1: That's great, but, uh, in the meantime, um, I have to say that living in Keller Dormitory is not a very pleasant experience. The smell is so awful that I feel like throwing up half of the time. You can't really expect me—and the other students—to stay in a place that smells like a garbage dump, can you?

M2: Not at all. Right now, we're working with a couple of local hotels to put every student in Keller Dormitory up until we get the problem solved. We'll make that announcement sometime in the next couple of hours. Oh, and we'll be running shuttle buses back and forth between the school and the hotels so that everyone will be able to get to their classes on time. If you show up for the dorm meeting that's scheduled for five in the evening today, you'll get all of that information.

M1: Ah, I've been in classes all day, so I wasn't aware that a meeting had been called. Okay, sir, it looks like you've got your hands full, so I won't take up any more of your time. I appreciate what you're doing for us. I know it's not your fault, and I like what you just told me about how the school is responding. See you at the meeting.

Translation

M1 Student: 죄송하지만, 제 주거 상황에 대해 이곳 사무실의 누군가와 정말로 이야기를 해야 해서요. 저를 도와주실 수 있는 분이신가요?

M2 Housing Office Employee: 그랬으면 좋겠군요. 그렇지 않으면, 학교에서는 제가 계속 이곳에서 일하는 것을 원치 않을 거예요. 어쨌든, 물론, 진담인데, 제가 학생의 문제에 관해 학생을 도울 수 있을 거예요.

M1: 잘 되었군요. 아시겠지만, 저는 *Kelly* 기숙사에서 단독으로 방을 쓰고 있어요. 어디인지 아시죠, 그렇죠?

M2: 물론이에요. *Bronwin Hall* 옆에 있죠. 오… 학생이 여기에 왜 왔는지 알 것 같아요.

M1: 아신다고요?

M2: 음, 제게 좋은 생각이 있지만, 학생이 먼저 말을 해보는 것이 어떨까요?

M1: 좋아요… 냄새 때문이에요. 그 기숙사에서는 끔찍한 냄새가 나요.

M2: 네, 학생이 말할 것이라고 제가 생각했던 바군요.

M1: 그러면 이미 그 문제에 대해 알고 계신 건가요?

M2: 오, 네. 여기 모든 사람들이 확실히 그 문제를 알고 있다는 점은 믿어도 좋아요.

M1: 그러면, 어, 어떤 일이 일어나고 있는 것이죠? 왜 그곳에서, 어, 솔직히 말씀드리면… 쓰레기 처리장과 같은 냄새가 나는 것인가요?

M2: 우리도 확실하게는 몰라요. 인정하기는 싫지만, 사실이에요. 알겠지만, 학생이 이미 알고 있으리라고 확신하는데, 갑자기 냄새가 나기 시작했어요… 어, 무엇이었을까요? 3일 전이었죠, 맞나요?

M1: 맞아요.

M2: 네, 그래요. 여기서 불만 사항이 처음으로 접수된 때도 3일 전이었어요. 어쨌든, 지하에서 일을 하고 있던 공사 인부가 하수관 같은 것을 건드렸다고 생각했지만, 그런 건 아닌 것 같아 보이고요. 단지, 음, 냄새가 난데없이 나타난 것처럼 보여요.

M1: 오, 제발요. 분명 이유가 있다고요.

M2: 저를 믿으세요. 냄새의 원인이 무엇인지 우리도 알아내려고 노력하고 있어요. 현재 원인을 알아내기 위해 두 명의 작업 인부들을 그곳으로 보냈어요. 원인을 찾아내면, 냄새를 제거할 수 있을 것이고, 그러면 모든 것이 다시 정상으로 돌아올 거예요.

M1: 그러면 좋겠지만, 어, 한편으로는, 음, *Kelly* 기숙사에서 사는 것은 정말로 유쾌한 경험이 아니라고 말씀드려야 할 것 같군요. 냄새가 너무나 지독해서 줄곧 속이 메슥거리는 것 같은 기분이 들어요. 제가 — 그리고 다른 학생들도 — 쓰레기 처리장과 같은 냄새가 나는 곳에서 계속 있게 될 것이라고 예상하는 것은 아니시죠, 그런가요?

M2: 전혀 그렇지 않아요. 현재, 저희는 문제가 해결될 때까지 *Kelly* 기숙사의 모든 학생들이 인근 두어 개의 호텔에 투숙할 수 있도록 노력하고 있어요. 몇 시간 후에는 그러한 공지 사항을 발표한 것이고요. 오, 그리고 학교와 호텔을 오가는 셔틀 버스를 운행할 것이기 때문에 모든 학생들은 제때에 수업에 참석할 수 있게 될 것이에요. 오늘 저녁 5시로 예정된 기숙사 회의에 참석한다면, 그에 대한 모든 정보를 얻을 수 있을 거예요.

M1: 아, 오늘 하루 종일 수업이 있어서, 회의가 소집되었다는 점은 몰랐네요. 좋아요, 선생님, 바쁘신 것 같아, 더 이상 시간은 뺏지 않을 게요. 저희를 위해 일을 하고 계신 점에 감사드려요.

선생님의 잘못이 아니란 것은 알고 있고, 학교가 어떻게 대응하고 있는지를 알려 주셔서 좋았어요. 회의에서 뵙기로 해요.

| 04-03 |

M Professor: One of the oldest stories in the Western world is that of the Trojan War. When it took place is unknown, but many historians estimate that it happened sometime between 1300 and 1200 B.C. According to legend, Troy was a city located on the coast of the land that is modern-day Turkey. The Greeks attacked Troy, and, following a ten-year siege, they overcame the city's defenses. They proceeded to sack the city, killed and enslaved most of the Trojans, and then burned Troy to the ground. Later, the Greek poet Homer wrote an epic poem about the siege. Most people thought Homer's tale was a legend and that Troy never existed, but others believed there was an element of truth to the story. They were proven right when, in the nineteenth century, the ruins of Troy itself were discovered right where Homer had said they were.

Prior to delving into the story of its discovery, I want to take a closer look at Troy's history. According to the archaeological evidence at the site where Troy was found, there were at least nine—yes, nine—different towns or small cities built there. Experts typically identify these remains with numbers, so, uh, Troy One is the oldest city while Troy Nine is the most recent one. The Troy site is believed to have first been occupied sometime around 3000 B.C. Some of the layers there contain evidence of cultures whose people engaged in trade, used bronze weapons and tools, and had pottery. They also constructed walls around the city. There is evidence of damage to these walls and many of the buildings. The damage was most likely caused by earthquakes, fire, or war. The initial excavations of the site led archaeologists to believe that Troy Two was the city that had been involved in the Trojan War. But this was proven wrong. Instead, it was probably Troy Seven that was attacked by the Greeks.

Archaeologists believe that Troy Seven had anywhere from five to ten thousand people living in it during its heyday around 1300 B.C. The city had several towers around its walls, and some of them exhibited battle damage. There was also evidence of fire damage in the city, and bronze weapons were found there as well. The evidence isn't conclusive, but, of all the remains found in the different layers, Troy Seven is definitely the leading choice for the Troy of the Trojan War.

During the time of Troy Seven, the Mycenaeans were the major force in the eastern Mediterranean Sea. They occupied Greece and the island of Crete and were warlike in nature. It's entirely conceivable that they attacked Troy and destroyed it sometime around 1200 B.C. Unfortunately for the Mycenaeans, they too were attacked and overrun around this time, which resulted in Greece entering a period known as the Greek Dark Ages. Historians use this term because of the lack of written records from Greece from around 1200 to 800 B.C. Later Greeks came to regard the time of the Mycenaeans as a period shrouded in myths and legends. Many Greek gods and goddesses and stories from Greek mythology, including that of the Trojan War, come from this period of time. The Greek legends of the time of the Trojan War were recorded in a number of epic poems, two of which were Homer's *Iliad* and *Odyssey*.

W Student: I've read the *Iliad*. How much of it is based on fact?

M: That's a question that may never be answered, Alice, since so much is unknown about the war and about Homer's sources. But I can say that the Greeks and Romans believed the stories were true. They even knew the general vicinity of Troy. When Alexander the Great led his army to attack the Persian Empire, he stopped at the ancient site of Troy and paid his respects to the dead Trojan and Greek warriors. The Romans also later founded a city near the site, but it later fell into decline.

It wasn't until the nineteenth century, when people once again became interested in Greek history and the archaeology of the Middle East, that Troy was discovered. Two men were responsible for that: an Englishman, Frank Calvert, and a German, Heinrich Schliemann. Calvert lived in Turkey, where he worked as a diplomat, and his family owned land near the area where Troy was thought to have existed. In 1866, he identified a hill on his land called Hisarlik as a possible site of Troy. He did some excavations there and discovered a few ancient ruins. He told his story to Schliemann, who was an amateur archaeologist. Schliemann proceeded to spend many years there, during which time he discovered ruins at varying levels. Schliemann is often credited with discovering Troy, but, if you ask me, I'd say that the credit should go to both men. Anyway, now let's take a look at a map of the site and look more closely at its excavation.

M Professor: 서구에서 가장 오래된 이야기 중의 하나는 트로이 전쟁에 관한 것입니다. 전쟁이 일어났던 시기는 알려져 있지 않으나, 많은 사가들은 트로이 전쟁이 기원전 1300에서 1200년 사이에 일어났다고 추정하고 있습니다. 전설에 따르면, 트로이는 오늘날 터키 지역의 해안가에 위치해 있던 도시였습니다. 그리스인들이 트로이를 공격했고, 10년간의 싸움 끝에, 도시의 방어를 무너뜨렸습니다. 그리스인들은 도시를 약탈하고, 대부분의 트로이 사람들을 죽이거나 노예로 삼았으며, 그리고는 트로이를 태워버렸습니다. 이후, 그리스 시인 호머는 이러한 공격에 대한 서사시를 썼습니다. 대부분의 사람들은 호머의 이야기가 전설이며 트로이는 결코 존재한 적이 없다고 생각했지만, 그 이야기에 사실적 요소가 있다고 믿었던 사람들도 있었습니다. 19세기, 트로이가 있다고 호머가 말했던 바로 그곳에서 트로이의 유적이 발굴됨으로써 그러한 의견은 옳았다는 것이 밝혀졌습니다.

트로이의 발굴에 대한 이야기를 살펴보기에 앞서, 트로이의 역사에 대해 보다 자세히 알아봤으면 합니다. 트로이가 발굴된 지점에서의 고고학적 증거에 따르면, 최소한 9개의 — 그래요, 9개입니다 — 크고 작은 도시들이 그곳에 세워져 있었습니다. 전문가들은 이러한 유적지들을 숫자로서 확인하고 있는데, 그래서, 어, 트로이 원이 가장 오래된 도시이고, 반면 트로이 나인이 가장 최근의 도시입니다. 트로이 유적지는 약 기원전 3000년쯤에 최초로 사람이 거주했다고 생각됩니다. 그곳의 몇몇 층에는 무역에 종사하고, 청동 무기 및 도구를 사용하고, 도기를 가지고 있었던 사람들의 문화에 대한 증거가 포함되어 있습니다. 또한 이들은 도시를 둘러싸는 벽을 건설했습니다. 이러한 벽과 많은 건물에는 손상의 흔적들이 있습니다. 이러한 손상은 아마도 지진이나, 화재, 혹은 전쟁에 의해 생긴 것 가능성이 높습니다. 유적지에 대한 최초의 발굴이 이루어지자, 고고학자들은 트로이 투가 트로이 전쟁과 관련되었던 도시라고 믿게 되었습니다. 하지만 이는 틀렸다고 입증되었습니다. 대신, 그리스인들의 공격을 받은 것은 아마 트로이 세븐이었을 것입니다.

고고학자들은 트로이 세븐이 전성기를 맞은 기원전 약 1300년쯤에 5천에서 만 명의 사람들이 살았던 장소가 그곳에 있었다고 믿고 있습니다. 그러한 도시의 벽 주위에는 몇 개의 탑이 있었으며, 그 중 일부는 전쟁에서 입은 피해를 보여 주고 있었습니다. 또한 이 도시에는 화재의 증거들도 있었으며, 청동 무기들 또한 그곳에서 발견되었습니다. 증거가 결정적인 것은 아니지만, 다양한 층에서 발견된 유적지 중, 트로이 세븐이 분명 트로이 전쟁의 그 트로이일 것입니다.

트로이 세븐이 있었던 당시, 지중해 동부의 주요 세력은 미케네인들이었습니다. 이들은 그리스와 크레타 섬을 차지하고 있었으며 특성상 호전적이었습니다. 이들이 트로이를 공격해서 기원전 1200년에 트로이를 파괴시켰다고 생각해 볼 수 있습니다. 미케네 사람들에게는 안타까운 일이었는데, 이들 역시 공격을 받아 비슷한 시기에 정복되었고, 그 결과 그리스는 그리스 암흑 시대라고 알려진 기간으로 들어가게 되었습니다. 기원전 1200년에서 기원전 800년까지, 그리스에서 문자 기록이 발견되지 않았기 때문에, 사가들은 그러한 용어를 사용하고 있습니다. 이후 그리스인들은 미케네인들의 시기를 신화와 전설로 감싸진 기간으로 여겼습니다. 그리스의 많은 신들과 여신들에 대한 이야기들과, 트로이 전쟁을 포함하여, 그리스 신화로부터 비롯된 이야기들은 수많은 서사시에 기록되어 있었는데, 그 중 두 개가 호머의 일리아드와 오디세이였습니다.

W Student: 일리아드는 읽어본 적이 있습니다. 그것의 얼마나 많은 부분이 사실에 기반하고 있나요?

M: 전쟁에 대해 그리고 호머의 출처에 대해 많은 부분이 알려져 있지 않으므로, 정답이 없을 수도 있는 질문이군요, *Alice*. 하지만 그리스인들과 로마인들은 그 이야기들이 사실이라고 믿었다고 말할 수 있을 것 같습니다. 그들은 심지어 트로이의 대략적인 위치도 알고 있었습니다. 알렉산더 대왕이 군대를 이끌고 페르시아 제국을 공격했을 때, 그는 고대 트로이 지역에서 멈춰, 사망한 트로이 전사들과 그리스 전사들에게 경의를 표했습니다. 로마인들 또한 이후 트로이 유적지 근처에 도시를 건설했는데, 하지만 이 도시는 차후 쇠퇴하게 되었습니다.

사람들이 다시 한 번 그리스의 역사와 중동 지역의 고고학에 대해 관심을 갖게 된 19세기가 되어서야, 트로이가 발견되었습니다. 그러한 발견은 두 사람이 이루어냈죠: 영국인인 프랭크 칼버트와 독일인인 하인리히 슐리만이었습니다. 칼버트는 터키에서 살았는데, 그는 그곳에서 외교관으로 일을 했고, 그의 가족들은 트로이가 존재했다고 생각되던 지역 근처의 땅을 소유하고 있었습니다. 1866년, 그는 자신의 땅에서 트로이의 유적지가 될 수도 있는 히사를리크라고 불리는 언덕을 확인해 보았습니다. 그곳에서 몇 차례의 발굴을 벌였고 몇 점의 고대 유물들을 발견했습니다. 그는 자신의 이야기를 슐리만에게 했는데, 슐리만은 아마추어 고고학자였습니다. 슐리만은 그곳에서 수년을 보내기 시작했고, 이 기간 동안 다양한 수준의 유적들을 발견했습니다. 트로이 발견의 공신은 슐리만이라고 종종 언급되지만, 여러분이 제게 묻는다면, 저는 두 사람 모두라고 말하고 싶군요. 어쨌든, 이제 유적지의 지도를 살펴보고 그에 대한 발굴에 대해 보다 자세히 알아보도록 하겠습니다.

Actual Test 05

Reading Section p.57

Answers

1. Ⓐ [Factual Question]

2. Ⓓ [Rhetorical Purpose Question]

3. Ⓑ [Reference Question]

4. Ⓒ [Negative Factual Question]

5. Ⓐ [Vocabulary Question]

6. Ⓐ [Rhetorical Purpose Question]

7. Ⓓ [Factual Question]

8. Ⓒ [Inference Question]

9. Ⓒ [Vocabulary Question]

10. Ⓐ [Sentence Simplification Question]

11. Ⓑ [Vocabulary Question]

12. Ⓒ [Factual Question]

13. 4ᵗʰ [Insert Text Question]

14. Ⓒ, Ⓓ, Ⓕ [Prose Summary Question]

Translation

독성 화학 물질이 환경에 미치는 영향

화학 물질이 다양한 산업, 교통, 그리고 농산 가공에 사용되면서, 사람들은 다량의 제품을 제조할 수 있고, 보다 먼 거리를 더 빠르게 이동할 수 있으며, 이전보다 많은 작물을 재배할 수 있게 되었다.

하지만, 이들 중 많은 화학 물질들은 환경에 피해를 입힐 수 있고 토양, 물, 그리고 공기에 해를 끼칠 수도 있다. 환경에 유출되면, 이러한 화학 물질들은 식물, 사람, 그리고 다른 동물들에 의해서 흡수된다. 단기적인 결과로 간혹 파괴적인 경우가 있다. 많은 화학 물질들은 또한, 통제가 가능하기까지 수십 년이 필요할 정도로, 장기적인 위협이 되기도 한다. 그 결과, 화학 물질을 통제하고 이들이 환경에 유입되지 않도록 하는 것이 주요한 관심사가 되었다.

화학 물질의 치명성은 그 물질의 독성에 의해 측정된다. 어떠한 소량의 화학 물질은 다량의 다른 화학 물질보다 유해하기 때문에 몇몇 화학 물질들은 다른 물질들 보다 독성이 강하다. 이러한 독성 화학 물질들이 생명체들만이 아니라 환경에 노출되는 주요한 방법에는 두 가지가 있다: 급성 노출과 만성 노출이다. 급성 노출은 많은 양의 독성 화학 물질에 한 번 노출되는 경우를 말한다. 이러한 화학 물질은 섭취, 흡입, 혹은 호흡을 통해서 직접적으로 흡수되는데, 이는 빠르게 질병이나 사망으로 이어지기도 한다. 하지만, 만성 노출은 장기간 동안 적은 양에 걸쳐서 일어난다. 환경 속에서, 만성 노출은 대부분 물, 토양, 그리고 공기 중에서 발견되는 화학 물질에 의해서 일어난다. 이러한 화학 물질들은, 일반적으로 다양한 과정에 의해 희석되어서, 환경으로 흘러 들어가게 되는데, 살아있는 유기체들이 이러한 물질에 노출된다. 노출은 직접적일 수도 있으며 간접적일 수도 있다. 예를 들어, 식물은 화학 물질에 직접적으로 노출될 것이지만 이 식물들의 잎을 먹는 동물들은 그 이후에 간접적으로 이러한 화학 물질에 노출된다.

독성 화학 물질들이 환경과 생물에 미치는 해로운 영향은 독성의 정도와 화학 물질에 노출된 기간에 따라서 다양하다. 마을 인근에 버려진 독성 화학 물질과 관련된 여러 유명한 사건들을 보면, 그 영향이 나타나기까지 오랜 시간이 걸리지만, 이러한 영향은 치명적이라는 사실이 증명되었다. 예를 들면, 뉴욕 주의 나이아가라 폭포 근처에 위치한 러브 운하 인근 지역과, 캘리포니아 주 힌클리 마을의 전 지역은 화학 물질이 환경에 유입되었을 때 발생할 수 있는 재앙에 관한 좋은 사례들이다. 이 두 마을 모두에서, 엄청난 양의 화학 물질이 그 지역의 수계에 유입되었다. 수 년 간에 걸쳐서, 마을의 거주자들은 정상 범위를 넘어선 유산, 기형아 출산, 그리고 암을 겪었다. 결국, 거주자들은 성공적으로 소송을 해냈지만, 피해는 이미 발생한 뒤였다.

최근 수십 년 동안, 화학 물질과 관련된 가장 큰 두 문제는 산성비와 표면 유출이다. 산성비는 전 세계의 산업화 및 인류가 교통 수단과 전력 생산을 위해서 내연 기관에 의존하게 된 결과이다. 현대 세계에서 사용되는 설비의 가동을 위하여 화석 연료를 연소시키게 되면서 상당한 양의 황과 질소가 대기 중으로 방출되었는데, 대기에서는 이 물질들이 계속해서 산성 화합물을 형성하게 된다. 이러한 화합물들은 수증기에 달라붙어서 비가 내릴 때 땅으로 떨어진다. (공기 중으로 오염 물질을 배출하지 않는 다른 국가에서도 산성비가 종종 내린다.) 이러한 과정에서, 산성비는 식물과 동물에 손상을 입히고 심지어 건물의 철근 콘크리트 구조를 침식시킬 수도 있다.

표면 유출에 관해 이야기하자면, 이와 관련된 주요한 문제는 비료에 사용되는 질산염이다. 이러한 질산염은 토양에 흡수되어 식물의 성장을 돕지만, 이 물질들은 수계에 흡수되어, 결국에는 강, 호수, 그리고 바다로 흘러든다. 농축된 양의 질산염은 조류대 번식을 일으킬 수 있는데, 이를 통해서는 물 속에서의 조류의 양이 갑자기 증가하게 된다. 조류는 수중의 대부분의 산소를 흡수하여, 물고기와 다른 수중 생명체들을 질식시켜서, 수중에는 생명체가, 혹시 있다 하더라도, 거의 존재하지 않는 죽음의 해역이 생성된다.

독성 화학 물질을 환경으로 흘러들지 못하게 하려는 노력은 전 세계적으로 진행되고 있지만, 사람들의 노력이 헛수고가 되는 경우가 많다. 게다가, 화학 폐기물을 관리하기 위한 많은 장비와 절차는 비용이 많이 들뿐만 아니라, 기업들은 그렇지 않다고 주장하지만, 많은 기업에서 이러한 것들은 우선적으로 고려되는 사안이 아니다. 또한, 화학 물질의 사용과 처리에 관한 규칙과 규제가 국가마다 서로 다르다; 몇몇 국가들은 강력한 규칙을 가지고 있지만 다른 국가들은 이에 보다 느슨하다. 하지만 환경에는 국경이 없으며, 화학 오염 물질들은 다른 지역의 사람들과 토지에 쉽게 영향을 줄 수 있기 때문에, 독성 화학 물질에 관한 엄격한 법안들이 보다 절실하게 필요하다.

Listening Section

p.63

Answers

1. (B) [Detail Question]

2. (C) [Understanding Attitude Question]

3. (A) [Understanding Attitude Question]

4. (C) [Making Inferences Question]

5. (D) [Understanding Function Question]

6. (A) [Gist-Content Question]

7. (A), (D) [Detail Question]

8. (C) [Gist-Content Question]

9.

	Gray Whales	Humpback Whales
(A)		X
(B)	X	
(C)		X
(D)	X	

[Connecting Content Question]

10. (A) [Detail Question]

11. (B) [Understanding Function Question]

Script

| 05-02 |

W1 Student: Professor Winfield, um, you didn't hand back my poem at the end of class today. Didn't you get the poem I submitted to you last week? I remember giving it to you when you asked everyone for them.

W2 Professor: Oh, I got the poem all right, Marcy. I just wanted to talk with you about it first. That's why I didn't return it to you when I handed the students back their poems.

W1: You wanted to talk about it?

W2: Yes, I did. I'm curious . . . You didn't follow the directions that I gave the class. You were supposed to write a short poem, but yours was about three pages long. What happened?

W1: Uh . . . I don't know. I guess I just got a little, uh, carried away. I had intended only to write about twenty lines—just like you asked—but I suppose that I was, uh, inspired or something because I suddenly discovered that I had about five times that many lines. I'm really sorry, Professor. If you will permit me, I can shorten the poem and resubmit it.

W2: Shorten it? Why would you want to do that?

W1: Er . . . Didn't you just say that the poem I turned in was supposed to be twenty lines? I didn't follow your instructions, so I figure that I ought to fix the poem.

W2: Marcy, you've totally misinterpreted why I called you here.

W1: I have?

W2: One hundred percent, I'd say. I was calling you here to compliment you on your poem, not to criticize you for making it too long.

W1: Oh . . .

W2: You see, I don't mind when students don't precisely follow directions in my class. When inspiration strikes, you have to go wherever it takes you. And, like you said, you were suddenly inspired. If you had cut off writing your poem after twenty lines, you wouldn't have written this poem right here, which is, I must say, quite brilliant.

W1: Oh, thank you. I wasn't aware that you liked it.

W2: Like it? No. I love it. In fact, I hope you don't mind, but I submitted the poem to The Penfeather. That's the name of the English Department's journal in case you don't know. So, anyway, the editor of the journal already contacted me and said that, if you give your approval, he'd like to print your poem in full in next month's edition of the journal. What do you think of that?

W1: Th-th-that would be . . . incredible. I never imagined getting my work published this early in my college career.

W2: Well, try imagining it because it's going to happen next month. Oh, and Marcy, if you don't mind a little advice . . .

W1: Yes?

W2: [5]Next year, why don't you take a creative writing class with Professor Killian? You're doing a great job in my poetry class, but Professor Killian would be able to help you polish your prose work tremendously. I've already spoken with him about you, and he's willing to hold a place open for you in one of his classes. **He normally only takes juniors and seniors, but he'll make an exception for you next semester.**

W1: Wow, I'd totally love that. I've heard so much about him from some of the other English majors. Should I go and introduce myself to him?

W2: That would be the prudent thing to do. He's in his office right now just so you know.

W1 Student: *Winfield* 교수님, 음, 교수님께서 오늘 수업이 끝날 때 제 시를 돌려주지 않으셨어요. 지난 주에 제가 제출한 시를 받지 못하셨나요? 교수님께서 모두에게 요청하셨을 때 제가 제출한 것으로 기억하고 있거든요.

W2 Professor: 오, 시를 잘 받았어요, *Marcy*. 다만 우선 그에 대해 학생과 이야기를 하고 싶었어요. 학생들에게 시를 다시 나누어 주었을 때 학생에게는 돌려주지 않은 이유죠.

W1: 그에 대해 이야기를 하고 싶으셨다고요?

W2: 네, 그랬어요. 궁금해서… 수업 시간에 알려 준 지침을 따르지 않았더군요. 짧은 시를 쓰도록 되어있었는데, 학생의 시는 3페이지의 분량이었어요. 무슨 일이 있었나요?

W1: 어… 모르겠어요. 제가 약간, 어, 정신이 나갔었나 봐요. 약 20행의 시를 — 교수님께서 요구하신 대로 — 쓰려고 했는데, 갑자기 그보다 5배가 많은 양의 시를 썼다는 걸 알게 되어서, 제가, 어, 영감 같은 것을 받았다고 생각했어요. 정말로 죄송해요, 교수님. 허락하신다면, 시를 줄여서 다시 제출할 수 있어요.

W2: 줄인다고요? 왜 그렇게 하려고 하죠?

W1: 어… 제가 제출한 시가 20행이 되어야 한다고 방금 말씀하지 않으셨나요? 교수님의 지침을 따르지 않아서, 제가 시를 고쳐야 할 것으로 알았는데요.

W2: *Marcy*, 제가 학생을 여기로 부른 이유를 완전히 잘못 이해하고 있군요.

W1: 제가요?

W2: 100%라고 말하고 싶네요. 학생의 시에 대해, 너무 길게 썼다고 비난하기 위해서가 아니라, 칭찬을 하기 위해 학생을 부른 거예요.

W1: 오…

W2: 알겠지만, 학생들이 수업에서의 지침을 정확하게 따르지 않는 것은 신경을 쓰지 않아요. 영감이 떠오르면, 영감에 따라야 하는 것이죠. 그리고, 학생이 말한 대로, 학생은 갑작스럽게 영감이 떠올랐어요. 20행으로 시를 줄여버리면, 여기에 있는 시와 같은 것은 쓰지 못할 텐데, 이 시는, 정말 굉장하다고 말해야 할 것 같군요.

W1: 오, 감사합니다. 마음에 드실 줄은 몰랐어요.

W2: 마음에 든다고요? 그게 아니에요. 정말로 좋아해요. 사실, 학생이 싫어하지 않았으면 좋겠는데, 이 시를 *The Penfeather* 에 보냈어요. 모르는 경우를 위해 말을 하면, 영문학과의 잡지 이름이죠. 그래서, 어쨌든, 그 잡지의 편집자자가 제게 전화를 해서, 학생이 승낙한다면, 다음 달 호에 시를 그대로 실었으면 하더군요. 이에 대해 어떻게 생각하나요?

W1: 그 – 그 – 그러면… 정말 믿을 수가 없을 것 같아요. 대학생이 된지 얼마 되지 않았는데 이처럼 빨리 제 글이 발표된다는 건 생각도 못해봤어요.

W2: 음, 다음 달에 일어날 일이기 때문에 한번 생각해 봐요. 오, 그리고 *Marcy*, 작은 충고를 하나 하면…

W1: 네?

W2: 내년에, *Killian* 교수님의 창의적 글쓰기 수업을 들어보는 것이 어때요? 제 시 수업 시간에 멋진 일을 해내고 있지만, *Killian* 교수님께서는 학생의 글을 다듬는데 많은 도움을 주실 수 있을 거예요. 학생에 대해서는 이미 그분과 이야기를 나누었고, 그분께서는 기꺼이 자신의 수업에 학생을 위한 자리 하나를 마련해 주실 거예요. 보통 3학년과 4학년 학생들만 받지만, 다음 학기에 학생은 예외로 해주실 거예요.

W1: 와, 그러면 정말 좋을 것 같아요. 그분에 대해서는 몇몇 영문학 전공자들에게 이야기를 많이 들었거든요. 그분께 가서 제 소개를 해야 하나요?

W2: 그렇게 하면 빈틈이 없을 것 같네요. 알겠지만 지금 사무실에 계세요.

| **05-03** |

M Professor: We looked at bird and mammal land migrations in our previous class, so today we're going to continue with that topic but move to animals that live in the ocean. We'll start with whale migrations. Whales migrate for two main reasons: to mate and reproduce and to find food-rich waters. They typically migrate from the Polar Regions and go toward the equator and then return to one of the poles when it's summertime in those places.

In order to understand whale migration better, I think it's best if we look at some different whale species and see how exactly they migrate. First up is the Eastern North Pacific gray whale. It spends its winters in the warm waters off Mexico's Baja Peninsula and its summers in the cool waters near Alaska. [11]This is a one-way journey of around 10,000 kilometers, and they do this every year. The gray whales in Alaska head for the warm waters in the fall, leaving Alaska sometime around October and arriving in the warm waters by December. Then, they begin to breed. **Some of the females are already pregnant from the previous year's mating season, so they give birth there.** The mothers nurse their babies with milk to ensure they will be big enough to survive the return trip north.

In February or March, the gray whales begin their journey north. The newly pregnant females and males depart first, and the new mothers and their babies leave last once their young are ready. They return to Alaskan waters as spring is arriving, and they proceed to spend the summer there. The cool waters off the Alaskan coast are full of nutrients, so they attract abundant marine life. The pregnant females eat as much as they can, which lets them fatten up to prepare for when their babies are born. This, of course, enables them to produce enough milk to feed their calves.

So you can see that gray whales migrate for the two reasons I mentioned, uh, breeding and giving birth as well as feeding. One interesting aspect of these gray whale migrations is that the whales always go to the same places to breed and follow the same routes year after year, so scientists, uh, and tourists, too, can see these creatures up close.

Now, how do scientists track the whales as they migrate . . . ? In the past, it wasn't very easy. Marine biologists used to get to know particular whales by their distinctive markings. Gray whales have mottled skin on their bodies and fins that results in spots which are unique to each whale. So, every year, the marine biologists would wait near the known breeding spots or transit points and track whales they'd seen in the past. But that's not necessary anymore. Instead, um, scientists use satellite tracking systems. The marine biologists approach a whale and tag it with an electronic device, usually on one of its fins. This device relays a signal that lets them track the whale for as long as it functions.

Most whale species follow a similar pattern of migration as the gray whale. For instance, humpback whales also follow the seasons. Humpback whales live in the Arctic and Antarctic regions. But because the seasons at each place are reversed, groups of whales from the different poles almost never meet or breed with one another. You see, uh, as the Arctic humpbacks are traveling south to breed in warmer waters, the Antarctic humpbacks are also moving south, but they're going from the equator back toward the Antarctic, where they will feed. Occasionally, the two groups come close to meeting. This happened once when a group of Antarctic humpbacks swam as far as the area around Costa Rica in Central America. That was one of the longest recorded migrations of any mammal species. Also, one group of northern humpbacks has made it a habit to visit the Hawaiian Islands every year, where they breed before swimming north again. No one knows why they visit Hawaii. The most likely reason is that sometime in the past, one group of humpbacks found its way there by accident, and the group simply started going to Hawaii year after year out of habit. Personally, I'd love to make that a personal habit of mine.

Anyway, um, that brings up a couple of questions. First . . . how do gray whales know when to go? Second . . . how do the whales know where to go? The most likely explanation to the first question is the one used for all migratory species. That is, uh, changes in the local environment trigger a migratory urge in the animals. For example, changes in the water temperature most likely induce the whales to migrate. Then, as they are traveling, the whales can tell where in the water they are by the changes in temperature, salinity, density, and maybe even the patterns of the currents and the marine life forms the whales feed on. Anyway, however they do it, every year, gray whales leave one place for another and always arrive at the right place at the right time.

M Professor: 이전 수업 시간에 조류와 포유류의 이동에 대해 살펴보았으므로, 오늘은 그러한 주제를 계속 이어나가 해양에 사는 동물들에 대해 알아보도록 하겠습니다. 고래의 이동으로 시작해 봅시다. 고래는 주로 두 가지 이유 때문에 이동을 합니다: 짝짓기와 번식을 하기 위해, 그리고 먹이가 풍부한 수역을 찾기 위해서죠. 일반적으로 고래들은 극지방에서 이동을 시작하여 적도 쪽으로 간 다음, 여름을 맞는 극지방 중 한 곳으로 돌아가게 됩니다.

고래의 이동을 보다 잘 이해하기 위해서는, 고래의 몇몇 다양한 종을 살펴보고 그들이 정확히 어떻게 이동을 하는지를 알아보는 것이 최선일 것이라고 생각합니다. 첫 번째는 귀신고래입니다. 이들은 멕시코의 바하 반도에서 약간 떨어져 있는 따뜻한 수역에서 겨울을 보내고, 알래스카 근처의 차가운 수역에서 여름을 보냅니다. 이는 편도로 약 10,000킬로미터에 이르는 여정이 되며 고래들은 매년 이러한 이동을 합니다. 알래스카의 귀신고래는 가을이 되면 따뜻한 수역으로 향하는데, 10월경에는 알래스카를 떠나 12월에는 따뜻한 수역에 도착하게 됩니다. 그런 다음, 새끼를 낳아 기르기 시작합니다. 몇몇 암컷 고래들은 그 이전 해의 짝짓기 시기에 임신을 하기 때문에, 그곳에서 새끼를 낳습니다. 어미 고래들은 새끼들이 충분히 자라 북쪽으로 돌아가는 동안 살아남을 수 있도록 하기 위해 새끼에게 모유를 먹입니다.

2월이나 3월에, 귀신고래는 북쪽으로의 여행을 시작합니다. 새로 임신한 암컷들과 수컷들이 먼저 출발을 하고, 새끼들이 준비가 되면 어미 고래들과 새끼 고래들이 마지막으로 출발합니다. 봄이 찾아오면, 이들은 알래스카의 수역으로 되돌아 가서, 그곳에서 여름을 보냅니다. 알래스카 근처의 차가운 수역에는 영양분이 풍부하기 때문에, 이곳에 많은 해양 생물들이 모이게 됩니다. 임신한 암컷 고래들은 가능한 많은 먹이를 먹는데, 이로써 아이가 태어날 때를 대비하여 충분한 지방을 축적하게 됩니다. 이는, 물론, 새끼들에게 먹일 충분한 모유를 만들어 낼 수 있도록 해주죠.

그래서 여러분들은 귀신고래가 제가 말씀드린 두 가지 이유로, 어, 먹이를 먹고 또한 새끼를 낳아 기르기 위해 이동을 한다는 점을 알 수 있을 것입니다. 이들 귀신고래의 이동에 있어서 한 가지 흥미로운 측면은 이 고래들이 항상 같은 장소로 가서 새끼를 낳아 기르며 매년 같은 루트를 이용한다는 점인데, 이로 인해 과학자들은, 어, 그리고 관광객들 역시, 이러한 동물들을 가까이에서 볼 수가 있습니다.

자, 고래들이 이동을 할 때 과학자들이 어떻게 이들을 추적할까요…? 과거에는, 그렇게 쉽지가 않았습니다. 해양 생물학자들은 고래의 특별한 표식으로 특정 고래들을 확인하곤 했습니다. 귀신고래는 몸통과 지느러미에 얼룩덜룩한 피부를 가지고 있는데, 이는 각각의 고래에게 고유한 반점이 됩니다. 따라서, 매년, 해양 생물학자들은 새끼를 낳는 곳으로 알려져 있는 장소나 통과 지점 근처에서 기다리고 있다가 이전에 보았던 고래들을 추적하곤 했습니다. 하지만, 이제 더 이상 그럴 필요가 없습니다. 대신, 음, 과학자들은 위성 추적 시스템을 이용합니다. 해양 생물학자들은 고래에 다가가서, 보통 지느러미의 한 곳에 전자 장치를 부착합니다. 이 장치는 작동을 멈추지 않는 한 고래를 추적할 수 있는 신호를 전달해 줍니다.

고래의 대부분의 종은 귀신고래와 유사한 이동 패턴을 따릅니다. 예를 들면, 혹등고래 또한 계절을 따르죠. 혹등고래는 북극과 남극 지역에서 서식합니다. 하지만 각 지역에서의 계절이 반대이기 때문에, 서로 다른 극지방의 고래들이 서로 만나거나 짝짓기를 하는 경우는 거의 없습니다. 아시겠지만, 어, 북극의 혹등고래들이 따뜻한 수역에서 새끼를 낳기 위해 남쪽으로 이동을 하는 것처럼, 남극의 혹등고래들 또한 남쪽으로 이동을 하지만, 이들은 적도에서 다시 남극 쪽으로 가서, 그곳에서 먹이를 먹게 될 것입니다. 때때로, 두 무리들이 거의 만날 뻔 하기도 합니다. 이러한 일은 남극의 혹등고래들이 중앙 아메리카 코스타리카 인근 지역까지 멀리 헤엄쳐 올 때 이루어집니다. 포유류의 종 중 가장 긴 이동으로 기록되어 있는 것 중 하나이죠. 또한, 북쪽의 혹등고래의 한 무리는 습관적으로 매년 하와이 섬들을 찾는데, 다시 북쪽으로 헤엄쳐 가지 전까지 이곳에서 새끼를 낳아 기릅니다. 이들이 왜 하와이를 방문하는지는 아무도 모릅니다. 가장 그럴듯한 이유는 과거 언젠가, 한 무리의 혹등고래들이 우연히 이곳으로 이어지는 길을 찾았고, 따라서 매년 하와이를 찾는 습성이 길러졌다는 것입니다. 개인적으로는, 저에게도 그런 습성이 있었으면 좋겠네요.

어쨌든, 음, 그럼으로써 두어 가지 질문이 제기됩니다. 첫째는… 귀신고래들이 가야 할 시기를 어떻게 알까요? 둘째는… 어디로 가야 할 지를 어떻게 알까요? 첫 번째 질문에 대한 가장 그럴듯한 설명은 이동을 하는 모든 종에게 적용되는 설명입니다. 즉, 어, 지역 환경의 변화로 동물들이 이동을 하겠다는 충동을 느끼게 되는 것이죠. 예를 들면, 수온의 변화가 고래로 하여금 이동을 하도록 만들 가능성이 가장 높습니다. 그러면, 이동을 하면서, 고래들은 온도, 염도, 밀도의 차이 및 심지어 해류의 패턴과 그들이 먹는 해양 생물들의 차이로 인해, 자신들이 어느 수역에 있는지를 알 수가 있습니다. 어쨌든, 어떻게 하던지 간에, 매년, 귀신고래들은 한 장소를 떠나 다른 곳으로 이동을 하면서 언제나 정확한 시기에 정확한 장소에 도착을 하고 있습니다.

Actual Test 06

Reading Section
p.69

Answers

1. Ⓒ [Reference Question]

2. Ⓒ [Inference Question]

3. Ⓑ [Factual Question]

4. Ⓑ [Reference Question]

5. Ⓓ [Negative Factual Question]

6. Ⓒ [Vocabulary Question]

7. Ⓐ [Factual Question]

8. Ⓑ [Factual Question]

9. Ⓓ [Vocabulary Question]

10. Ⓐ [Vocabulary Question]

11. Ⓒ [Rhetorical Purpose Question]

12. Ⓒ [Sentence Simplification Question]

13.

	EARLY WRITING SYSTEM
Sumerian	Ⓐ, Ⓒ, Ⓕ
Egyptian, Chinese, and Mayan	Ⓓ, Ⓔ

[Fill in a Table Question]

Translation

초기 문자의 형태

문자는 의사소통의 수단이자 기록을 유지하고, 이야기로써 사람들을 즐겁게 하며, 역사적인 기술로 과거를 보존하는 방법이다. 인류는 과거의 서로 다른 시기에 각기 다른 지역에서 문자를 발명했다. 수천 년 전, 사람들은 어느 정도의 구어를 사용했으며 이러한 단어들을 나타내는 상징을 만들었다. 역사 언어학자들은 문자를 발명해 낸 문화가 있었던 네 지역을 확인했다: 수메르(현재의 이라크), 이집트, 중국, 그리고 마야 제국(중앙 아메리카)이다. 다른 문화에서도 문자를 발명하기는 했지만, 그들의 문자 체계는 직간접적으로 이들 4개의 원형 문자의 하나로부터 비롯되었다. 천천히, 하지만 끊임없이, 문자는 현재까지 전파되고 진화되었으며, 사실상 모든 곳에서 일정한 형태로 존재하고 있다.

최초의 문자는 설형 문자였는데, 이는 기원전 3000년경 수메르 문명에 그 기원을 두고 있다. 수메르인들은 수백 년 동안 계산에 사용했던 그림 기호 체계를 보유하고 있었다. 이러한 기호들은 설형 문자로 발달했다. 이 문자는 수메르인들의 평범한 일상 생활의 면면을 보여주는 그림으로 시작되었다. 이는 수메르어 단어의 소리에 바탕을 두고 있지 않았고, 여기에는 문법적인 측면도 거의 없었다. 이러한 그림들은 부드러운 진흙판에 철필을 사용하여 그려졌다. 그리고 나서 이 쐐기 모양의 기호들은 부드러운 진흙에서 굳어졌다. 이 진흙판들은 보존이 잘 되었기 때문에, 수천 년 후, 고고학자들은 예전 수메르 지역의 다양한 장소에서 수백여 점의 진흙판들을 발굴했다. 점차적으로, 수메르인들이 새로운 단어를 만들기 위해서 그림들을 결합하면서, 설형 문자는 수메르인들의 언어의 소리에 바탕을 둔 음성 표기 문자 체계가 되었다.

보다 발달된 형태에서, 설형 문자는 구두 언어를 표현하는 세 가지 형태의 기호들을 포함하고 있었다. 첫째로, 표어 문자가 있었는데, 이는 완전한 단어를 나타내는 기호들이다. 둘째는 음성 표기 기호였는데, 이는 음절, 문자, 단어의 일부분, 또는 문법적인 요소를 나타낸다. 마지막으로, 기호의 의미가 다소 애매한 경우에 추가되었던 특수한 부호들이 있다. 이들은 특정한 기호나 기호들의 조합이 한 가지 이상의 의미를 가질 때 활용되었다. 수메르인들은 또한 그들의 문자를 체계화했다. 그들은 윗줄에서 아랫줄로, 왼쪽에서 오른쪽으로 글을 읽었는데, 이는 서구 세계의 대다수의 문자 체계에서 적용되고 있는 패턴이다.

수메르 문자의 발전이 하룻밤 사이에 일어났던 것은 아니었다. 문자의 발달에는 기나긴 시간이 걸렸으며, 수메르인들에게는 다행스럽게도, 그들이 세운 문명 덕분에 수메르인 학자들이 언어를 연구하기에 충분한 시간을 확보할 수 있었다. 게다가, 수메르 사회의 특성상, 사람들과 생산물들을 계속적으로 파악할 수 있는 문자 체계가 필요했다. 수메르에는, 지배 계층 엘리트, 성직자, 그리고 군인들이 있었는데, 상당히 많은 수의 농부들이 노동을 통해서 이들을 부양했다. 따라서, 식량과 그 밖의 물품들을 파악하는 관료 제도가 생겨났다. 최초의 회계 시스템을 만들어 낸 사람들이 바로 이러한 관료들이었다.

이집트, 중국, 그리고 마야 제국에서도 이와 비슷한 사건들이 일어났는데, 이들은 모두 지속적이고 안정적인 문명을 보유하고 있었다. 이집트에서는, 상형 문자가 — 즉, 표어 문자 체계가 — 수천 년 동안 사용되었다. 언어 학자들은 중국의 문자 체계가, 부드러운 조개 껍질과 거북이 등껍질에 새겨진, 점을 치기 위해 사용되었던 기호들로부터 발달했다고 생각한다. 수메르인들과 마찬가지로, 마야인들 또한 표어 문자들과 음성 표기 기호들을 사용했다. 하지만, 유럽인들이 이들의 영토를 정복함에 따라 그에 대한 견본이 거의 남아있지 않았기 때문에 언어학자들은 마야인들의 문자 체계의 기원과 발달을 알아내는데 힘든 시간을 보냈으며, 이 문자들을 완전히 해독하지 못하고 있다.

이러한 네 지역으로부터, 문자는 그 후 두 가지 방법들 중 하나의 방법으로 퍼져 나갔다: 그 방법은 청사진 복사이거나 전파이다. 청사진 복사는 한 집단이 다른 문자 체계를 직접적으로 채택해서 그들의 문화에 알맞도록 변형시키는 것이다. 자신들의 언어에 라틴어 알파벳을 채택한 대부분의 문화들은 청사진 복사를 이용했으며, 라틴어 알파벳 자체도 그리스어와 몇몇 중동의 알파벳으로부터 유래되었다. 전파는 조금 더 복잡한 문자 체계 발명의 방법이다. 전파의 경우, 어떤 문화의 사람들은 문자의 발명이 가능하다는 것을 알고 있었고 이를 어떻게 만들어야 하는지에 대한 기본적인 개념도 가지고 있었지만, 다른 문화의 문자 체계나 사용되었던 기호에 대한 완전한 지식을 가지고 있지는 않았다. 그래서, 시행 착오를 통하여, 다른 문자 체계와 유사하지만 이를 완전히 모방한 것은 아닌, 새로운 문자 체계가 발명되었다.

Listening Section

p.75

Answers

1. (A) [Detail Question]
2. (C) [Understanding Attitude Question]
3. (D) [Gist-Purpose Question]
4.

	Fact	Not a Fact
(A)	X	
(B)		X
(C)		X
(D)	X	

[Detail Question]

5. (A) [Making Inferences Question]
6. (B) [Gist-Content Question]

7.

	Home Countries	Colonies
(A)		X
(B)	X	
(C)	X	
(D)		X

[Connecting Content Question]

8. (D) [Detail Question]
9. (B) [Making Inferences Question]
10. (C) [Understanding Attitude Question]
11. (D) [Understanding Function Question]

Script

| 06-02 |

M Dean of Students: Carrie Smith, I've been looking forward to this. I've heard so much about you. I must say that it's a real pleasure to meet you.

W Student: Thank you, Dean Carter. It's a pleasure to meet you as well.

M: Please, make yourself comfortable and have a seat right here . . .

W: Thank you very much.

M: Well, first, Carrie, let me congratulate you on your academic performance ever since you enrolled here. You're the only student in your class who has received all A's in every class during your freshman and sophomore year. That's quite an accomplishment you know.

W: Oh, thank you, sir. But it really wasn't anything special. All I did was, you know, go to all of my classes and study all the time.

M: In actuality, what you've accomplished is special. You're the only student in your class to have a perfect 4.0 GPA. That makes you tops in your class going into your junior year. You're leading the race for class valedictorian when you graduate in two years. And that's why you received that award yesterday. You should be proud of having won it.

W: I am, sir. I definitely am. And so are my parents.

M: Excellent, excellent. So, anyway, I invited you here to my office today because . . .

W: Yes?

M: Well, I'd like to talk to you about the Furman Prize.

W: The Furman Prize? What's that?

M: It's a special prize that we've only started awarding to students in the past three years. Your major is history, right?

W: That's correct. I'm specializing in the history of the Mediterranean region with an emphasis on Italian history during the Renaissance. It's a rather fascinating period of history.

M: I totally agree with you. Anyway, since that is your area of specialty, then the Furman Prize is something that you definitely need to be aware of.

W: Why is that, sir?

M: Here's why . . . The Furman Prize is a special scholarship that covers the cost of tuition for one year at any school in Europe for one student here. Depending on which school the student attends, it can be worth tens of thousands of dollars.

W: Oh, that sounds wonderful, but I don't think I could afford the housing and other fees. Europe is quite expensive these days.

M: You didn't let me finish. Not only does the scholarship pay for one year's tuition, but it also covers housing, food, and airfare, and it provides a small stipend of, oh, five hundred dollars a month. Interested?

W: That's one way of saying it. How I do to apply?

M: You don't. You just need to let it be known to someone like me that you're interested in the prize. I'll make sure that your name is considered when the committee decides who gets awarded the prize. There will be an announcement in, um, I believe it's two weeks from today.

W: That's it? I don't have to do anything? No essay?

M: Nope. You don't have to do anything more than you've already done. Pretty easy, huh? The committee will consider your academic background and speak with your advisor. That's the entire process. There are, hmm . . . four other students in the running I believe. But between you and me, I'd say that you've got an outstanding chance of receiving the prize.

Translation

M Dean of Students: *Carrie Smith*, 이 순간을 기다리고 있었어요. 학생에 대해서는 많은 이야기를 들었죠. 만나게 되어 정말 기쁘다고 말하고 싶군요.

W Student: 감사합니다, *Carter* 학장님. 저 또한 만나 뵙게 되어 기쁩니다.

M: 편하게 이쪽으로 와서 앉으세요.

W: 정말 고맙습니다.

M: 음, 우선, *Carrie*, 이곳에 입학한 이후로 학생이 보여 준 학업 성적에 축하의 말을 전할게요. 학생은 1학년과 2학년 동안 모든 수업에서 A를 받은 유일한 학생이에요. 알겠지만 상당히 훌륭한 성과죠.

W: 오, 감사합니다, 학장님. 하지만 정말로 특별한 것은 아니었어요. 제가 한 것은, 어, 아시겠지만, 모든 수업에 참석해서 공부를 꾸준히 한 것이 전부였거든요.

M: 실제로, 학생이 거둔 성과는 특별한 것이에요. 학생은 학급에서 평점이 4.0 만점인 유일한 학생이죠. 그래서 3년이 되는 학급에서 학생이 최우수 성적을 갖게 되는 것이고요. 2년 후 졸업을 하게 될 때에는 수석 졸업생 후보 중 선두가 되겠죠. 그리고 그것이 어제 학생이 상을 수상한 이유고요. 상을 탔다는 점에 대

해서는 자랑스럽게 생각해야 해요.

W: 자랑스럽게 생각해요, 학장님. 정말로요. 그리고 부모님들도 마찬가지시고요.

M: 좋아요, 좋아요. 그러면, 어쨌든, 오늘 제 사무실로 학생을 부른 건…

W: 네?

M: 음, Furman 상에 대한 이야기를 하고 싶어서요.

W: Furman 상이요? 그게 무엇이죠?

M: 3년 전에 처음으로 학생들에게 수여하기 시작한 특별한 상이에요. 학생의 전공이 역사학이죠, 맞나요?

W: 맞아요. 르네상스 시대 이탈리아의 역사에 초점을 맞춘, 지중해 지역의 역사를 전공하고 있어요. 역사상 정말 멋진 시기죠.

M: 정말 그래요. 어쨌든, 그것이 학생의 전공 분야이기 때문에, Furman 상에 대해서는 학생이 꼭 알아야 할 필요가 있어요.

W: 왜 그렇죠, 학장님?

M: 이유는… Furman 상은 이곳 학생들을 위해 유럽의 어느 학교에서라도 일 년간의 학비 전체를 책임져 주는 특별한 장학금이에요. 어느 학교에 다니는지에 따라, 수천 달러의 비용이 될 수도 있겠죠.

W: 오, 정말 멋지게 들리지만, 주거비와 기타 비용을 제가 감당할 수 있을 것 같지는 않아요. 요즘 유럽의 물가가 꽤 비싼 편이라서요.

M: 아직 말이 끝나지 않았어요. 이 장학금은 일 년간의 학비를 대 줄 뿐만 아니라, 주거비, 식비, 그리고 항공 요금도 지급해 주며, 소정의 생활비로, 오, 한 달에 500달러를 제공해 주죠. 관심이 있나요?

W: 물론이에요. 어떻게 신청을 하면 되나요?

M: 하지 않아도 돼요. 학생이 그 상에 관심이 있다는 것을 저와 같은 사람에게 알려주기만 하면 되죠. 위원회에서 누구에게 상을 줄 것인가를 결정할 때, 제가 확실히 학생의 이름이 거론되도록 할 거에요. 오늘부터 2주 후라고 생각하는데, 음, 공지 사항이 나갈 것이고요.

W: 그런가요? 아무 것도 할 것이 없다고요? 에세이도 필요 없고요?

M: 없어요. 학생이 이미 한 일 이외에 더 해야 할 것은 없어요. 꽤 간단하죠, 그렇죠? 위원회에서 학생의 학력을 검토하고 학생의 지도 교수님과 이야기를 나누게 될 거에요. 그것이 전체 과정이죠. 제 생각에는, 흠… 후보 학생이 4명 더 있어요. 하지만 학생과 저 사이의 이야기인데, 학생이 수상하게 될 가능성이 확실히 높다고 말을 하고 싶군요.

Script

| 06-03 |

M Professor: [10]So, uh, I've mentioned the term mercantilism a couple of times in class, but I've seen a few blank stares. This is something you need to know, so let me cover it for a few minutes. Mercantilism was a system of trade involving a home nation and its colonies. It reached its height during the great colonial empires the Europeans built between the fifteenth and the eighteenth centuries. The main nations that practiced mercantilism were Great Britain, Spain, Portugal, and France. The purpose of this system was to establish a protected trade system with little outside interference.

Countless books and articles have been written about mercantilism. While economists disagree on some of its minor aspects, they are virtually all in agreement about its main points. Here they are . . .   First, all economic activity was designed to improve the home country at the expense of other nations and even the home country's own colonies. Second, there were high tariffs on imports and laws that prohibited the importing of specific products manufactured by protected domestic industries. If certain products couldn't be obtained in the home country, they were expected to be furnished by the colonies. As a last resort, the products could be imported from foreign nations or colonies, but they had to be transported on ships flying the flag of the home country. For example, Great Britain used to import coffee from the Spanish empire's colonies, but that coffee had to be carried on British ships. Also, in some nations, such as Great Britain, all raw materials from the colonies that were destined for foreign lands first had to be shipped to the home country. There, the goods were taxed, and only then could a merchant ship transport them to another nation.

Third, raw materials had to be converted into finished products since those fetched higher prices than the raw materials did. These raw materials were supplied either by the home country or its colonies. This led to many colonies becoming centers of raw material production. Again, the raw materials had to be sent to the home country in ships belonging to either the home country or its colonies. From there, they could be shipped elsewhere.

W Student: [11]If you don't mind, Professor Chandler, I have a question. Is this what the North Atlantic triangular trade was all about?

M: Ah, that's very perceptive of you, Denise. Some of you may remember learning about the triangle trade in the North Atlantic Ocean when you were in high school. In case you don't recall, let me describe it in brief. Okay . . . Great Britain imported raw materials such as timber, sugar, cotton, and tobacco from its North American colonies. British companies then converted the raw materials into finished products like rum and textiles. These products were then sold back in the colonies or to people in other lands. Part of the triangle trade also involved slavery. Black Africans were captured, enslaved, and shipped to the American colonies, where they provided labor on the plantations that produced various raw materials. So raw materials went to Britain, finished products went to North America, Europe, Africa, and other places, and slaves went from Africa to North America, uh, hence the name triangle trade.

All right. Now for the third . . . oops, I mean the fourth, yeah, the fourth aspect of mercantilism. This involved the control of precious metals, especially gold and silver. Merchants had to pay for imports with trade goods, not with gold or silver. But they were encouraged to accept gold and silver for their exports. This led to the home country accumulating a large supply of precious metals. This happened because people strongly believed in the necessity of their country gaining more wealth than other countries. This would give them more power and prepare them for future wars. So, uh, those are the four basic aspects of mercantilism.

W: Didn't the colonies resent being controlled so strictly?

M: Yes, but the level of resentment varied from colony to colony and from era to era. For example, the Spanish and Portuguese firmly ruled their colonies. They exploited the natives, utilized large numbers of slaves, and basically turned Central and South America into gigantic centers for raw materials. They became fabulously wealthy thanks to their colonies, but both—especially the Spanish—squandered it on lavish spending and wars that they lost. The British, on the other hand, had a looser policy regarding their colonies. In the American colonies, the people processed lots of raw materials themselves in order to meet local needs. The British were okay with this so long as the finished products weren't shipped to Britain to compete against domestic industries and so long as the supply of raw materials shipped home wasn't adversely affected.

Eventually, however, the British began to tighten their grip on the American colonies. They sought greater control and taxed the people more heavily. This led to the American Revolution. But that's a topic for a history class, not an economics class, so let's get back to some of the minor aspects of mercantilism.

M Professor: 그러면, 어, 수업에서 두어 차례 중상주의란 용어에 대해서 언급을 했는데, 몇 분이 멍한 눈빛을 보이고 있군요. 여러분들이 알아야 하는 것이기 때문에, 잠시 그에 대해 다루어 보도록 하겠습니다. 중상주의는 본국 및 식민지와 관련된 무역 시스템입니다. 이는 15세기와 18세기 사이에 유럽인들이 거대한 식민 제국을 건설했던 당시, 정점에 도달했습니다. 중상주의를 실행한 대표적인 나라로는 영국, 스페인, 포르투갈, 그리고 프랑스가 있습니다. 이러한 시스템의 목적은 외부의 간섭이 거의 없는, 보호 무역 시스템을 구축하는 것이었습니다.

수많은 책들과 글들이 중상주의에 관해 쓰여져 있습니다. 일부 사소한 측면에 대해서는 경제학자들 사이에서 의견이 일치하지 않고 있지만, 사실상 중요한 점에 있어서는 의견이 일치해 있습니다. 알려드리면… 우선, 모든 경제 활동은 다른 나라 및 심지어 자국의 식민지를 희생시켜서라도 본국을 발전시키도록 고안되었습니다. 둘째, 높은 수입 관세가 존재했으며, 보호를 받는 국내 산업이 제조하는 것과 같은 특정 상품은 법으로 수입이 금지되었습니다. 본국에서 특정 제품을 구할 수 없으면, 식민지에 의해 조달될 수 있을 것으로 예상되었습니다. 최후의 수단으로서만, 외국이나 식민지로부터 제품이 수입될 수 있었으나, 이는 기국이 본국인 선박들로만 운송되어야 했습니다. 예를 들면, 영국은 스페인 제국의 식민지로부터 커피를 수입하곤 했는데, 그러한 커피는 영국 선박에 의해서만 수송되어야 했습니다.

또한, 영국과 같은 일부 국가의 경우, 식민지에서 생산되어 해외로 보내질 모든 원재료들이 영국 본국에 먼저 운송되어야 했습니다. 그곳에서, 제품에 세금이 매겨졌고, 그런 후에야 상선이 이를 싣고 다른 나라로 갈 수 있었습니다.

셋째, 완제품에는 원료보다 더 높은 가격이 책정되었기 때문에, 원료는 완제품으로 전환되어야 했습니다. 이러한 원료들은 본국이나 식민지에 의해 공급되었습니다. 이로써 많은 식민지들이 원료 생산의 중심지가 되었죠. 또 다시, 원료는 본국이나 본국의 식민지에 소속된 선박에 의해 본국으로 보내져야 했습니다. 그곳에서, 원료는 그 밖의 다른 곳으로 운반될 수 있었습니다.

W Student: 괜찮으시다면요, *Chandler* 교수님, 질문이 하나 있습니다. 대서양 삼각 무역도 그러한 것이었나요?

M: 아, 통찰력이 뛰어나군요, *Denise*. 여러분 중 일부는 고등학교 때 북대서양의 삼각 무역에 대해 배웠던 것을 기억하실 수 있을 것입니다. 기억이 나지 않는 경우를 위해, 짧게 설명해 드리죠. 좋아요… 영국은 목재, 설탕, 면, 그리고 담배를 북미의 식민지로부터 수입했습니다. 그러면 영국 기업들이 원료를 가지고 럼과 직물과 같은 완제품을 만들었습니다. 그런 다음 이러한 제품들은 다시 식민지나 다른 지역의 사람들에게 판매되었습니다. 삼각 무역의 일부는 또한 노예제와 관련이 있었습니다. 아프리카 흑인들이 붙잡혀서, 노예가 되고, 배를 타고 미국으로 이동하여, 그곳의 다양한 원료들을 생산해 내는 농장에서 노동력을 제공해 주었습니다. 그래서 원료는 영국으로, 완제품은 북미, 유럽, 아프리카, 그리고 기타 지역으로, 노예는 아프리카에서 북미로 이동해 갔는데, 어, 따라서 삼각 무역이라는 이름이 생긴 것이었죠.

좋아요, 이제 세 번째에 대해 말씀드리면… 이런, 중상주의의 네 번째, 그래요, 네 번째 측면입니다. 여기에는 귀금속, 특히 금과 은에 대한 통제가 관련되어 있었습니다. 상인들은, 금이나 은이 아니라, 무역 상품으로 수입에 대한 대가를 지불했습니다. 하지만 수출에 있어서는 금이나 은도 받아들여졌습니다. 이로써 본국에는 많은 양의 귀금속이 축적될 수 있었습니다. 자신의 나라가 다른 나라들보다 더 많은 부를 얻어야 한다고 믿었기 때문에 그렇게 된 것이었죠. 이로써 보다 많은 힘을 얻고 미래의 전쟁에 대비를 할 수가 있었습니다. 그래서, 어, 이들이 중상주의의 네 가지 기본적인 측면입니다.

W: 그렇게 엄격히 통제되는 것에 대해 식민지들이 분노하지 않았나요?

M: 그렇기는 했지만, 분노의 수준은 식민지마다 달랐고 또한 시기마다 달랐습니다. 예를 들면, 스페인과 포르투갈은 식민지를 엄격하게 통치했습니다. 원주민들을 착취했고, 많은 양의 노예를 활용했으며, 기본적으로 중미와 남미를 거대한 원료 중심지로 바꾸어 놓았습니다. 자신들의 식민지 덕분에 이들은 막대한 부를 이루게 되었지만, 양 국가 모두 — 특히 스페인은 — 사치와 패션으로 부를 탕진해 버렸습니다. 영국은, 반면, 식민지에 대해서 보다 느슨한 정책을 펼쳤습니다. 미 식민지에서, 사람들은 지역적 수요를 충족시키기 위해 스스로 원료들을 처리했습니다. 영국은 완제품이 영국으로 들어와서 국내 산업과 경쟁을 하지 않는 이상, 그리고 본국으로 들어오는 원료가 역효과를 일으키지 않는 이상, 위와 같은 사실을 문제 삼지 않았습니다.

하지만, 결국, 영국인들은 미국 식민지에 대한 통제를 강화하기 시작했습니다. 보다 많은 규제를 원했고 보다 무거운 세금을 매겼습니다. 이로써 미국 혁명이 일어난 것이었죠. 하지만 이는 역사 수업의 주제이지 경제학 수업의 주제는 아니기 때문에, 중상주의의 몇몇 세세한 측면들로 다시 돌아가보도록 하겠습니다.

Actual Test 07

Reading Section p.81

Answers

1. Ⓒ [Vocabulary Question]

2. Ⓒ [Negative Factual Question]

3. Ⓐ [Rhetorical Purpose Question]

4. Ⓐ [Reference Question]

5. Ⓑ [Factual Question]

6. Ⓓ [Vocabulary Question]

7. Ⓒ [Negative Factual Question]

8. Ⓑ [Inference Question]

9. Ⓓ [Vocabulary Question]

10. Ⓒ [Reference Question]

11. Ⓐ [Factual Question]

12. Ⓑ [Vocabulary Question]

13. Ⓓ [Factual Question]

14. Ⓒ, Ⓔ, Ⓕ [Prose Summary Question]

Translation

화성의 물

지구상의 생물들은 대부분 생존을 위해서 물을 필요로 하기 때문에, 과학자들은 다른 세계에 존재하는 탄소 기반 생물도 동일하게 물을 필요로 할 것이라고 생각한다. 21세기 초반에 화성의 물을 발견하게 되면서, 몇몇 과학자들은 그곳에 생명체가 존재할 것이라고 추측했다; 하지만, 아직까지 화성 주변을 비행하거나 화성에 착륙했던 위성들은 살아있는 생명체의 어떠한 흔적도 발견하지 못하였다. 화성의 물은 극지방에 빙원의 형태로 얼어있거나 지하 깊은 곳에 있지만, 과거 화성의 표면에 물이 자유롭게 흘렀다는 증거를 통하여 현재 과학자들은 이 행성에 한때 생명체가 존재했을지도 모른다는 희망을 가지게 되었다.

화성에 물이 존재한다는 점에 대한 첫 번째 증거는 이 행성의 표면에 인접해 있었던 위성들이 촬영한 사진으로부터 나왔다. 이러한 사진들을 통하여 물에 의한 침식의 흔적을 보여 주는 지형이 드러났다. 하곡 및 수많은 지류가 있는 강의 수계와 유사한 광범위한 구조가 수백 킬로미터에 걸쳐 화성의 모든 지형에 뻗어 있었다. 그 후, 1970년대 중반 바이킹호 탐사선들이 화성에 착륙했을 당시, 탐사선들이 수행했던 몇몇 실험을 통해서 과학자들은 한때 화성의 표면에 물이 막힘없이 흘렀었다는 결론을 내렸다. 두 번째 *바이킹호* 탐사선은 마치 지표면에 서리가 있는 것 같아 보이는 사진을 전송하기도 했는데, 이는 엷은 대기에 수증기가 포함되어 있다는 사실을 암시하고 있었다. 불행하게도, 이 탐사선은 어떠한 견본도 확보하지 못했고, 따라서 사진들은 확실한 증거가 되지 못하였다.

화성에 북극과 남극에 존재했다는 것에 대한 차후의 사진 증거는 눈과 얼음으로 덮여 있는 것으로 보이는 광대한 흰 색의 지역에 있었다. 두 극지방에 있는 빙원들은 3킬로미터 정도의 두께일 것으로 생각된다. 주변을 돌고 있는 위성들의 기록에 따르면, 이 하양 지역들은 실제로 얼음이며 얼어 있는 이산화탄소와 얼어 있는 물로 구성되어 있다. 가장 위의 층들은 주로 얼어 있는 이산화탄소인 반면, 그 아래에는 거대한 얼어 있는 물의 층이 있다. 그러나, 빙원에 착륙했던 위성은 없었기 때문에, 화성의 극지방에 있는 빙원의 정확한 구성 성분은 수수께끼로 남아 있다. 하지만, 과학자들은 화성의 계절이 변화함에 따라서 양 극의 빙원들이 수축과 팽창을 계속한다는 사실을 알게 되었다. 화성의 축은 지구의 축과 마찬가지로 기울어져 있기 때문에, 때때로, 이 행성이 태양 주위를 도는 동안, 한쪽 극지방은 완전한 암흑 상태인 반면에 다른 극지방은 거의 계속적으로 햇빛을 받는다. 햇빛이 자주 비치는 극지방에서는 이산화탄소가 녹는 경우가 종종 있지만 또 다른 극지방에서는 얼어 있는 이산화탄소의 양이 증가하게 된다.

그렇지만, 화성에서 1년 동안 이산화탄소가 얼고 녹는 것을 반복함에도 불구하고, 액체 상태의 물은 존재하지 않는다. 그 주요 원인은 화성의 온도와 압력에 의해서 어떠한 물도 사실상 즉시 얼어 있는 상태나 기체 상태가 되기 때문이다. 하지만, 한때 이 행성의 지면에서 물이 막힘없이 흘렀었다는 증거가 있다. 과학자들은 화성에서, 지구에서와 마찬가지로, 수백만 년 전에 수많은 화산 폭발이 있었다고 생각한다. 이렇게 엄청난 화산 활동으로 인하여 수증기로 가득한 두껍고 따뜻한 대기가 생겨났다. 비가 내리고, 물이 쌓여서, 강, 호수, 그리고 아마도 바다가 생겨났을 것이다. 하지만, 시간이 흐르면서 대기가 변화하였다. 화성의 약한 자기장은 대기를 유지할 수 없었을 것인데, 대기는 태양풍에 의해서 점차 제거되었을 것이다. 이 태양풍으로 인해 높은 수치의 복사에너지와 낮은 온도에 수면이 노출되어, 물은 점차 증발하거나 얼어붙게 되었다.

한때 화성의 표면에서 물이 흘렀었기 때문에, 천문학자들은 이곳에 생명체가 존재하지 않았을까 생각하고 있다. 대부분의 학자들은 아마도 탄소 기반 생명체가 화성에 살지는 않았을 것이라고 결론을 내렸다. 그 이유는 천문학자들이 화성이 생명 지대라고 부르는 지역의 경계에 위치하고 있기 때문인데, 생명 지대란 태양에 너무 가까이 있지도 않고 너무 멀리 있지도 않아서 생명체가 존재하는 우주상의 지역이다. 수성과 같은 행성은, 태양에 너무 가까이 있어서, 태양으로부터 엄청난 양의 열과 복사에너지를 받기 때문에, 이곳에서는 생명체가 생존할 수 없다. 반면에, 목성과 토성 같은 행성들은 태양에서 너무 멀리 떨어져 있기 때문에, 이 행성들에는 생명체가 살아갈 수 있기에 충분한 정도의 열이 미치지 않는다. 물론, 화성에 생명체가 존재하는 것이 가능하기는 하지만, 그렇다고 하더라도, 지구에서 살고 있는 탄소 기반 생명체와는 다를 것이다. 화성에 대한 미래의 임무들이 수행되기 전까지는, 과학자들은 진실을 알아

낼 수 없을 것이다.

Listening Section p.87

Answers

1. (A) [Gist-Content Question]
2. (A) [Detail Question]
3. (C) [Making Inferences Question]
4. (D) [Understanding Attitude Question]
5. (B) [Understanding Function Question]
6. (C) [Gist-Content Question]
7. (A) [Understanding Attitude Question]
8. (D) [Understanding Organization Question]
9. (B) [Detail Question]
10. (B) [Understanding Organization Question]
11. (A) [Making Inferences Question]

Script

| 07-02 |

W1 Professor: Laura, what a pleasant surprise. I haven't seen you in, uh, what . . . it must have been three weeks since you've been in class. Have you been all right?

W2 Student: To be completely honest, Professor Eagleton, no, I haven't been all right.

W1: Goodness. What's wrong?

W2: I was in the hospital for the past three weeks. I just got out a couple of days ago.

W1: The hospital? That must have been a serious illness you had.

W2: Actually, um, I wasn't really ill. You see, I went to have a routine knee surgery . . . I'm on the volleyball team, and I hurt my knee in practice . . . but there were some, um . . . complications from the surgery. So I had to stay in the hospital until I got better.

W1: That's awful. Ah . . . I suppose that's why you never responded to any of my emails either, right?

W2: Yes, ma'am. That's correct. I didn't have Internet access while I was there. So, uh . . . I'm here to talk about class. I know we've got the final exam coming up next week, but, well . . .

W1: You're not ready to take it, are you?

W2: I don't see how I could. Well, okay, I could take the test, but I would almost definitely fail it. And it's too late for me to drop the class. So, um . . . what am I supposed to do about this?

W1: Well, first, don't worry too much. The school has

a policy for situations like this. You're not the first student to get hospitalized in the middle of the semester after all. What I can do is give you an "I" in the class.

W2: An eye?

W1: Not an eye that you see with. I mean the letter I. It stands for incomplete.

W2: Oh, okay . . . And then what?

W1: Well, you'd need to complete the work for the course within a certain period of time. It's usually a month, but it could be longer. After you finish the course, then you'd get a real letter grade.

W2: [4]Hmm . . . That sounds good. But, uh, what about the classes I missed? How am I supposed to catch up on the lectures and stuff?

W1: There's no need to stress out about that, Laura. You see, I record all of my lectures. I don't have them on video, but I have them on audio. I can send you the computer files for the classes you missed, and then you can listen to them. When you feel like you're ready, you can take the final exam. Uh, you live here in the city, right?

W2: Yes, that's correct. So even though it's winter break, I will still be in the neighborhood. Taking the final during vacation won't be a problem. Okay . . . This sounds like a good plan. Can you send me the files so that I can start listening to them?

W1: No problem. And if you feel up to it, try to make it to the last couple of classes. Obviously, you don't need to attend the final exam. But it would be nice to see your face in class again.

W2: [5]I'll try, Professor. Well, I've got to go and find my other professors now. Oh, and thanks a million for letting me know about incompletes. I guess I'm going to have lots of I's on my transcript this semester.

Translation

W1 Professor: *Laura*, 정말 놀랐어요. 학생을 보지 못했는데, 어… 수업에서 마지막으로 본 지 틀림없이 3주가 지났군요. 괜찮나요?

W2 Student: 정말 솔직하게 말씀드리면요, *Eagleton* 교수님, 아니에요. 괜찮지가 않아요.

W1: 이런. 무슨 문제인가요?

W2: 지난 3주 동안 병원에 있었어요. 이틀 전에 퇴원을 했고요.

W1: 병원이요? 틀림없이 심각한 병이었겠군요.

W2: 실은, 음, 정말로 아팠던 것은 아니었어요. 아시겠지만, 일상적인 무릎 수술을 받으러 갔는데… 저는 배구부인데요, 연습을 하다가 무릎을 다쳤어요… 하지만, 음… 수술로 합병증이 생겼어요. 그래서 회복이 될 때까지 병원에 있어야만 했죠.

W1: 안 되었군요. 아… 그래서 제 이메일에 아무런 답장도 하지 못했을 것이라는 생각이 드네요. 맞나요?

W2: 네, 교수님. 맞아요. 그곳에 있는 동안 인터넷에 접속을 하지 못했어요. 그래서, 어… 수업에 대해 이야기하기 위해 제가 여기에 온 것이고요. 다음 주에 기말고사가 있다고 알고 있는데,

하지만, 음…

W1: 시험을 볼 준비가 안 되었군요, 그런가요?

W2: 어떻게 해야 할지 모르겠어요. 음, 좋아요, 시험을 볼 수는 있겠지만, 거의 틀림없이 낙제를 하게 될 거예요. 그리고 수강 신청을 취소하기에는 너무 늦었고요. 그래서, 음… 이에 대해 제가 어떻게 해야 할까요?

W1: 음, 먼저, 너무 걱정 말아요. 이러한 상황을 대비해서 학교에서는 방침을 세워두고 있죠. 어쨌든 학기 중간에 입원을 한 사람은 학생이 처음은 아니니까요. 제가 할 수 있는 일은 수업에서 학생에게 "I"를 주는 거예요.

W2: 'eye'요?

W1: 보는 눈은 아니고요. 글자 'I'를 말하는 거예요. '불완전 이수'를 의미하죠.

W2: 흠… 좋아요. 하지만, 어, 제가 빠진 수업은 어떻게 하죠? 강의와 수업 내용을 따라잡으려면 제가 어떻게 해야 할까요?

W1: 그 점에 대해서는 걱정할 필요가 없어요, *Laura*. 알겠지만, 저는 제 모든 강의를 녹음해 두고 있죠. 비디오는 없지만, 오디오로 가지고 있어요. 듣지 못한 수업에 대해 컴퓨터 파일을 보내 줄 수 있고, 그러면 학생이 그것을 들을 수 있을 거예요. 준비가 되었다고 생각이 들면, 기말고사를 볼 수도 있고요. 어, 여기 시내에서 살죠, 맞나요?

W2: 네, 맞아요. 그래서 겨울 방학에도, 이곳 근처에 있을 거예요. 방학 동안 기말 시험을 치르는 것은 문제가 되지 않을 거예요. 좋아요… 좋은 계획으로 들리는군요. 제가 들어볼 수 있도록 파일을 보내 주실 수 있나요?

W1: 문제 없죠. 그리고 여력이 되면, 마지막 두 수업에는 들어오도록 해봐요. 물론, 기말시험 시간에는 들어오지 않아도 되지만요. 하지만 수업 시간에 다시 학생의 얼굴을 보게 된다면 좋을 것 같아요.

W2: 그렇게 해볼게요, 교수님. 음, 이제 나가서 다른 교수님들을 찾아뵈어야 할 것 같아요. 오, 그리고 불완전 이수에 대해 알려 주셔서 정말 감사합니다. 이번 학기의 성적표에는 'I'가 많이 있게 될 것 같네요.

Script

| 07-03 |

M Professor: Today, we shall continue our examination of the great European filmmakers and theater directors of the twentieth century. I think we'll move away from Western Europe and focus on Eastern Europe. Right now, we're going to look at how artists fared under the communist regimes in that part of Europe. We'll start with one of the greats of the era as well as one of my personal favorites, Jerzy Grotowski of Poland. He was a theater director who transcended the restrictions placed on artists by communist governments and also established a school of acting that won him renown both at home and abroad.

First, let me give you a few details about his life. Grotowski was born in 1933 and graduated from university in 1955. He was a student of acting, and, after graduating, he went to Moscow, Russia, in the late 1950s to study the acting methods of some great Russians. This included Konstantin Stanislavsky, whom we've already looked at a bit and will talk about in more detail in a few minutes. Grotowski next took a position as an assistant theater director in the Polish city of Krakow. It was there that he began to develop his unique style of theatrical performing. Over the next fifteen years, Grotowski directed numerous plays, both by foreign and Polish writers. Some plays were famous while others were new productions. Around this time, Grotowski began experimenting. He was trying to erase the line that divided the performers on stage from the audience watching them. He wanted the members of the audience to feel like they were a part of the performance.

W Student: I'm sorry, Professor Kimball, but I don't exactly understand what you mean.

M: Oh, uh, in that case, let me give you some examples. Hopefully, that will clarify matters. Let me think . . . Okay, as you know, in traditional plays, the stage is where the actors perform while the audience sits in seats and doesn't take part in the performance. But Grotowski wanted the audience to have its own role. In one play, *Faust*, the lead actor used the audience members like they were priests and he was confessing to them. In another one, uh, *Kordian*, the audience members were considered to be patients in a mental hospital. In addition, many of the stage directions Grotowski gave called for the actors to move through the audience. In theatrical terms, this is known as "breaking the fourth wall." Ah, you see, the first three walls are the sides and rear of the stage while the fourth wall is the invisible one between the stage and the audience. It's like when, uh, in a movie, an actor looks at the camera and seems to talk to the audience. See what I mean . . . ? Good . . . So by acknowledging the presence of the audience, Grotowski was breaking the fourth wall. Grotowski wrote about this in his book entitled *Toward a Poor Theater*. It and Grotowski's other writings became the basis for avant-garde theater in the West during the 1960s and 1970s.

As you can no doubt imagine, Grotowski's fame grew in the late 1960s. His Poor Theater Group, as his acting troupe was called, traveled abroad and performed in Great Britain and the United States. Ah, please remember that during this time in Eastern Europe, there were all sorts of restrictions, so it was a big deal for a troupe of actors to travel to the West to perform. As proof of this, while Grotowski's writings on acting and the theater were published in the West, they weren't available in Poland, his native land, because of restrictions placed on the publishing industry.

Now, uh, throughout the 1970s, Grotowski traveled extensively and sought to expand his methods by studying theater in various cultures. Then, in the 1980s, his life underwent a dramatic change. While he was abroad, Polish workers desiring democratic reform demonstrated, and the government declared martial

law. Grotowski sought political asylum and eventually settled in the U.S., where he taught theater at some universities. A few years later, he moved to Italy to work on a grand project called "Art as Vehicle." Later, in 1999, while Grotowski was still working on this project, he died.

As for his legacy . . . Well, there are his writings and the principles that he applied to his actors and their performances. At his school, which he referred to as a theater laboratory, Grotowski made a list of ten principles of acting. All the students there had to learn and emulate these principles during the initial part of their training. Until they embraced these principles in their entirety, they weren't able to become full members of his acting company. These ten principles became a crucial part of his writings and teachings that made it to the West and are rightly regarded as a major contribution to theater acting. Since I'm sure you're all wondering what they are, I've got a handout that lists them right here. Would someone help me pass these out to the class, please?

M Professor: 오늘은, 20세기 유럽의 위대한 영화 제작자들과 연극 연출가들에 대해 계속 알아보도록 하겠습니다. 서유럽을 벗어나 동유럽에 초점이 맞추어 질 것 같군요. 이제, 공산주의 정권 하의 동유럽 지역에서 예술가들이 어떻게 살아갔는지를 살펴보도록 하겠습니다. 당대의 위대한 인물 중 한 명이자, 제가 개인적으로 가장 좋아하는 사람 중 한 명인, 폴란드의 예지 그로토프스키로 시작해 보도록 하겠습니다. 그는 공산주의 정부가 예술가들에게 부여했던 제한 조치들을 뛰어넘은 연극 연출가였으며, 고국과 해외 모두에서 그에게 명성을 안겨다 준 연기학교도 설립했습니다.

우선, 그의 삶에 대해 몇 가지 자세한 내용을 알려드리도록 하죠. 그로토프스키는 1933년에 태어나서 1955년에 대학을 졸업했습니다. 그는 연기를 전공한 학생이었고, 졸업 후에는 러시아의 모스크바로 가서, 1950년대 후반에 몇몇 위대한 러시아인들의 연기 훈련법을 공부했습니다. 여기에는 콘스탄틴 스타니슬랍스키가 포함되어 있었는데, 이 사람에 대해서는 이미 약간 살펴보았으므로 잠시 후에 보다 자세히 이야기해 보도록 하겠습니다. 그 다음 그로토프스키는 폴란드의 크라쿠프 시에서 조연출의 자리를 맡았습니다. 그가 독특한 스타일의 무대 연기를 발전시키기 시작한 곳이 바로 그곳이었습니다. 이후 15년 동안, 그로토프스키는 외국 작가와 폴란드 작가가 쓴 수많은 연극들을 연출했습니다. 일부 연극은 유명한 것이었던 반면, 일부는 새롭게 만들어진 것이었습니다. 이 시기에, 그로토프스키는 실험을 시작했습니다. 무대 위의 연기자들과 연기자들을 바라보는 관객들을 구분해 주던 선을 없애려고 했던 것이었죠. 관객들이 스스로 공연의 일부인 것처럼 느끼도록 하고자 했습니다.

W Student: 죄송하지만, *Kimball* 교수님, 무슨 말씀인지 정확히 이해가 가지 않는군요.

M: 오, 어, 그러면, 몇 가지 예를 들어보도록 하겠습니다. 명확해졌으면 좋겠네요. 생각해 봅시다… 좋아요, 아시겠지만, 전통 연극에서, 무대는 배우들이 공연을 하는 장소이고, 관객들은 좌

석에 앉아 공연에는 참여하지 않습니다. 하지만 그로토프스키는 관객들이 자신들의 역할을 갖기를 원했습니다. 파우스트라는 한 연극에서, 주인공은 관객들을 성직자로 여기고 그들에게 고해를 합니다. 다른 경우, 어, 코르디안이라는 연극에서는, 관객들이 정신 병원에 있는 환자로 간주되었습니다. 또한, 그로토프스키가 했던 많은 무대 지시들은 배우들이 관객들 사이를 지나갈 것을 요구했습니다. 연극 용어로, 이는 "제4의 벽을 무너뜨리는 것"이라고 알려져 있습니다. 아, 알겠지만, 처음 3개의 벽은 무대의 양쪽 면과 뒷면인 반면, 4번째 벽은 무대와 관객 사이에 존재하는, 눈에 보이지 않는 벽입니다. 마치, 어, 영화에서, 배우가 카메라를 보고 관객들에게 말을 하는 것과 같은 경우죠. 제가 말씀드리는 바를 알겠나요…? 좋습니다… 그래서, 관객들의 존재를 인정함으로써, 그로토프스키는 제4의 벽을 무너뜨리고 있었던 것입니다. 그로토프스키는 자신의 책, 가난한 연극을 향하여라는 제목의 책에서 이에 대한 글을 썼습니다. 이 책과 그로토프스키의 다른 글들은 1960년대와 1970년대 서구에서 아방가르드 연극의 기초가 되었습니다.

틀림없이 여러분도 짐작할 수 있듯이, 그로토프스키의 명성은 1960년대 후반에 커졌습니다. 그의 '푸어 시어터 그룹'은, 그의 극단은 그렇게 불렸는데, 해외를 돌아다니며 영국과 미국에서 공연을 했습니다. 아, 이 시기 동안 동유럽에서는, 온갖 종류의 제한 조치들이 실시되어, 연극 단원들이 서방으로 공연을 하러 가는 것은 커다란 모험이었다는 것을 기억해 두십시오. 이에 대한 증거로, 연기와 연극에 대한 그로토프스키의 글이 서구에서는 출판되었지만, 그의 고향 폴란드에서는 구할 수가 없었는데, 그 이유는 출판 업계에 내려진 제한 조치 때문이었습니다.

자, 어, 1970년대를 통해, 그로토프스키는 많은 곳을 여행하고 다양한 문화권에서 연극을 공부함으로써 자신의 방법을 확장시키려고 했습니다. 그런 다음, 1980년대에, 그의 삶은 극적인 변화를 겪습니다. 그가 해외에 있는 동안, 민주주의 개혁을 바라던 폴란드 노동자들이 시위를 벌였고, 정부는 계엄령을 선포했습니다. 그로토프스키는 정치적 피난처를 찾았고, 결국 미국에 정착했는데, 여기서 그는 몇몇 대학에서 연극을 가르쳤습니다. 몇 년 후, 그는 이탈리아로 가서 "운송 수단으로서의 예술"이라는 대규모 프로젝트에 참여했습니다. 이후, 1999년, 그로토프스키가 이 프로젝트의 일을 계속 하고 있는 시기에, 그는 사망했습니다.

그가 남긴 것들에 대해 말씀을 드리면… 음, 그가 쓴 글들이 있고 그가 연기자와 공연자들에게 적용시켰던 원칙들이 존재합니다. 학교에서, 그는 학교를 연극 실험실이라고 불렀는데, 그로토프스키는 연기의 10가지 원칙을 만들었습니다. 그곳의 모든 학생들은 연기 연습의 첫 부분에서 이러한 원칙들을 익히고 직접 체험해 보았습니다. 이러한 원칙들을 자기의 것으로 만들 때까지, 학생들은 정규 단원이 될 수 없었습니다. 이러한 10가지 원칙은 서방으로 전파되었고, 당연하게도, 연극 연기에 대한 주요한 공헌으로 간주되고 있는 그의 글과 가르침에서 중요한 부분이 되었습니다. 여러분 모두가 틀림없이 그것이 무엇인지에 대해 궁금할 것이라고 생각하기 때문에, 여기 원칙들이 적혀 있는 유인물을 가지고 왔습니다. 누가 나누어 주는 것을 도와주시겠어요?

Reading Section
p.93

Answers

1. B [Rhetorical Purpose Question]
2. C [Reference Question]
3. C [Vocabulary Question]
4. D [Vocabulary Question]
5. B [Factual Question]
6. C [Inference Question]
7. A [Factual Question]
8. A [Vocabulary Question]
9. A [Negative Factual Question]
10. B [Inference Question]
11. C [Factual Question]
12. B [Rhetorical Purpose Question]
13. 2nd [Insert Text Question]
14. A, D, E [Prose Summary Question]

Translation

신고전주의 건축

18세기의 전반, 서구의 건축은 로코코 시대의 한 가운데에 있었다. 하지만, 한 세기가 흐르면서, 사람들은 무엇인가 다른 것을 갈망하기 시작했다. 그들은 이탈리아에서 르네상스가 일어나서 그리스와 로마의 양식이 인기를 끌었던 15세기와 16세기로 관심을 돌렸다. 게다가, 서기 79년 베수비우스 화산이 폭발했을 때 파묻혔던 로마의 도시 폼페이와 헤르쿨라네움이 1700년대 중반에 재발견되었다. 이 도시들의 모습은 많은 건축가들의 마음을 사로잡았고, 고전주의 건축은 다시 한 번 인기를 끌게 되었다. 1700년대 중반부터 1800년대에 이르기까지, 신고전주의 시대가 유럽과 미국의 건축을 지배했다.

신고전주의에 대한 사실상 즉각적인 인기는 주로 로코코 양식의 사치스러움에 대한 반발로부터 비롯되었는데, 로코코 양식은 후기 바로크 양식에 속하였다. 로코코 양식은 디자인에 있어서 대칭을 채택하지 않았던 대신, 복잡하고 정교하게 만들어진 화려하고 흐르는 듯한 패턴에 의존했다. 하지만 유럽인들은 1700년대 중반 로코코 양식에 싫증을 느끼기 시작했다. 고대 그리스와 로마에 대한 향수도 함께 일어났는데, 다수의 유럽인들은 이러한 두 문명의 잃어버린 웅대함을 회복하기를 희망하고 있었다. 많은 위대한 그리스와 로마의 작품들이 — 아테네의 파르테논 신전과 로마의 콜로세움을 포함하여 — 여전히 그대로 남아 있었기 때문에, 사람들은 이러한 작품들의 간결함과 위풍당당한 모습에 감탄하였다. 그리하여 신고전주의 시대에 상당한 영향을 주었던 과거에 대한 동경이 시작되었다.

동시에, 로마의 잃어버린 두 도시, 폼페이와 헤르쿨라네움이 수십 미터의 재속에서 재발견되었다. 이 도시들은 대략 1,700년 전에 베수비우스 화산 분출로 인하여 완전히 파괴되었다. 차츰, 이 도시들은 사람들의 기억 속에서 사라졌지만, 발견되자마자, 두 도시는 많은 유럽인들을 매혹시켰다. 중요한 것은, 이 도시들이 용암에 의해 파괴되었던 것이 아니라 재속에 파묻혔다는 사실이었다. 그 결과, 많은 건물들이 잘 보존되어서, 로마인들의 삶, 예술, 그리고 건축 양식에 대한 있는 그대로의 세세한 부분들이 재발견 되었다. (예를 들면, 원형 그대로의 로마 벽화들이 이곳에서 발견되었는데, 이를 통해서 로마 시대의 삶의 많은 부분들에 대한 세세한 부분들도 알 수 있게 되었다.) 두 도시의 모습은 유럽 전역에 센세이션을 일으켰고, 수많은 건축가들이 고대 양식을 직접 목격하기 위해 이 도시들을 방문했다. 특히 로마 가옥 내부의 디자인이 감탄을 자아냈으며, 이러한 디자인들은 곧바로 부유층의 가옥에 그대로 옮겨졌다.

하지만 고대 그리스와 로마의 디자인들이 1700년대 이전에 익숙하지 않았던 것은 아니었다. 유럽인들은 르네상스 이후로 이러한 것들에 대해서 많이 알고 있었다. 이 때는 베네치아의 건축가 안드레아 팔라디오가 살고 있었던 시기였다. 팔라디오는 고대 건축에 대해 가르치며 집필도 했는데, 그의 작품들은 신고전주의 시대 동안 많은 유럽과 미국의 건축가들에게 주요한 모범이 되었다. 팔라디오는 건물의 전체적인 디자인에서 대칭과 균형을 강조했으며, 원주와 화려한 정면을 선호했다. 그는 원주가 건물에 심오하고 강인한 느낌 및 장엄함을 부여해 준다고 생각했다.

하지만 원주가 신고전주의 시대에 활용된 그리스와 로마의 모습들 가운데 유일한 것은 아니었다. 로마 양식의 아치와 돔 역시 여러 신고전주의 건축물에서 활용되었다. 건축가들은 석재 또한, 특히 건물 외부에는 화강암과 석회암이, 그리고 내부에는 대리석을 주로 사용하였다. 신고전주의 시대 동안, 건물의 내부는 상당히 간결해졌는데, 특히 로코코 양식과 비교했을 때 그러했다. 신고전주의 건물들은 공간과 빛을 강조했기 때문에, 건물의 내부는 강렬한 느낌을 주었다. 하지만, 이러한 최소 표현주의 양식은 도서관, 대학교 학사 건물, 그리고 정부 건물에는 효과적이었으나, 그 목적이 가정용 주택의 경우에는 거의 부합되지 못했다. 이러한 이유로, 로마 가옥의 디자인을 모방하려는 시도는 실용적인 이유로 인하여 중지되었다.

신고전주의 시대의 건축은 유럽에서 시작되었지만, 1700년대가 끝날 무렵, 미국에도 영향을 주었다. 아마도 사실상 미국 최초의 건축가였던 토마스 제퍼슨은 새로운 양식을 연구하기 위해 파리에서 많은 시간을 보냈으며, 그 후 모든 지식을 가지고 본국으로 돌아왔다. 그가 설계하고 건설했던 몇몇 건물들, 특히 버지니아 대학의 건물들은 오늘날까지도 여전히 사용되고 있다. 신고전주의 시대는 1800년대 동안 줄곧 인기가 있었지만, 그 세기의 후반에 콘크리트와 철골로 건설된 건물들이 들어서면서 영향력을 잃기 시작했다. 그럼에도 불구하고, 신고전주의 시대의 여러 가지 측면들은 1900년대에도 그대로 남아있었으며, 1900년대 중반 소련의 건축물들과 북미 전역의 많은 대학 캠퍼스에서 그 영향력을 찾아볼 수 있다.

Answers

1. (B) [Gist-Purpose Question]

2. (A) [Making Inferences Question]

3. (D) [Understanding Function Question]

4. (D) [Detail Question]

5. (C) [Understanding Function Question]

6. (B) [Gist-Content Question]

7.

	Fact	Not a Fact
(A)	X	
(B)		X
(C)	X	
(D)	X	

[Detail Question]

8. (D) [Detail Question]

9. (A) [Making Inferences Question]

10. (B) [Understanding Organization Question]

11. (C) [Understanding Function Question]

Script

| 08-02 |

M Student: Excuse me, but I need to return this equipment here. It was borrowed from the library a couple of days ago I think. To be honest, uh, I'm not quite sure exactly when it was borrowed, but I know that it's not overdue.

W Librarian: Ah, the movie projector. Great. I was wondering when we were going to get it back. Someone else has been asking about it. I'll have to give her a call and let her know it's here.

M: Ah, well, you must be glad that I decided to bring it back this evening. I had considered waiting until tomorrow, but I thought it would be better to return it tonight instead since I've got a busy day tomorrow.

W: Thanks a lot for being considerate. We only have a couple of these movie projectors since almost everyone uses computers to watch videos nowadays. So when we get multiple requests for our movie projectors, we always hope that they get returned quickly.

M: You shouldn't have anything to worry about now that you've got it.

W: That's true. Okay. Let me just check this in, and you can be on your way.

M: Sure thing.

W: You are . . . um, David Jenkins?

M: Er, no. That's the professor. My name is Eric Showman. I'm a teaching assistant in Professor Jenkins's class, so I get stuck with duties like returning the projector here. It's all part of being a graduate student.

W: Yeah, I remember those days as well. All right. The projector appears to be in good working order, so I'd say that we're done. Thank you very much and have a great evening.

M: Oh, um, if you don't mind, I have a quick question for you concerning the equipment you have here.

W: Sure. What do you need to know about it?

M: Is anyone at the university allowed to check out the projectors? I mean, film is kind of a hobby of mine, and I'd love to be able to screen some films with a projector for my friends. Is it possible for me to check this machine out sometime?

W: Hmm . . . Not exactly.

M: What do you mean?

W: Students—both undergraduate and graduate—are generally not allowed to remove the film projectors from the library. Only faculty and staff are permitted to check them out for the most part.

M: You said for the most part. How come?

W: All right, it is possible for a student to check one out, but there is one condition. The student needs to have a note from either a faculty or staff member basically, uh, taking responsibility if anything happens to the projector. This equipment is expensive, and too many students damaged various items in the past. That's why we no longer permit students to take this kind of equipment out of the library.

M: I see.

W: [5]Basically, if you can talk one of your professors—Professor Jenkins perhaps—into writing a note for you, I'd be glad to let you borrow a projector if one is available at the time.

M: Excellent. In that case, I can pretty much guarantee that you'll be seeing me again in a few days. Thanks for the information. I appreciate it.

W: It's my pleasure. Good luck getting a note.

Translation

M Student: 실례지만, 여기 이 장비를 반납해야 해서요. 제 생각에 이틀 전에 도서관에서 빌린 것 같아요. 솔직히 말씀드리면, 어, 정확히 언제 빌렸는지는 확실하지 않지만, 기한이 지나지 않았다는 점은 알고 있어요.

W Librarian: 아, 영사기군요. 잘 되었네요. 언제 돌려받게 될 것인지 궁금했어요. 누군가가 이에 대한 요청을 해두었거든요. 그녀에게 전화를 해서 여기 있다고 알려 줘야겠어요.

M: 아, 음, 제가 오늘 저녁에 다시 가지고 오기로 해서 틀림없이 기쁘시겠네요. 내일까지 기다려 볼까 생각했지만, 내일은 바쁠 것 같아 오늘밤에 돌려드리는 것이 낫겠다고 생각했어요.

W: 신경을 써 줘서 정말 고맙군요. 요즘 거의 모든 사람들이 컴퓨터를 이용해서 비디오를 보기 때문에, 영사기는 두 대뿐이에요.

그래서 영사기에 대한 요청이 여러 개 들어오면, 항상 빨리 반납되기를 바라고 있죠.

M: 이게 받게 되었으니 걱정할 것이 없으시겠어요.

W: 맞아요. 좋아요. 반납을 받을 게요, 그러면 가셔도 좋아요.

M: 그래요.

W: 학생이… 음, *David Jenkins*인가요?

M: 어, 아니에요. 그분께서는 교수님이세요. 제 이름은 *Eric Showman*이고요. *Jenkins* 교수님 수업에서 제가 조교를 맡고 있기 때문에, 여기 영사기를 반납하는 것과 같은 일은 제가 하고 있어요. 모두가 대학원생이 되면 해야 하는 일이죠.

W: 네, 저도 마찬가지로 그러한 시기가 기억나네요. 좋아요. 영사기의 상태가 좋은 것 같아 보여서, 다 되었다고 말하고 싶네요. 정말 고맙고 좋은 저녁 보내세요.

M: 오, 음, 괜찮으시면, 이곳에 있는 장비에 대해 간단히 물어볼 것이 있는데요.

W: 그러세요. 무엇을 알아야 하나요?

M: 대학에 있는 사람이면 누구라도 영사기를 대출할 수가 있나요? 제 말은, 영화는 제 취미인데, 몇몇 영화를 친구들에게 영사기로 보여 줄 수 있으면 좋을 것 같아서요. 제가 추후에 이 기기를 대출하는 것이 가능한가요?

W: 흠… 꼭 그렇지는 않아요.

M: 무슨 말씀이시죠?

W: 학생들은 — 학부생과 대학원생 모두 — 일반적으로 도서관에서 영사기를 밖으로 가지고 나가지 못해요. 주로 교수님들과 교직원 분들만이 대출을 하실 수 있죠.

M: 주로라고 말씀하셨군요. 어째서죠?

W: 좋아요. 학생이 대출하는 것도 가능하지만, 한 가지 조건이 있어요. 학생은 원칙적으로 어, 영사기에 무슨 일이 생기면 책임을 지겠다는 교수님이나 직원 분의 노트를 가지고 있어야 해요. 이 장비가 고가이고, 너무 많은 학생들이 예전에 다양한 기기에 손상을 입혔거든요. 더 이상 학생들에게 이와 같은 장비를 도서관 밖으로 가져가지 못하게 한 이유죠.

M: 알겠어요.

W: 원칙적으로, 교수님 중 한 분께 말씀을 드려서 — 아마 *Jenkins* 교수님이 되겠네요 — 노트를 써 달라고 하면, 제가, 그 시기에 이용 가능한 영사기가 있는 경우, 기꺼이 학생에게 빌려 줄 게요.

M: 정말 잘 되었군요. 그런 경우라면, 며칠 후에 다시 뵙게 될 것이라고 확실히 말씀드릴 수 있어요. 정보를 주셔서 고마워요. 정말로 감사합니다.

W: 제가 기쁘죠. 노트를 얻는데 행운이 있기를 바랄게요.

Script

| 08-03 |

M Professor: Ever since humans first ventured into space and, eventually, explored the moon in the 1960s and 1970s, people have dreamed of building a permanent base on the moon. One of the biggest obstacles in doing so is power. Namely, uh, where would the energy needed to power a moon base come from? The answer seems to be from the moon itself in the form of helium-3, which is a helium isotope.

Helium is an element with two protons and two neutrons and appears most commonly in its gaseous form. Interestingly, on occasion, during nuclear reactions such as, uh, such as those which take place both in the sun and in nuclear reactors, some helium atoms lose a neutron. As a result, they have two protons but only one neutron. This is helium-3. Helium-3 is incredibly rare on Earth and typically appears due to the decay of another isotope, called, uh, tritium, which is a form of hydrogen. But it takes more than twelve years for tritium to decay into helium-3, and the amount of tritium needed to produce even a tiny amount of helium-3 is great. Tritium's also quite rare on Earth. It's mostly found in nuclear reactors that use lithium. Anyway, these factors all make the commercial production of helium-3, well, impractical.

But that raises another question . . . Why would anyone want to make helium-3 . . . ? Well, uh, here's a good answer: It could be a source of clean energy. You see, when helium-3 reacts with another isotope of hydrogen, called deuterium, it releases energy in a process called fusion. Small amounts of helium-3 and deuterium can produce massive amounts of energy that can be controlled in reactors and converted to electrical power.

Unfortunately, there are currently fewer than 200 kilograms of helium-3 on Earth. That's so little that it doesn't justify the expense of conducting research into designing and building a nuclear fusion reactor that could run on helium-3 and deuterium. It's simply not viable. However, there's one place we know of where there is an abundance of helium-3: the moon.

Due to its prolonged exposure to solar winds thanks to its lack of an atmosphere, the surface of the moon contains a large amount of helium-3 in its dusty soil. In fact, scientists estimate that the moon contains more than, uh, get this, one million tons of helium-3. All that needs to be done is for the helium-3 to be separated from the dust and rocks through a chemical process. Then, it would be able to be used in fusion reactions to produce power. How much power . . . ? We estimate that only twenty-five tons of helium-3 converted by fusion into electricity could serve all the power needs of the United States for an entire year . . . Ah, now you're starting to see why it's so appealing, aren't you?

So, anyway, the goal of many now is to construct a base on the moon where helium-3 fusion reactors would be utilized to provide power. [11]NASA, the European Space Agency, and the Russians are all working on plans to build a moon base in the next few decades. Meanwhile, engineers and scientists are trying to design a helium-3 fusion reactor that could operate on the moon. **Unfortunately, this won't happen for several decades in the future.** However, when completed, it will guarantee that any moon base will have a supply of power for many years. It might also be able to serve as a fuel source for interstellar flights that would use the

moon base as their starting point.

W Student: Why don't they just mine the dust and rocks and bring them back to Earth?

M: That's a possibility. However, there are many logistical problems. For instance, this would require large cargo-carrying rockets that could take off from Earth, land on the moon, take off again, return here, and land safely with the cargo. To make this financially feasible, each rocket would have to make several trips. There's also the issue of price. If oil and other fossil fuels can be used to make electricity much cheaper than moon dust with helium-3, no one will pay for electricity made from helium-3. Still, it's definitely an appealing option for the future, both when we start depleting our fossil fuel supply further and when our technology makes traveling to the moon easy and frequent.

Now, what about the environmental impact of clean nuclear fusion . . . ? Isn't it worth spending extra money on helium-3? Well, think for a second . . . Since the 1940s, we've known how to make electricity from nuclear reactions. And it's very clean, especially when compared to fossil fuels. Despite that, we still haven't totally replaced fossil fuels with nuclear energy. For one, people worry about the danger of radiation from nuclear power plants. Yet experts claim that helium-3 fusion reactors would be much safer and cleaner. Of course, it's all theoretical since no one has done it yet. But helium-3 is potentially one of the greatest power sources available to us. We merely lack the technology to take full advantage of it.

M Professor: 인간이 처음 우주로 모험을 시작하여, 마침내, 1960년대와 1970년대에 달을 탐사한 이후로, 인간은 달에 영구적인 기지를 세우겠다는 꿈을 꾸어 왔습니다. 그렇게 하는데 가장 큰 문제 중의 하나는 전력입니다. 즉, 어, 달 기지에 전력을 공급해 줄 에너지는 어디에서 얻을 수 있을까요? 그 답은 헬륨3라는 형태로 달 자체로부터 얻어질 수 있는 것처럼 보이는데, 헬륨3는 헬륨의 동위 원소입니다.

헬륨은 두 개의 양성자와 두 개의 중성자를 지닌 원소로, 기체 형태로 존재하는 경우가 가장 일반적인 것으로 보입니다. 흥미롭게도, 때때로, 예컨데, 어, 예컨데 태양과 원자로에서 일어나는 것과 같은 핵반응이 일어나는 동안, 일부 헬륨 원자들은 중성자를 잃게 됩니다. 그 결과 양성자는 두 개이지만, 중성자는 하나만 있게 되죠. 이것이 헬륨3입니다. 지구상에서 헬륨3는 매우 희귀하며 일반적으로는 또 다른 동위 원소, 즉, 어, 트리튬이 붕괴됨으로써 나타나는데, 트리튬은 수소의 한 형태입니다. 하지만 트리튬이 붕괴되어 헬륨3가 되는 데는 12년 이상이 걸리고, 매우 적은 양의 헬륨3를 만들어 내기 위해서는 막대한 양의 트리튬이 필요합니다. 지구상에서 트리튬 또한 매우 희귀합니다. 주로 리튬을 사용하는 원자로에서 찾아볼 수 있죠. 어쨌든, 이러한 요인들 모두가 헬륨3의 상업적 생산을, 음, 비현실적인 것으로 만듭니다.

하지만 또 다른 문제가 제기됩니다… 왜 헬륨3를 만들고자 하는 것일까요…? 음, 어, 여기 적절한 답이 있습니다: 헬륨3는 청정 에너지의 원천이 될 수 있습니다. 아시겠지만, 헬륨3가, 듀테륨이라고 불리는 수소의 또 다른 동위 원소와 반응을 하면, 융합이라고 불리는 과정을 통해 에너지를 방출하게 됩니다. 적은 양의 헬륨3와 듀테륨으로도, 원자로에서 제어되어 전력으로 전환될 수 있는 막대한 양의 에너지를 생산해 낼 수가 있습니다.

안타깝게도, 현재 지구상에는 헬륨3가 200킬로그램 이하로 존재합니다. 너무나 적은 양이어서 연구를 통해 헬륨3와 듀테륨을 처리할 수 있는 핵융합로를 설계하고 제작하는 일을 감당할 수가 없습니다. 실행 가능성이 없는 것이죠. 하지만, 우리는 헬륨3가 풍부한 곳 중 하나를 알고 있습니다: 바로 달입니다.

대기가 없어서 태양풍에 장기간 노출되기 때문에, 달의 표면에는 많은 양의 헬륨3가 먼지와 같은 흙 속에 포함되어 있습니다. 실제로, 과학자들은 달에, 어, 보시면, 백만 톤의 헬륨3가 포함되어 있다고 추정하고 있습니다. 해야 할 일은 화학적 처리를 통해 헬륨3를 먼지와 암석 속에서 분리해 내는 것이 전부입니다. 그러면, 핵융합로에서 전력을 생산해 내는데 사용될 수 있을 것입니다. 얼마나 많은 전력을요…? 단 25톤의 헬륨3가 융합을 통해 전기로 변환된다면 이는 일 년 동안 미국의 전력 수요 모두를 충당시킬 수 있을 것으로 생각되고 있습니다… 아, 이제 여러분들은 왜 그것이 그렇게 매력적인지 깨닫기 시작하는 것 같군요, 그렇지 않나요?

그래서, 어쨌든, 현재 많은 기관들의 목적은 헬륨3 핵융합로를 활용하여 전력을 공급받을 수 있는 달 기지를 건설하는 것입니다. NASA, 유럽 우주 기관, 그리고 러시아 사람들 모두 다음 수십 년 후에 달 기지를 건설하려는 계획에 참여하고 있습니다. 반면, 기술자들과 과학자들은 달에서 가동될 수 있는 헬륨3 핵융합로를 설계하기 위해 노력하고 있습니다. 안타깝게도, 차후 수십 년 동안 이러한 일은 이루어지지 않을 것입니다. 하지만, 완성이 되면, 어떠한 달 기지라도 수년 동안 전력을 공급받게 될 것이 확실합니다. 또한 출발점으로서 달 기지를 이용하게 될 항성간 우주 비행에 있어서도 연료를 공급하는 기능을 담당할 수 있을 것입니다.

W Student: 토지와 암석을 채굴해서 지구로 가져오는 것은 어떨까요?

M: 가능합니다. 하지만, 여러 수송상의 문제가 있습니다. 예를 들면, 지구에서 이륙하여, 달에 착륙하고, 다시 이륙해서, 이곳으로 돌아와서는, 화물을 실은 채 안전하게 착륙할 수 있는 거대한 화물용 로켓이 필요할 것입니다. 이를 재정적으로 실행 가능한 것으로 만들기 위해서는, 각 로켓이 수 차례의 왕복을 해야 할 것입니다. 또한 비용적인 문제도 있습니다. 헬륨3를 가지고 있는 달의 토양보다 훨씬 더 저렴하게 석유와 기타 화석 연료들이 전기를 만드는데 이용될 수 있다면, 아무도 헬륨3로 만들어진 전기에 대해 요금을 지불하려 하지 않을 것입니다. 하지만, 화석 연료가 고갈되기 시작하고 기술 발전으로 달 여행이 쉽고 빈번하게 될 미래에 있어서는, 분명 매력적인 방안이 될 것입니다.

자, 청정 핵융합의 환경적 영향은 어떨까요…? 헬륨3에 추가적인 비용을 지불할 가치는 없을까요? 음, 잠시 생각해 보세요… 1940년대 이후로, 우리는 핵융합으로 어떻게 전기를 만들수 있는지를 알아냈습니다. 그리고 특히 화석 연료와 비교해 볼 때, 이는 매우 깨끗한 편입니다. 그러한 점에도 불구하고, 우리는 여전히 화석 연료를 핵에너지로 완전히 대체하고 있지는 못

합니다. 우선, 사람들은 핵발전소에서 나오는 방사선의 위험성에 대해 우려를 합니다. 하지만 과학자들은 헬륨3 핵융합로가 훨씬 더 안전하고 훨씬 더 깨끗할 것이라고 주장합니다. 물론, 아무도 아직 그렇게 한 적이 없기 때문에, 모두 이론적인 것이긴 합니다. 하지만 헬륨3는 잠재적으로 우리가 이용할 수 있는 가장 멋진 에너지원 중 하나입니다. 단지 그것을 충분히 활용할수 있는 기술이 없을 뿐이죠.

Actual Test 09

Reading Section p.105

Answers

1. C [Vocabulary Question]

2. D [Negative Factual Question]

3. B [Vocabulary Question]

4. A [Rhetorical Purpose Question]

5. B [Factual Question]

6. A [Rhetorical Purpose Question]

7. C [Factual Question]

8. B [Negative Factual Question]

9. B [Vocabulary Question]

10. D [Vocabulary Question]

11. D [Factual Question]

12. A [Sentence Simplification Question]

13. C [Factual Question]

14. B, C, E [Prose Summary Question]

Translation

알츠하이머병

때때로, 사람들은 무엇인가를 잊어버린다. 하지만 자신의 이름을 잊어버리거나, 사랑하는 사람들을 알아보지 못하며, 사실상 그들의 삶에 있는 모든 것을 기억하지 못하는 경우도 있다. 이것이 바로 알츠하이머병을 앓고 살아가는 경우이다. 과거에, 이 질병은 치매나 노망으로 불렸지만, 오늘날에는 잠행성 뇌질환으로 인식되고 있다. 알츠하이머병의 정확한 원인은 알려져 있지 않지만, 과학자들은 유전적 요인과 환경적 요인 모두를 발병의 원인으로 추측하고 있다. 발병의 원인을 모르기 때문에 그 치료법을 찾기가 힘든데, 이로 인하여 이 질병을 앓고 있는 사람들은 현재 거의 사망에 이르고 있다. 전 세계적으로 대략 2천 5백만 명의 사람들이 이 질병을 앓고 있다

고 생각되지만, 전 세계의 인구가 노령화 될수록, 앞으로 이러한 문제는 결국 악화될 것이다.

알츠하이머병은 1906년에 이 질병의 존재를 처음으로 이론화했던 독일의 정신과 의사의 이름을 따서, 그 명칭이 붙여졌다. 수십 년에 걸친 연구 덕분에, 의사들은 현재 이 질병이 뇌에 영향을 주는 신체적인 질병으로 이해하고 있다. 알츠하이머병을 일으키는 위험 인자들은 사람이 나이가 들수록 증가하는데, 이는 병세의 대부분이 60세 이상의 사람들에게서 발생한다는 사실로 증명된다. 하지만 나이가 든 모든 사람들이 알츠하이머병에 걸리는 것은 아니므로, 분명히 노화 이외의 다른 관련 요인들이 있을 것이다. 알츠하이머병을 앓았던 부모나 형제가 있는 사람은 알츠하이머병이 발병했던 가족력이 없는 사람에 비해서 이 병에 걸리는 경우가 보다 많았기 때문에, 의사들은 발병의 원인을 유전적인 것으로 추측하고 있다. 최근의 연구는 또한 유전자 내의 특정한 단백질 결합이 알츠하이머병에 걸릴 가능성을 증가시킨다는 것을 보여주었다. 또 다른 위험 인자들로는 고혈압과 두부 외상이 있으며, 남성보다 여성이 이 질병에 걸리기 쉽다.

알츠하이머병의 주요 증상들은, 기억력, 언어, 지각, 감정, 그리고 인지 능력을 포함하는 정신적인 능력의 다양한 측면에서, 어려움을 보이는 사람과 관련이 있다. 이 질병의 발병의 첫 번째 경고증상은 최근의 일들을 기억하지 못하는 경우, 문제 해결 능력에 이상이 있는 경우, 그리고 동시에 여러 가지 일을 하지 못하는 경우에 나타난다. 병이 진행되면서, 환자들은 자신이 있는 장소가 어디인지 잊어버리고, 익숙한 길에서도 방향을 잃으며, 예전에 즐겼던 활동에 흥미를 잃기도 하고, 약간의 복잡한 일을 하는 경우에 어려움을 느낀다. 질병의 정도가 심해지면, 환자들은 자신의 과거에 대해서 기억하지 못하며, 사랑하는 사람들을 더 이상 알아보지 못하고, 망상 장애를 앓게 되며, 문장을 뒤죽박죽으로 말하거나 언어를 완전히 잊어버리기도 하고, 삼키는 능력을 포함한 여러 가지 신체 기능을 상실하게 된다. 대개는 폐렴과 같이 몇몇 질병의 결과로 조기에 사망하게 되는 경우가 종종 있는데, 환자들은 이러한 질병들을 극복할 수 없다.

알츠하이머병에는 두 가지 형태가 있다: 조기 발현과 후기 발현이 그것이다. 조기 발현 알츠하이머병은 사람이 60세가 되기 전에 발생한다. 드물기는 하지만 때때로 40대의 사람들에게서 발병하기도 한다. 이러한 종류의 질병은 빠르게 진행되며, 일반적으로 동일 가정 내의 여러 구성원들에게서 발생하기 때문에 유전적인 질병으로 생각된다. 반면에, 후기 발현 알츠하이머병은 60세 이상의 사람들에게서 발병하며 보다 흔한 형태이다. 이는 비교적 느린 속도로 진행되며, 가족 내력이라고 볼 수가 없기 때문에, 이 질병이 유전적인 요인에 의해서 발병할 가능성은 낮다. 후기 발현 알츠하이머병은 다른 정신 질환과 비슷하고 나이가 들면서 건망증에 걸리기 쉽다는 사람들의 인식 때문에, 조기에 진단해 내지 못하는 경우가 종종 있다.

지금까지는, 어떤 사람이 알츠하이머병에 걸렸는지를 알 수 있는 유일한 방법은 그 사람이 사망한 후에 뇌를 검사하는 것이다. 이러한 검사를 통하여 신경 세포의 집단 괴사 흔적을 밝혀낼 수 있는데, 이는 알츠하이머병의 징후가 된다. 베타–아밀로이드라는 비정상적인 단백질로 인하여 뇌에 반이 축적되기 때문에 이러한 세포들이 괴사하는 것이다. 이러한 현상의 발생 원인은 현재까지 알려져 있지 않다. 과학자들은 한때 이 질병이 납이나 수은을 포함하여, 과도한 양의 화학 물질로 인하여 발병한다고 생각했지만, 더 이상 그렇

게 생각하지는 않는다. 알츠하이머병의 원인에 대해서 보다 잘 이해하지 못한다면, 치료법도 있을 수 없다. 최근 이 질병의 진행 속도를 지연시키는 약물을 활용하려는 시도를 통하여 제한적이나마 성과가 나타나고 있다. 현재 할 수 있는 유일한 것은, 결국 환자들이 사망할 것이기 때문에 가능한 한 환자를 편안하게 해주고, 이렇게 힘든 정신적인 상황에 대처할 수 있도록 가족들이 환자를 도울 수 있도록 해주는 것뿐이다.

Listening Section   p.111

Answers

1. B [Gist-Purpose Question]
2. A [Detail Question]
3. C [Making Inferences Question]
4. D [Understanding Function Question]
5. C [Understanding Attitude Question]
6. B [Gist-Purpose Question]
7. D [Understanding Attitude Question]
8.

	Fact	Not a Fact
A		X
B	X	
C		X
D		X

[Detail Question]

9. A [Understanding Organization Question]
10. B [Making Inferences Question]
11. B [Understanding Function Question]

Script

| 09-02 |

W Professor: Donald, I'm pleased to see you. Come on into my office and take a seat right there, please.

M Student: Yes, ma'am.

W: I'm sure you're wondering why I requested this meeting, aren't you?

M: Yes, ma'am. I-I-I . . . I haven't ever had a professor send me an email insisting that I go to her office as soon as possible. Am I in some kind of trouble or something?

W: Hmm . . . I wouldn't say that you're in any kind of trouble in the literal meaning of the word. However, I would say that you've got some issues in my class.

M: I do?

W: You do . . . Donald, is there any reason that you haven't been submitting your daily homework assignments? [4]I mean, it's clear from your grades on the first two exams that you understand how to solve all of the problems in this class. So why haven't you been turning in your homework to me?

M: I don't know.

W: You're going to have to do better than that, Donald.

M: Okay . . . I, well, I'm not that great at getting my homework done on time. It's kind of a problem that I have in all of my classes.

W: Why is that? Do you have a part-time job or something that's keeping you from doing your homework on time?

M: No, ma'am. I don't have a job. I just spend most of my free time in the library reading books and stuff. I totally love doing personal research on various topics.

W: Well, Donald, it's great that you are doing extra reading, but you really ought to focus on the work that you're supposed to be doing right now. I mean, you got a 98 on your first exam and a 95 on your second exam.

M: Right.

W: So I know that you're capable of doing the work. But you've turned in fewer than ten percent of your homework assignments, and those were all at the beginning of the semester. You've got to do better than that.

M: But I've got an A in the class because of my test grades.

W: On the contrary, you don't have an A in the class.

M: Huh? But you just mentioned my test scores.

W: True, but homework is a part of your grade, Donald. In fact, it's twenty percent of your grade, which means that if you continue not to turn in any homework assignments, there's a high likelihood that you will get a C in my class.

M: A C? Oh my goodness. I've never gotten one of those in my life.

W: Then you'd better start turning in your homework. All right?

M: Yes, ma'am. I see your point. [5]Um . . . If I turn in my homework assignments for the rest of the semester and get an A on the last test, can I still get an A in this class?

W: I doubt it . . . But an A⁻ is a distinct possibility. I'm sorry, Donald, but you really have no one to blame but yourself. Perhaps you will learn something about personal responsibility from this. That could serve you well in the future.

M: Yes, ma'am, I see what you're talking about. Thank you for the lesson.

Translation

W Professor: *Donald*, 만나서 기뻐요. 사무실 안으로 들어와서 저쪽에 앉으세요.

M Student: 네, 교수님.

W: 왜 제가 보자고 했는지 틀림없이 궁금해 할 거예요, 그렇지 않나요?

M: 맞아요, 교수님. 저-저-저는 어느 교수님으로부터도 가능한 빨리 사무실로 오라는 이메일은 받아본 적이 없었거든요. 어떤 문제 같은 것이라도 있나요?

W: 흠… 말 그대로의 어떠한 문제가 있다고는 말할 수는 없을 것 같군요. 하지만, 수업과 관련해서 학생에게 몇 가지 이야기해야 할 것들이 있다고 말하고 싶네요.

M: 제게요?

W: 학생에게요… *Donald*, 매일 제출해야 하는 과제를 제출하지 않은 이유가 있나요? 내 말은, 첫 두 차례 시험에서의 학생의 성적으로 보면, 학생은 이번 수업에서의 모든 문제들을 푸는 방법을 알고 있다는 점이 확실해요. 그런데 왜 과제를 제출하지 않고 있나요?

M: 잘 모르겠어요.

W: 그 보다는 더 잘 설명해야 해요, *Donald*.

M: 알겠습니다… 저는, 음, 저는 제때에 과제를 마치는 것을 그다지 잘 하지 못해요. 모든 수업에서 제가 가지고 있는 일종의 문제죠.

W: 왜 그렇죠? 아르바이트나 혹은 제때에 숙제를 하지 못하게 만드는 다른 일이라도 있나요?

M: 아니에요, 교수님. 아르바이트는 하고 있지 않아요. 도서관에서 책 등을 읽으며 남는 시간 대부분을 보낼 뿐이죠. 다양한 주제에 대해 개인적으로 조사를 하는 것을 정말 좋아하거든요.

W: 음, *Donald*, 학생이 따로 책을 읽는다는 것은 좋은 일이지만, 지금 해야 하는 일에 정말로 집중을 해야 해요. 제 말은, 학생은 첫 시험에서 98점을 받았고 두 번째 시험에서는 95점을 받았다는 것이죠.

M: 맞아요.

W: 그래서 학생에게 과제를 수행할 능력이 있다는 것을 알고 있어요. 하지만 과제의 10%도 안 되는 과제만을 제출했을 뿐이고, 그러한 과제들은 모두 학기 초반에 한 것이었죠. 그 보다는 더 잘해야 해요.

M: 하지만 시험 성적으로 수업에서 A를 받았는데요.

W: 그 반대예요, 학생은 수업에서 A를 받지 못했어요.

M: 네? 하지만 제 시험 성적을 방금 언급하셨잖아요.

W: 그렇지만, 과제는 성적의 일부예요, *Donald*. 실제로, 성적의 20%에 해당되는데, 이는 학생이 과제를 계속 제출하지 않으면, 학생은 내 수업에서 C를 받게 될 가능성이 높아지게 되죠.

M: C요? 이런 세상에. 평생 그러한 성적은 받아본 적이 없는 걸요.

W: 그러면 숙제를 제출하기 시작하는 것이 좋겠네요. 괜찮겠죠?

M: 네, 교수님. 무슨 말씀인지 알겠어요. 음… 학기의 나머지 기간 동안 과제를 제출하고 마지막 시험에서 A를 받는다면, 제가 이번 수업에서 A를 받을 수 있을까요?

W: 확실하지는 않아요… 하지만 A⁻는 확실히 가능할 거예요. 유감이지만, *Donald*, 자기 자신 말고는 아무도 비난할 사람이 없어요. 아마 이번 일로 개인의 책임에 대해 무언가를 배우게 될 거에요. 그러면 미래에 학생에게 도움이 될 것이고요.

M: 네, 교수님, 무슨 말씀인지 알겠어요. 알려 주셔서 감사합니다.

| 09-03 |

W1 Professor: Let's turn our attention to *Walden*, a book written by American author Henry David Thoreau. Thoreau wrote the book while living at Walden Pond outside Concord, Massachusetts, between the years 1845 and 1847. The total amount of time Thoreau spent there, as he wrote, was two years, two months, and two days. *Walden* actually wasn't published until 1854, but, over time, it gained popularity and today serves as a primary source for the environmental movement. The main point of the book was to describe a return to nature as it details the time Thoreau spent living alone in the woods. While there, Thoreau spent his time reflecting on life and man's place in nature.

Before we talk about *Walden*, you need to know a bit about its author. Thoreau was born in 1817 and died of a respiratory illness in 1862. He had several siblings, and his family ran a pencil-making business. He went to school at Harvard and later became a teacher and writer. Thoreau became interested in the philosophy of transcendentalism, which posited that a person's spiritual state goes beyond the physical world based on his or her intuition, not because of any religious beliefs or doctrines. Transcendentalists also believed there was a connection between man and nature. Thoreau became immersed in transcendentalism primarily on account of his associating with a group of writers in the Concord area. Among them was Ralph Waldo Emerson, one of the greatest of all American writers and a leading advocate of transcendentalism. Thoreau actually lived in Emerson's home for nearly three years, where he taught Emerson's children. It was during that time when he became influenced by both Emerson and his philosophy. Yes? You have an observation?

W2 Student: A question actually. Is that why Thoreau chose to live alone in the woods?

W1: In part. You see, after Thoreau left the Emerson family in 1844, he got involved in the family business. Thoreau, unsurprisingly I might add, had no interest in the pencil-making business, yet he felt an obligation to assist his family. After some time though, he rebelled against that life. He sought a place of solitude where he could have the quiet he required to write. Also, he was seeking a connection to nature. These factors drove him to the woods near Walden Pond. Oh, the forest where he lived was owned by the Emerson family, so I'm sure Emerson had something to do with Thoreau's adventure. Anyway, Thoreau built a cabin there and meticulously recorded the costs of the materials he used to make it. It came out to around, oh, twenty-eight dollars. This might seem like a small amount to us today, but to a struggling writer back then, it was quite a lot. The cabin was small—only ten by fifteen feet—and Thoreau dwelled there for two years.

There's one crucial thing to remember: Don't be under the impression that Thoreau was roughing it by living alone in the forest or think that he survived by hunting and farming. [11]In reality, he was just a few miles out of town, received many visitors, and often left his cabin to visit his friends and family members. These people also helped supply him with necessities such as food. Thoreau's cabin was not far from town at all. **In fact, he often complained about the noise from train whistles and church bells.** That's the reality of his life there. It was only in later years that Thoreau's time there took on something of a . . . mythological aspect as nature lovers and environmentalists came to envy how he, er, got away from civilization. But Thoreau wasn't really trying to do that. He just wanted a quiet place where he could think and write. And write he did. He not only wrote the main manuscript for *Walden* there, but he also worked on some other books and a few poems.

Yet the main product from that period in Thoreau's life is *Walden*, the book you all should have finished reading by now. As you should know, it's filled with tales of how he built his cabin, his purpose in going there, his daily life in the cabin, his trips to the nearby town of Concord, his experiences with nature, and his philosophy, especially his views on life and man's connection with nature. A common theme throughout the book that I hope you noticed was the notion of abandoning all luxuries in life and leading a quiet, simple existence.

It's the last thing that I just mentioned that has given *Walden* its exalted place in both American literature and the modern environmentalist movement. *Walden* has been accepted by many environmentalists as a sort of Bible, uh, a source of their movement in which they would have man live in harmony with nature. Again, that's not really what Thoreau was writing. So that's why I want you to write a five-page essay on what *Walden* was really about. I expect those papers two weeks from today. Are there any questions before I dismiss you for the day . . . ? No . . . ?

Translation

W1 Professor: 미국인 작가 헨리 데이비드 소로가 쓴 책인 월든에 대해 주의를 돌려보도록 하죠. 소로는 1945년과 1847년 사이에, 매사추세츠 콩고드 외곽의 월든 호수 근처에서 살고 있던 당시, 이 책을 썼습니다. 소로가 그곳에서 글을 쓰며 보낸 시간은 총 2년 2개월 그리고 이틀이었죠. 월든은 실제로 1854년까지는 출판이 되지 못했지만, 시간이 지나면서, 인기를 얻고 오늘날에는 환경 운동의 주요한 원전으로 사용되고 있습니다. 이 책의 주제는 자연으로의 회귀를 설명하는 것이었는데, 책에서는 소로가 숲에서 혼자 살며 보냈던 시간이 자세히 묘사되어 있습니다. 그곳에서, 소로는 삶과 자연에서의 인간의 위치에 대해 생각하며 시간을 보냈습니다.

월든에 대한 이야기에 앞서, 책의 작가에 대해 약간 알아야 할 것 같군요. 소로는 1817년에 태어났고 1862년에 호흡기 질환으로 사망했습니다. 그에게는 형제 자매들이 몇 명 있었고, 그의 가족들은 연필 제조 업체를 운영했습니다. 그는 Harvard 대학에 다녔으며 이후에는 교사이자 작가가 되었습니다. 소로는 철학의 초월론에 흥미를 갖게 되었는데, 초월론은 개인의 정신

상태가, 종교적인 믿음이나 교리 때문이 아니라, 직관에 근거하여 물리적 세계를 뛰어넘게 된다고 주장했습니다. 초월론자들은 또한 인간과 자연 사이에 연결 부분이 존재한다고 믿었습니다. 주로 소로는 콩고드 지역의 작가 모임에 참여함으로써 초월론에 빠져들게 되었습니다. 모임에는 미국 작가 중 가장 뛰어났던 작가이자 초월론의 주요 지지자였던 랄프 왈도 에머슨이 있었습니다. 소로는 실제로 거의 3년 동안 에머슨의 집에서 살았는데, 여기에서 소로는 에머슨의 아이들을 가르쳤습니다. 그가 에머슨과 그의 철학 모두에 의해 영향을 받게 된 때가 바로 이 시기였습니다. 네? 하고 싶은 말이 있나요?

W2 Student: 실은 질문인데요. 그것이 소로가 숲에서 혼자 살기로 했던 이유였나요?

W1: 부분적으로는요. 아시겠지만, 1844년에 에머슨의 집을 나온 후, 소로는 가업을 맡았습니다. 소로는, 놀라운 일이 아니라고 말하고 싶은데, 연필 제조 사업에 전혀 관심이 없었지만, 가족을 도와야겠다는 의무감을 느꼈습니다. 하지만 얼마 후, 그는 그러한 생활에 반감을 가지게 되었습니다. 그는 글을 쓰는데 필요한 조용한 외딴 곳을 찾았습니다. 또한, 자연과의 연관성도 모색했습니다. 이러한 요인들로 인해 그는 월든 호수 근처의 숲으로 가게 되었습니다. 오, 그가 살았던 숲은 에머슨 가의 소유였기 때문에, 소로의 그러한 모험에 에머슨이 관련되어 있었다고 확신합니다. 어쨌든, 소로는 그곳에서 오두막집을 짓고, 오두막집을 짓는데 사용했던 자재들의 가격을 자세히 기록해 두었습니다. 약, 오, 28달러 정도가 나왔죠. 오늘날 우리에게는 적은 금액처럼 보이지만, 당시 고분 분투하던 작가에게는, 꽤 큰 금액이었습니다. 이 오두막집은 작았고 — 가로가 10피트, 세로는 15피트 밖에 되지 않았습니다 — 소로는 그곳에서 2년 동안 머물렀습니다.

기억해야 할 한 가지 중요한 점이 있습니다: 숲에서 혼자 살았다고 해서 소로가 고생을 했다고 느끼거나 그가 사냥과 농사로 살아갔다고 생각하지는 마십시오. 실제로, 그는 시내에서 몇 마일 떨어지지 않은 곳에 있었으며, 그를 찾아오는 사람도 많고, 그는 종종 오두막을 떠나 친구와 가족들을 찾아가기도 했습니다. 이러한 사람들 역시 그에게 식품과 같은 필수품들을 가져다 주었습니다. 소로의 오두막집은 결코 시내에서 멀리 떨어져 있지 않았습니다. 실제로, 그는 기차의 기적 소리와 교회 종소리에서 비롯되는 소음에 대해 종종 불평을 하곤 했습니다. 그것이 바로 그곳에서의 실제 생활이었죠. 자연을 사랑하고 환경을 보호하고자 하는 사람들이, 어, 그가 문명으로부터 벗어나 있었다는 점을 부러워하게 되었기 때문에, 불과 몇 년 후에 그곳에서 소로가 보낸 시간은, 어, 신화적인 측면을 갖게 되었습니다. 하지만 소로가 실제 그렇게 하려고 노력한 것은 아니었습니다. 단지 사색을 하며 글을 쓸 수 있었던 조용한 장소를 원했을 뿐이었죠. 그리고 실제로 글을 썼습니다. 그곳에서 월든의 원고를 썼을 뿐만 아니라, 다른 책들과 시도 몇 편 썼습니다.

하지만 소로의 인생에서 그러한 기간 동안 만들어진 주요 작품은 월든이었는데, 여러분 모두가 지금쯤이면 다 읽어보셨을 것 같군요. 알아야 하는 점인데, 이 작품은 그가 자신의 오두막집을 지은 과정과 그곳으로 간 목적, 오두막에서의 일상 생활, 그리고 인근 콩고드 시로 나갔던 일, 자연에서 겪은 경험, 그리고 그의 철학, 특히 삶과 인간 대 자연의 관계에 대한 자신의 견해에 대한 이야기로 채워져 있습니다. 여러분이 주목하길 바라

는 책 전체에 걸쳐져 있는 공통된 주제는, 삶에서 모든 사치스러운 것들을 버리고 조용하고 편안한 삶을 이어가야 한다는 생각입니다.

미국 문학과 현대 환경 보호 운동 모두에 있어서 월든이 높은 위치에 있게 된 것은 제가 방금 말씀드렸던 마지막 내용 때문이었습니다. 월든은 많은 환경 보호론자들에게 일종의 성경, 어, 즉 인간으로 하여금 자연과 조화롭게 살도록 해야 한다는 운동의 원전으로서 받아들여지고 있습니다. 또 다시, 소로가 실제로 그러한 내용을 썼던 것은 아니었습니다. 그래서 월든이 실제로 무엇에 관한 글이었는지에 대해 여러분들이 5페이지짜리 에세이를 쓰기를 바랍니다. 오늘부터 2주 후에 받도록 하겠습니다. 오늘의 수업을 마치기 전에 질문이 있나요…? 없습니까…?

Actual Test 10

Reading Section   p.117

Answers

1. Ⓐ [Vocabulary Question]
2. Ⓑ [Vocabulary Question]
3. Ⓒ [Factual Question]
4. Ⓓ [Rhetorical Question]
5. Ⓓ [Vocabulary Question]
6. Ⓐ [Factual Question]
7. Ⓐ [Reference Question]
8. Ⓑ [Vocabulary Question]
9. Ⓒ [Factual Question]
10. Ⓐ [Inference Question]
11. Ⓑ [Factual Question]
12. 3rd [Insert Text Question]
13.

PERIOD OF TIME	
During Charlemagne's Life	Ⓐ, Ⓓ, Ⓕ
After Charlemagne's Life	Ⓑ, Ⓖ

[Fill in a Table Question]

샤를마뉴

15세기 로마 제국의 몰락은 서유럽에서 수세기 동안 지속되었던 권력의 공백을 가져왔다. 시간이 흐르면서, 로마를 침략했던 작은 부족의 사람들이 예전에 로마의 영토였던 지역에 왕국들을 세웠다. 이러한 왕국들 중에서 가장 성공적이었고 중요했던 왕국은 카롤링거 왕조의 프랑크족 통치자들이 세운 왕국이었다. 이 왕국의 영토는 결국 현재의 프랑스, 독일의 서부, 이탈리아, 스위스, 벨기에, 네덜란드, 그리고 룩셈부르크 지역을 포함하고 있었다. 샤를마뉴는 모든 프랑크족 통치자들 중에서 가장 강력했다. 그는 전쟁터에서 삶의 대부분을 보낸 전사 왕이었고, 자신의 아버지로부터 넓은 왕국을 물려받았으며, 그 후에는 자신의 제국의 규모를 확장시켰다. 그러나 샤를마뉴는 선견지명이 있는 통치자였기 때문에, 그의 통치 기간 동안, 서유럽에서는 문화 부흥이 시작되었다. 하지만, 그가 사망한 후, 샤를마뉴의 후계자들은 서로 다투었고 제국은 분할되었는데, 이로써 천 년 이상 서유럽을 지배하게 된 다수의 근대 민족 국가의 탄생을 위한 길이 열렸다.

샤를마뉴는 742년에 태어났으며 프랑크족 통치자 피피누스 단구왕의 아들이었다. 샤를마뉴의 어린 시절에 대해서는 거의 알려진 바가 없다. 그의 아버지가 768년에 사망했을 때, 그에게는 자신과 함께 왕국을 통치했던 남동생이 적어도 한 명 — 샤를로망 — 이 있었다. 두 형제는 그들의 계승 문제를 놓고 충돌이 있었던 것으로 보이지만, 771년에 샤를로망이 사망한 뒤, 샤를마뉴가 유일한 통치자가 되었다. 그는 통치 기간 초반을 자신의 통치에 대한 반란을 진압하고 영토를 확장하는데 보냈다. (그들은 이슬람교도 무어인들을 물리치려는 시도를 계속 했는데, 이들은 스페인을 점령하고 있었다.) 778년에 스페인을 공격했을 때 오직 한 번의 패배를 경험한 것을 제외하면, 샤를마뉴의 군대는 항상 승승장구했다. 스페인의 국경은 샤를마뉴의 통치 기간 동안 분쟁 지역으로 남아있었다. 프랑크인들은 종종 스페인의 무어인 통치자들에게 도전했지만 피레네 산맥의 북쪽 지역을 넘어서까지 이동할 수는 없었다.

동쪽에서, 샤를마뉴는 많은 어려움을 겪었는데, 특히 색슨족과 그 밖의 독일 부족들을 정복하려고 했을 당시, 이들은 그의 권위에 대항하여 자주 반란을 일으켰다. 보다 큰 성공은 이탈리아에서 이루어졌는데, 그곳에서 샤를마뉴는 로마 가톨릭교회와 좋은 관계를 유지했다. 교황 레오 3세는 800년 크리스마스날 샤를마뉴에게 "로마 제국의 황제"의 대관식을 해주었고, 이는 고중세 시대에 사용되던 "신성 로마 제국의 황제"라는 칭호의 전신이 되었다. 교황이 그의 머리에 왕관을 씌워주고 황제라고 칭했을 때는 로마에서 열린 예배식이 진행되던 도중에 샤를마뉴가 무릎을 꿇고 기도를 하고 있었던 때였다. 샤를마뉴가 교황의 의도를 알고 있었는지에 대해서는 역사학자들 사이에서 의견이 일치하지 않지만, 그는 이러한 칭호를 받아들였고 그로 인하여 신성 로마 제국이 설립되었는데, 이 제국은 19세기 초반까지 지속되었다.

샤를마뉴의 통치가 전쟁과 유혈 사태와 관련되었던 것만은 아니었다. 그는 또한 역사학자들이 카롤링거 르네상스라고 부르는 운동과도 관련이 있다. 이는 문화, 미술, 건축, 문학, 언어, 교육, 그리고 종교 연구에 대한 관심의 부흥기였다. 그 중심은 아헨의 샤를마뉴의 왕궁에 있었으며, 성직자, 지식인, 그리고 귀족들에게만 국한되어서 일반 대중들은 이를 통하여 별다른 혜택을 보지 못했다. 샤를마뉴는 이러한 부흥을 적극적으로 장려하였다; 그는 학문을 지원

하여 로마 제국을 모방하려고 했지만, 그의 통치 기간 이후에도 오랫동안 지속되었던 것은 거의 없었다. 몇몇 예외적인 것들은 건축과 관련된 다수의 성과물들과 카롤링거 소문자라고 불리는 표준화된 문자이다. 하지만, 샤를마뉴는 경제와 통화 개혁, 거래의 표준화 시도, 그리고 제국의 주화를 주조한 것 등 보다 많은 성과를 이루기도 했다.

샤를마뉴는 최소한 4명의 부인과 20명의 자손을 두었다. 이들의 대부분은 샤를마뉴보다 먼저 사망했으며, 814년에 그가 72세의 나이로 사망했을 때 생존해있었던 유일한 적자는 루도비쿠스 경건왕이었다. 루도비쿠스는 권력을 이어받았고, 자신을 권력에서 쫓아내려는 많은 시도에도 불구하고 제국을 그대로 유지시켰다. 840년에 루도비쿠스가 사망했을 때, 그의 세 아들들이 계승권을 놓고 다투었으며, 결국 카롤링거 제국은 여러 지역으로 분리되었다. 843년에 베르됭 조약으로 인하여 그들의 분쟁은 해결되었다. 그 결과, 한 명의 아들은 동쪽의 독일 영토를 차지하였고, 다른 아들은 서쪽의 프랑스 영토를 차지하였으며, 셋째 아들은 중부 영토를 차지하였다. 이는 한때 샤를마뉴가 통치했던 제국으로부터 결국 독일, 프랑스, 그리고 여러 다른 국가들의 등장하게 된 현대 유럽의 청사진을 마련해 주었다.

Listening Section   p.123

Answers

1. (B) [Content Question]

2. (A) [Gist-Purpose Question]

3.

	Fact	Not a Fact
(A)	X	
(B)		X
(C)	X	
(D)		X

[Detail Question]

4. (C) [Making Inferences Question]

5. (C) [Understanding Attitude Question]

6. (B) [Gist-Content Question]

7. (C), (D) [Detail Question]

8. (D) [Understanding Function Question]

9. (A) [Connecting Content Question]

10. (B) [Making Inferences Question]

11. (C) [Understanding Attitude Question]

| 10-02 |

M Financial Aid Office Employee: Good afternoon. May I presume that you are Sandy Fitzgerald?

W Student: Yes, that's me. It's a pleasure to meet you, Mr. Daniels.

M: The pleasure is all mine, Sandy. So, uh, why don't you take a seat and then tell me why you requested this meeting with me?

W: Thank you. Okay. I wanted to meet with you because I am curious about how and, um, when I am supposed to start paying back my student loans.

M: All right. Why don't you give me the details of your loans first?

W: Sure. I have taken out around, hmm . . . approximately one thousand dollars in loans each semester for the past four years. Oh, this is my final semester of school. That's pretty much why I'm here. I'm going to be graduating next month, so I'd like to know when I need to begin repaying everything.

M: That's logical. And it's good that you're on top of this matter. A lot of students pretty much ignore the fact that they have accumulated several thousand dollars in loans over the course of their time here. When they graduate, well . . . I must say that it comes as something of a shock to them when they have to start paying huge sums of money to the bank.

W: Yes, I see. So, uh, about paying back my loans . . .

M: Right . . . Okay. Let me see if I have this straight. You have roughly eight thousand dollars in student loans, and you will be graduating next month. That's correct?

W: Precisely.

M: What are your plans for after you graduate? Will you be getting a job, attending graduate school, or doing something else?

W: Actually, I'm going to be attending graduate school in another state.

M: Is that a fact? In that case, you don't have to start paying your loans back until you are no longer a full-time student. So you don't have to worry about them until you're done with graduate school.

W: Really? That's a relief. I thought I was going to have to start paying them back starting in June.

M: Normally, that would be the case. But since you're going to continue your studies at the graduate level, you can fill out this form here . . . It will inform the bank that issued your loans that you aren't going to be paying them back yet.

W: [5]And if I don't fill out the form?

M: Then the bank will be expecting your first check one month after this year's graduation ceremony is held.

W: Er, right. I'll take that form, please.

M: I thought you might say that.

W: So, uh, is this everything I need? I just fill out the form and send it in?

M: Well, be sure to read the form carefully. It explains what kinds of documents you need to attach along with it. After all, the bank has to see proof that you're actually going to be a graduate student. However, once you submit all of the information, there shouldn't be any problems at all.

W: Thank you very much for your time. You've been a great help. If I have any more questions, I will be sure to come back here and ask them.

M Financial Aid Office Employee: 안녕하세요. 학생이 *Sandy Fitzgerald*인가요?

W Student: 네, 저예요. 만나서 반갑습니다, *Daniels* 선생님.

M: 제가 기쁘죠, *Sandy*. 그러면, 어, 앉아서 왜 저랑 만나려 했는지 말을 해줄래요?

W: 고맙습니다. 좋아요. 제 학자금 대출을 어떻게 그리고, 음, 언제부터 상환하기 시작해야 하는지가 궁금해서 만나 뵙고자 했어요.

M: 그래요. 우선 학생의 학자금에 대해 자세히 말을 해줄래요?

W: 물론이에요. 지난 4년 동안 매 학기마다 약, 흠… 대략 천 달러를 받았어요. 오, 이번이 마지막 학기고요. 제가 여기에 온 주된 이유죠. 다음 달에 졸업을 할 예정이어서, 언제 상환해야 하는지에 대해 알고 싶어요.

M: 말이 되는군요. 그리고 이 문제에 대해 잘 대처하고 있는 것 같아 보기가 좋군요. 많은 학생들이 여기에서 수업을 듣는 동안 수천 달러의 대출금이 쌓여 가고 있다는 사실을 잘 모르고 있죠. 졸업을 할 때, 음… 많은 금액의 돈을 은행에 갚기 시작해야 할 때가 되면 학생들이 충격을 받는다고 이야기해야 할 것 같아요.

W: 네, 알겠어요. 그래서, 어, 제 대출금을 갚는 것에 대해…

M: 맞아요… 좋아요. 제가 제대로 이해했는지 볼게요. 학생은 학자금 대출로 약 8,000달러를 받았고, 다음 달에는 졸업을 하게 될 거예요. 맞나요?

W: 정확해요.

M: 졸업 후의 계획이 어떻게 되나요? 취직을 할 건가요, 대학원에 진학할 건가요, 아니면 다른 일을 할 건가요?

W: 실은, 다른 주의 대학원에 다닐 거예요.

M: 사실인가요? 그런 경우라면, 더 이상 정규 학생이 아니게 될 때까지 대출금을 갚을 필요는 없어요. 그래서 대학원을 마칠 때까지는 그에 대한 걱정을 하지 않아도 되고요.

W: 정말이요? 안심이 되는군요. 6월부터 대출금을 갚기 시작해야 한다고 생각했거든요.

M: 보통은, 그렇죠. 하지만 학생이 대학원 공부를 계속할 것이기 때문에, 여기 양식에 내용을 기입해 주기만 하면 돼요… 대출을 해준 은행에게 학생이 아직 상환할 때가 아니라는 점을 알려 주게 될 거예요.

W: 그러면 이 양식에 기입을 하지 않으면요?

M: 그렇게 하면 은행에서는 올해 졸업식이 끝나고 한 달 후에 학생의 첫 상환금이 들어올 것이라고 예상을 하겠죠.

W: 어, 맞아요. 양식에 기입을 할 게요.

M: 그렇게 말할 줄 알았어요.

W: 그러면, 어, 제가 해야 할 것은 이것이 다인가요? 양식에 기입을 해서 제출하기만 하면 되는 건가요?

M: 음, 반드시 양식을 주의해서 읽어 보세요. 어떤 서류들을 거기에 첨부해야 하는지 설명이 되어 있어요. 어쨌거나, 은행으로서는 학생이 정말로 대학원생이 될 것이라는 증거를 확인해야 하니까요. 하지만, 모든 정보를 제출하고 나면, 전혀 문제가 될 것이 없을 거에요.

W: 시간을 내주셔서 정말 감사합니다. 많은 도움이 되었어요. 질문이 더 생기면, 이곳으로 와서 여쭤 보도록 할 게요.

Script

| 10-03 |

M1 Professor: In nature, there's constant competition between organisms for resources in their ecosystems. These resources include water, food, air, soil, and light, uh, things that most organisms need to survive. The resources in most ecosystems are often limited, so an area can only support a limited number of organisms. For instance, in a single patch of forest, there may only be so many plants, predators, and prey animals because many of these organisms are competing for the same resources, most particularly water and food sources. There are also external factors that act on ecosystems. Some of these include human influences. We might upset the balance of an ecosystem by introducing chemicals to it or by overfishing an area in an ocean. Severe weather and temperature changes are two other external factors that can disrupt an ecosystem, too.

You should understand that ecosystems are undergoing constant changes as a result of both competition and outside factors. But what would happen if these outside influences were removed? What if all of the factors in an ecosystem remained constant and the same amount of resources were present from day to day? And what if we were further to examine this idea by stressing that every species in an ecosystem has the same requirements, so they all need the same amounts of water, food, and other resources? What would the end result be? Well, if these things happened, then organisms would survive or die depending upon their own skills. Ultimately, one species would outcompete and, um, out-survive the others.

A Russian scientist, Georgii Gause . . . That's G-A-U-S-E . . . theorized this in 1932. He stated that if all of the factors in an ecosystem were constant and two species had the same resource requirements, then one species would outcompete the other. The species that outcompeted the other would somehow be more efficient at using the resources in its environment. This became known as Gause's Hypothesis, or the competitive exclusion principle. Gause tested his hypothesis in a simple way. He took two different strains of the same protozoan—that's a microscopic life form—and he placed them together in the same microecosystem. One was the Paramecium aurelia protozoa while the other was the Paramecium caudatum protozoa. Both protozoa had similar food and water requirements. Gause made the same amount of fresh water and food available to the two strands. In the experiments he ran, Paramecium aurelia dominated the ecosystem and outcompeted the other species.

M2 Student: What happened to the protozoa that were outcompeted?

M1: They died. Gause then repeated the experiment but used two strains of yeast. The results were the same: One type of yeast outcompeted the other. Now, let me stress that Gause's experiments were conducted in a laboratory with tiny organisms and under ideal conditions. Could this experiment actually be repeated in a natural environment? Most likely, the answer is, well, no. [11]A person's ability to control various factors in the experiment would be limited due to the unstable natures of many organisms as well as the influences of various external factors. I mean, can you imagine trying to control the food and water supplies of numerous organisms in a small part of a forest? **Talk about a nightmare.**

A further problem with Gause's theory is that there are many cases in nature where it has been proven false. One instance involves various types of plankton that live in the ocean. All planktons need sunlight and nutrients found in the water to survive. Yet many species of plankton coexist in the same regions. This seems to go against Gause's hypothesis that one type of plankton should outcompete the others for the same resources and thereby cause the other species to die.

Another limitation of Gause's theory is that it only deals with two species that are virtually identical. In nature, many different species live in the same ecosystem. It's unusual for two species from two different groups to have the exact resource requirements. For example, uh, some plants need less food than others whereas others need less sunlight. Some animals are omnivorous, some are carnivorous, and many are herbivorous. Even herbivores often don't eat the same vegetation. Different animals eat different plants. See what I mean . . . ?

Some scientists have suggested that Gause's Hypothesis should be altered to take competition between groups of organisms, such as bears and wolves, into account. But this would still be difficult to prove through experimentation. There are simply too many variables. And, in nature, there are alternatives to extinction. When faced with death because, say, there isn't enough food, many animals merely migrate to other areas. And numerous plants and animals evolve to overcome resource problems. Over time, most ecosystems become balanced as the organisms live in harmony with one another. Each takes what it needs to survive from its ecosystem, but it doesn't take so much that the ecosystem gets disrupted. So, while Gause's Hypothesis may have some applications in a controlled environment, in nature, it doesn't seem very applicable.

M1 Professor: 실제로, 생태계에서는 생물들이 자원을 두고 끊임없이 경쟁을 합니다. 이러한 자원에는 물, 먹이, 공기, 토양, 그리고 빛이 포함되는데, 어, 대다수의 생물들이 생존하기 위해 필요로 하는 것들입니다. 대부분의 생태계에서는 그러한 자원들이 종종 한정되어 있기 때문에, 일정 지역에서는 한정된 수의 생물들만이 살아갈 수 있습니다. 예를 들면, 숲의 한 부분에서는, 주로 생물들이, 특히 물과 먹이가 되는, 동일한 자원을 두고 경쟁을 하기 때문에 한정된 수의 식물, 포식자, 그리고 피식 동물만이 존재합니다. 또한 생태계에 영향을 미치는 외부 요인들도 있습니다. 이 중 일부에는 인간의 영향이 포함됩니다. 인간은 생태계에 화학 물질을 유입시키거나 혹은 바다의 일정 수역에서 남획을 함으로써 생태계의 균형을 파괴시킬 수 있습니다. 심각한 날씨 변화 및 온도 변화 역시 생태계를 교란시킬 수 있는 또 다른 외부 요인이 됩니다.

생태계는 경쟁과 외부 요인들로 인해 끊임없는 변화를 겪고 있다는 점을 이해하셔야 합니다. 하지만 그러한 외부 요인들이 제거된다면 어떤 일이 일어날까요? 생태계 내의 모든 요인들이 변하지 않고 매일 동일한 양의 자원이 존재한다면 어떻게 될까요? 그리고 더 나아가 생태계 내의 모든 종들이 동일한 것을 필요로 한다고, 즉 모두가 동일한 양의 물, 먹이, 그리고 기타 자원들을 필요로 한다고 강조함으로써 그러한 아이디어를 검증하고자 한다면 어떻게 될까요? 최종 결과는 무엇이 될까요? 음, 이러한 일이 일어나면, 생물들은 자기 자신의 능력에 따라 살거나 죽게 될 것입니다. 결국, 하나의 종이 경쟁에서 이겨서, 음, 다른 생물들을 제치고 살아남게 될 것입니다.

러시아 과학자인 게오르기 가우제는… G–A–U–S–E입니다… 1932년에 이를 이론화했습니다. 그는 특정 생태계에서 그러한 모든 요인들이 변하지 않고, 두 개의 종이 동일한 자원을 필요로 한다면, 하나의 종이 경쟁을 통해 다른 종을 물리칠 것이라고 주장했습니다. 다른 종을 경쟁에서 이긴 종은 환경 내의 자원을 보다 효율적으로 사용하게 될 것입니다. 이는 가우제의 가설, 혹은 경쟁적 배제 원칙이라고 알려지게 되었습니다. 가우제는 간단한 방법으로 자신의 가설을 검증했습니다. 그는 동일한 원생동물의 — 이는 미생물입니다 — 서로 다른 두 종을 가져다가 같은 미소 생태계에 놓았습니다. 하나는 P. aurelia라는 짚신벌레였고 다른 하나는 P. caudatum이라는 짚신벌레였습니다. 두 원생동물 모두 필요로 하는 먹이와 물이 비슷했습니다. 가우제는 동일한 양의 신선한 물과 먹이를 두 종이 이용할 수 있도록 했습니다. 그가 진행한 실험에서는, P. aurelia가 생태계를 지배하여 다른 종을 경쟁에서 내몰았습니다.

M2 Student: 경쟁에서 진 원생동물에게는 어떤 일이 일어났나요?

M1: 죽었습니다. 그 후 가우제는 실험을 반복했는데, 이번에는 두 개의 효모를 이용했습니다. 결과는 동일했습니다: 하나의 효모가 다른 효모를 경쟁에서 물리쳤습니다. 자, 가우제의 실험은 미세한 생물을 가지고 이상적인 조건을 갖춘 실험실에서 진행되었다는 점을 강조하고자 합니다. 이러한 실험이 실제 자연 환경에서 되풀이될 수 있을까요? 거의 확실히, 그에 대한 대답은, 음, '아니오'입니다. 다양한 외부 요인들의 영향뿐만 아니라 여러 생물들의 일정치 않은 특성으로 인해, 실험에서의 다양한 요인들을 통제할 수 있는 개인의 능력은 제한될 것입니다. 제 말은, 숲의 작은 부분에서 수많은 생물들의 먹이와 물 공급을 통제한다는 상상을 할 수가 있을까요? 끔찍합니다.

가우제의 이론에 있는 또 다른 문제는 실제로 그것이 잘못되었음을 판명해 주는 많은 사례들이 존재한다는 점입니다. 한 가지 경우는 바다에 사는 다양한 종류의 플랑크톤과 관련이 있습니다. 모든 플랑크톤들은 생존을 위해 햇빛과 물 속의 영양분들을 필요로 합니다. 하지만 많은 종의 플랑크톤들이 동일한 장소에서 공존하고 있습니다. 이는 동일한 자원을 두고 한 종류의 플랑크톤이 다른 플랑크톤을 내몰 것이며 따라서 다른 종은 소멸하게 될 것이라는 가우제의 가설에 반하는 것처럼 보입니다.

가우제 이론의 또 다른 한계는 그것이 사실상 동일한 두 개의 종을 다루고 있을 뿐이라는 점입니다. 실제로, 여러 다양한 종들이 동일한 생태계 내에서 서식합니다. 두 개의 다른 그룹에 속하는 두 종이 정확히 동일한 자원을 필요로 한다는 것은 특이한 경우입니다. 예를 들면, 어, 일부 식물들은 다른 식물들보다 먹이를 덜 필요로 하는 반면, 다른 식물들은 햇빛을 덜 필요로 합니다. 일부 동물들은 잡식성인데 비해, 일부 동물들은 육식을 하고, 많은 동물들은 초식을 합니다. 심지어 초식 동물들도 같은 식물을 먹는 경우는 많지 않습니다. 다양한 동물들이 다양한 식물들을 먹습니다. 제 말 뜻을 이해하셨나요…?

일부 과학자들은 가우제의 가설이 수정되어, 예컨대 곰과 늑대와 같은 생물들 간의 경쟁이 고려되어야 한다고 주장합니다. 하지만 이 역시 실험을 통해 입증하기가 어렵습니다. 변수가 너무나 많습니다. 그리고, 실제, 멸종에 대한 대안이 존재합니다. 가령 먹이가 충분치 않아서 죽음에 직면하게 되는 경우, 많은 동물들은 단지 다른 지역으로 이동을 할 뿐입니다. 그리고 많은 식물들과 동물들은 자원 문제를 극복하도록 진화하고 있습니다. 시간이 지나면서, 생물들이 서로 조화를 이루고 살아감에 따라 대부분의 생태계에는 균형이 존재하고 있습니다. 각각의 생물들은 자신의 생태계에서 생존에 필요한 것을 가져갈 뿐, 너무 많이 가져가서 생태계가 교란되도록 하지는 않습니다. 따라서 가우제의 가설이 통제된 환경 하에서는 응용성을 가질 수도 있겠지만, 실제로는, 적용성이 그렇게 높아 보이지는 않습니다.

Compact Actual iBT Reading & Listening has been designed to be used both in the classroom and by test takers working on an individual basis. Each compact test consists of one Reading passage, one Listening conversation, and one Listening lecture. All three of them are the standard length of actual TOEFL® iBT passages, conversations, and lectures. In addition, they all have the same number of questions and the same types of questions that are found on the actual test. By using this book, test takers will be more prepared for the test when they actually take it.

<Compact Actual iBT Reading & Listening Book 2> Components

- Main Book
- Answers, Listening Scripts, and Translations
- MP3 CD
- For More Student and Teacher Support Materials, Free Downloads at http://www.darakwon.co.kr